Literary
NORFOLK

JULIAN EARWAKER & KATHLEEN BECKER

Literary
NORFOLK

An Illustrated
Companion

Foreword by Malcolm Bradbury

Chapter 6 Publishing

With love and grateful thanks to our families,
without whom this guide would never have become reality

First published in England 1998
by Chapter 6 Publishing
134 London Road
Ipswich, Suffolk, IP1 2HQ

Text © Julian Earwaker & Kathleen Becker 1998
Illustrations © Julian Earwaker (Unless otherwise acknowledged) 1998
Foreword © Malcolm Bradbury 1998

A CIP record of this book is available from the British Library

ISBN 1 870707 01 X

Design by Ben Cracknell Studios, Norwich, Norfolk

Production Consultant: Grapevine Publishing Services Ltd, London
Printed in Great Britain by Butler & Tanner, Frome, Somerset

Contents

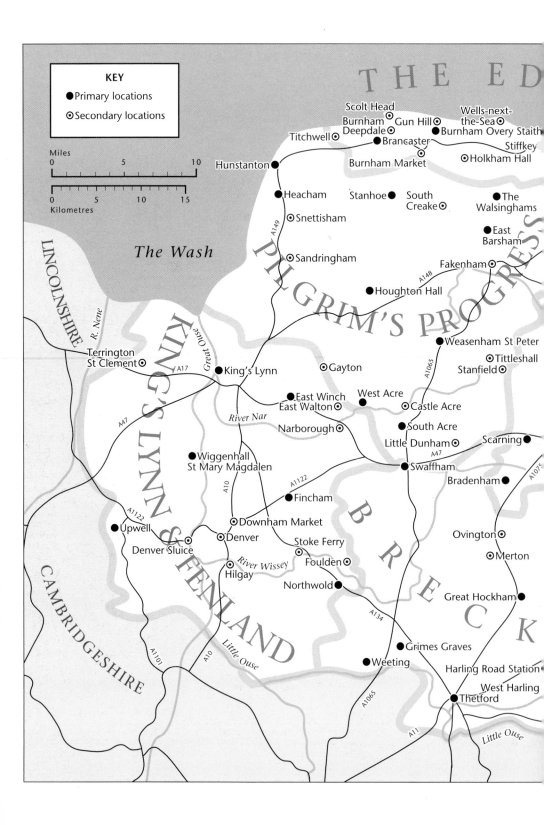

KEY

● Primary locations

⊙ Secondary locations

Miles
0 ___ 5 ___ 10

Kilometres
0 _ 5 _ 10 _ 15

THE ED

Scolt Head

Burnham ● Gun Hill⊙   Wells-next-
Deepdale⊙   the-Sea⊙

Titchwell⊙   ● Brancaster   Burnham Overy Staith●

Stiffkey

Burnham Market   ⊙Holkham Hall

Hunstanton ●

Heacham ●   Stanhoe●   South   ● The
                         Creake⊙   Walsinghams

⊙Snettisham

The Wash   ⊙Sandringham   ● East
                              Barsham

Fakenham⊙

● Houghton Hall

PILGRIM'S PROGRESS

LINCOLNSHIRE

R. Nene

Great Ouse

KING'S LYNN

● Weasenham St Peter

Terrington
St Clement⊙   A17   ⊙Gayton   ⊙Tittleshall
                                   Stanfield⊙

● King's Lynn

A47   River Nar   ● East Winch   West Acre●
                    East Walton⊙   ⊙Castle Acre

Narborough⊙   ● South Acre

                Little Dunham⊙   Scarning●

● Wiggenhall
St Mary Magdalen   A47   ● Swaffham

A10   A1122   Bradenham●   A1075

● Fincham

⊙Downham Market   Ovington⊙

Upwell●   ⊙Denver   Stoke Ferry
Denver Sluice⊙   ⊙Foulden⊙   ⊙Merton

River Wissey
Hilgay⊙

Northwold●   ● Great Hockham

KING'S LYNN & FENLAND

CAMBRIDGESHIRE

A1101   A10   Little Ouse   A134   BRECK

● Grimes Graves

● Weeting   Harling Road Station

West Harling
● Thetford

A1065   A11   Little Ouse

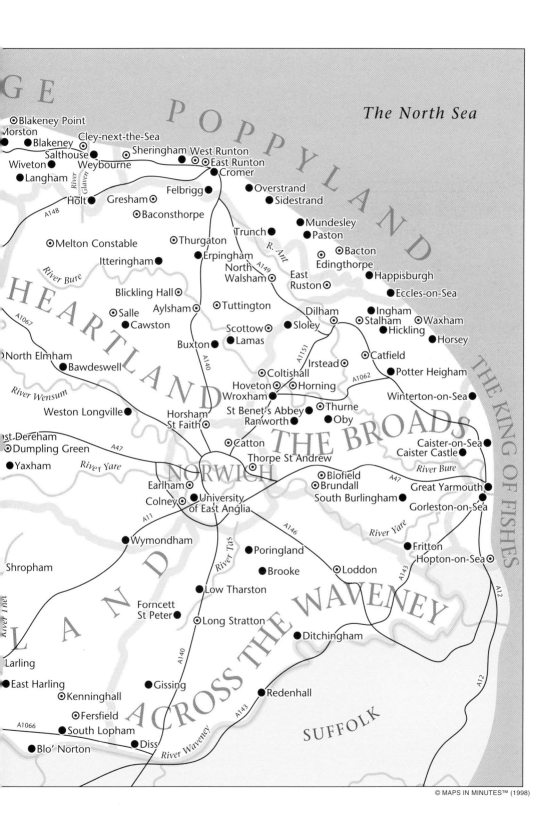

The North Sea

POPPYLAND

⊙Blakeney Point
Morston
●Blakeney ⊙ Cley-next-the-Sea
Salthouse● ⊙Sheringham West Runton
Wiveton● Weybourne ● ⊙●⊙East Runton
●Langham ⊙Cromer
Holt● Gresham⊙ Felbrigg● ●Overstrand
●Sidestrand
⊙Baconsthorpe Trunch● ●Mundesley
⊙Melton Constable ⊙Thurgaton ●Paston
Itteringham● ⊙Erpingham ⊙ ●Bacton
North Edingthorpe
Walsham⊙ East ●Happisburgh
Blickling Hall⊙ Ruston⊙ ●Eccles-on-Sea
⊙Salle Aylsham⊙ ⊙Tuttington Dilham● ●Ingham
●Cawston Scottow⊙ ●Sloley ● ⊙Stalham ⊙Waxham
North Elmham Buxton● ●Lamas ●Hickling ●Horsey
●Bawdeswell Irstead⊙ ●Catfield
⊙Coltishall ●Potter Heigham
River Wensum Hoveton⊙ ⊙Horning
Weston Longville● Wroxham● ●Winterton-on-Sea
Horsham St Benet's Abbey ⊙Thurne
St Faith⊙ Ranworth● ●Oby
st Dereham ⊙Catton Caister-on-Sea●
⊙Dumpling Green Thorpe St Andrew Caister Castle●
●Yaxham NORWICH ⊙Blofield River Bure
Earlham⊙ ⊙Brundall Great Yarmouth●
Colney⊙ ●University South Burlingham● Gorleston-on-Sea
of East Anglia
Shropham ●Wymondham ●Poringland ●Fritton
●Brooke Hopton-on-Sea⊙
Larling ●Loddon
●East Harling ●Low Tharston Ditchingham
⊙Kenninghall Forncett ●
St Peter● ⊙Long Stratton
⊙Fersfield ●Gissing
South Lopham ●Redenhall
●Blo' Norton ●Diss SUFFOLK

GE
HEARTLAND
A1067
River Bure
A148
River Glaven
R. Ant
A149
A1151
A1062
THE BROADS
THE KING OF FISHES
A140
A47
River Yare
A11
A146
River Yare
A143
River Tas
A12
LAND
ACROSS THE WAVENEY
River Thet
A1066
River Waveney
A140

© MAPS IN MINUTES™ (1998)

Foreword

BY MALCOLM BRADBURY

It was a good while back, in 1966, that I first came to Norfolk, a county I scarcely knew except through the promising pages of books. I knew it through John Skelton, Sir Thomas Browne, Parson Woodforde, George Borrow, Charles Dickens, Anthony Trollope, Rider Haggard, L P Hartley, Arnold Wesker, especially through the Broadland stories of a favourite author of my childhood, Arthur Ransome. I had come from one literary county, Yorkshire, to another – except that Norfolk is far less well-sung. Yorkshire boasts about its writers, proudly promoting Brontë Country, Herriot Country, Larkin Country. Norfolk does not, and still has to capitalise on a dense literary history which still continues. For there is scarcely a city, town, village in this amiable county that doesn't serve as home to several writers now.

Perhaps this shyness in cultural self-promotion goes with the sense of separateness, retreat and 'du different' that was always part of the Norfolk and East Anglian spirit – and still provides an attraction for those who come here to get on quietly with their own work. Yet over many generations the big, varied county of Norfolk, with its grand historical houses (and their fine private libraries), rolling agricultural estates and rural poverty and protest, strange isolated rectories with their strange isolated rectors, folk tales and pub storytellers, Broads and waterlands, Dutch-gabled ports (like Fanny Burney's King's Lynn) and extensive sea connections, its chilly north coast beaches for sharp summer holidays and great bird reserves, served as patron, producer and muse for a very large number of writers. Its connections were international. It sent off many of the Pilgrim Fathers, and got back Pocahontas. It lay on a crucial trade route, for once much of the traffic of Britain came down the coast from port to port.

Norwich itself was a great medieval city, the second in England: a place of learning, cultural activity, religious and political dissent. It too felt itself close to the continent, and was always enriched by 'Strangers'. The many Huguenots, and émigrés from the French Revolution, joined with some of the great, often dissenting and reforming local families – the Frys, Bacons, Barclays, Gurneys, Martineaus – to make it one of the key regional capitals, like Exeter and York. Well into the nineteenth century it boasted a thriving artistic culture, with the Norwich School of painters (Crome, Cotman), a fine musical and theatrical heritage, a major printing and publishing industry, and a good many writers, from George Borrow to Anna Sewell, Amelia Opie to Harriet Martineau. Martineau worried that in the industrial age Norwich was losing out: 'Its bombazine manufacture has gone to Yorkshire, and its literary fame to the four winds,' she wrote.

It was true that in the nineteenth century the region lost some of its historical place as the Industrial Revolution shifted social energies north and west. One thing it needed for cultural focus was a university, but not until 1962 did it get one. Then the 'new' University of East Anglia was established on the edge of Norwich, in the Yare Valley, and began to pull together some of the region's cultural and artistic life. It had the sense to appoint a very distinguished – and local – writer, Angus Wilson, as Professor of English. That had everything to do with bringing me here. Like Angus, I was a writer as much as an academic, and wanted to be in an institution and region where writing seemed to matter.

It was a happy choice. I soon found myself in a thriving local community of writers: Anthony Thwaite, George MacBeth, Correlli Barnett, Edwin Brock and more. With its strong literary emphasis, the university quickly began attracting as students many would-be writers, including Rose Tremain, Clive Sinclair and Snoo Wilson. By 1970 we were able to put this onto a formal footing, starting a postgraduate creative writing programme, the first of its kind in Britain. Its first student was Ian McEwan, soon followed by Kazuo Ishiguro. The programme, now run by Andrew Motion, is a major centre for new and modern writing, and is world-famous.

This is by way of reminder that literature is both a heritage – a form of imaginative history that gives meaning and presence to a region's history – and a vigorous, continuous living thing. Writers all come from somewhere, live some-where, form into communities, relate to their places. Sometimes our place is our real subject, the basic material we work with, providing our vision, setting, landscape and theme. Sometimes it is a culture which stimulates our writing and lets it happen, whatever its setting and subject-matter might be.

Norfolk has always been a profitable mixture of both kinds of author. Its writers, from the Pastons to the Walpoles, have kept the record well. There have been many vividly descriptive writers, like Rider Haggard, Henry Williamson, John Middleton Murry and R H Mottram, who have drawn on Norfolk landscapes, seascapes, agriculture, characters, social experiences. Others – sometimes, the same ones, like Rider Haggard, writing tales of African adventure – have chosen to live here, but set their books elsewhere, anywhere at all.

I belong to the second breed. My fictional world is spread very widely, even to imaginary lands – my imagination has caught up Norfolk from time to time. Like many writers I see writing as a constant intersection between the local and the universal, things near-at-hand and events far away. Yet even in our globalised age 'regional' writing still survives, indeed flourishes. Of course each generation defines place, region and bigger world afresh; but that too is part of the story.

As for myself, though I do not necessarily write about Norfolk, I am a Norfolk writer. I've loved my thirty years here, write here, and have put down my roots (literally, since I've taken on a farm). Place is important for writers – and readers too, which is why I welcome this book. It is extremely well-researched, telling me much I never knew. It lovingly reveals what remains a quite distinctive regional landscape, and the literary associations and landmarks, many unexpected, that fill it. I had forgotten that C P Snow set a mystery story on the Broads, though I did remember that Robinson Crusoe came ashore here. A landscape comes to life through what has been written in it; writers come to life when we follow in their steps. This companion is an excellent way to track down an undersung literary heritage.

Introduction

> Norfolk provides the 'still centre' when all around is turmoil. The air has a different quality to it the moment you cross the border. You can smell when you are entering Norfolk. There is a softness and a sweetness in the air.
>
> Edward Storey, *Spirit of the Fens*, 1985

Isolated geographically and independent spiritually, Norfolk is good at keeping secrets. With some of the most beautiful and varied landscape in Britain, this is an out-of-the-way sort of place – insular, though not unwelcoming. You don't pass through Norfolk, you *arrive* here. This guide, journeying from the Middle Ages to the millennium, arrives at one of Norfolk's best-kept secrets – its literary heritage.

Following in the footsteps of generations of writers, the temptation is to head straight for the coast – the much-altered 'strangeness' of David Copperfield's Yarmouth, the famed sea-bathing and faded grandeur of Jane Austen's Cromer or the shelter of L P Hartley's striped Hunstanton cliffs, where you might still expect to find Eustace poking around the rock pools. Further along this defiant coast, the cliffs give way to what Richard Mabey dubs 'The Edge'; part-land, part-sea, this is a 'waterslain' place in a constant state of flux, epitomised by the poetry of Kevin Crossley-Holland. Here, amidst the salt marsh and solitude, some of E F Benson's finest 'Spook' stories and Jack Higgins' *The Eagle Has Landed* took shape.

> I sometimes wondered if the closeness of these unstable edges of the land was part of the secret of Norfolk's appeal to us, a reflection of a half-conscious desire to be as contingent as spindrift ourselves, to stay loose, cast off, be washed up somewhere unexpected. Down among these shifting sands the world seems to be all possibility.
>
> Richard Mabey, *Home Country*, 1990

From its embattled coastline, Norfolk's literary landscape extends far inland. The wild and often barren beauty of the Brecks is lovingly re-created in the pages of Michael Home's novels, a lost world recognised by Virginia Woolf as a 'strange ... undulating, dreaming, philosophising & remembering land'. In the heartland of Norfolk the 'Romany Rye' George Borrow 'first saw the light' in the market town of Dereham, where the gentle but anguished William Cowper endured his final years, while some years later a young Brian Aldiss clambered out onto the rooftops from his first-floor flat. A short horse-ride across the fields is Dudwick Park where Black Beauty once grazed with his siblings before Anna Sewell bequeathed her children's classic to the waiting world. Over to the east, the reed-rimmed Broads conceal Arthur Ransome's delightful adventures, George MacBeth's anxious and honest poetry, and Gladys Mitchell's murder and mayhem. Westwards, the waterland of the Fens is a more distant and elusive landscape still: Graham Swift's 'low and liquid world' so familiar to Dorothy L Sayers – and so loathed by Anthony Trollope.

The preponderance of murder mysteries from these parts would suggest something sinister at work in Norfolk; ghostly apparitions, the devilish Black Shuck roaming the night, and shadowy strangers with murder in mind. Whether Alan Hunter's pipe-puffing Inspector Gently, Brian Cooper's Tench and Lubbock twosome, P D James' Adam Dalgliesh, or Sherlock Holmes himself, Norfolk retains an irresistible sense of mystery.

Norfolk is a land of the elements; wide skies, fierce winds and scouring tides. Punctuating this stoical landscape are its weather-beaten sentinels – the distinctive skeletal frames of windmills and pumps, and the solidity and certainty of hundreds of churches, with more round towers here than in any other county. These bastions of religious expression, representing continuity and remembrance, have long lured writers to their flinty magnitude; John Betjeman, writing of the 'soaring majesty of Norfolk', Kate Charles, combining church visits with the plotting of ecclesiastical mysteries, and centuries earlier, Julian of Norwich, retreating to the sanctuary of her church cell to meditate the meaning of her *Divine Revelations* for over thirty years. And let us not forget the writing rectors – John Skelton exercising his acerbic wit at Diss, Parson Woodforde meandering through many meals at Weston Longville and Augustus Jessopp immersing himself in local lore at Scarning.

> Every land and every sea
> Have I crossed, but much the worst
> Is the land of Norfolk cursed.
> That the land is poor and bad
> I the clearest proof have had
> If you plant the choicest wheat
> Tares and darnel you will meet.
> Satan on the road to Hell
> Ruined Norfolk as he fell.

> Anon. 12th C, 'The Soil and Climate of Norfolk'

Visible in all directions from the church towers, are the agricultural lands – the feeding grounds that have sustained generations of Norfolk communities. For the famous literary farmers, reading the land was often more important than writing a book. Rider Haggard stalked the fields at Ditchingham with a great dynastic sense, Henry Williamson struggled with his unyielding acres at Stiffkey, while both Mary Mann and Doreen Wallace extracted richer harvests from their lands.

If there has to be a capital of literary Norfolk, where better to find it than in the medieval streets of its cathedral city, described by J B Priestley as that 'grand, higgledy-piggledy, sensible old place'. Here, in Norfolk's wool and weaving capital, Shakespeare's contemporaries Robert Greene and the 'balletting silk-weaver of

Norwich', Thomas Deloney, plied their trade amongst immigrant 'Strangers'. Centuries later, Ralph Mottram and David Holbrook watched the inexorable spread of the city around them and the development of a one-way system Sylvia Haymon notes must 'surely be the longest distance between two points ever devised'.

If Norwich is the undisputed literary capital, still shrouded in a distinctly Dickensian atmosphere, then the University of East Anglia with its prestigious Creative Writing course might be said to be its literary Vatican. World-famous authors regularly grace the stage here, and many of its academics have busied themselves in outputting their own fiction: from the seminal works of Malcolm Bradbury and Angus Wilson to the rich and distinctive prose of Christopher Bigsby and W G Sebald. The creative process continues across town at the city's Art & Design college, occupying the combined talents of George Szirtes, Peter Scupham and Elspeth Barker.

> 'All England may be carved out of Norfolk.'
>
> Thomas Fuller, 1662

This guide is a celebration of Norfolk's literature in all its manifest variety. Haggard, Shakespeare, Skelton, Dickens, Trollope – these are the more familiar names of Norfolk's heritage, safely enshrined in the literary canon. But Norfolk is a landscape of lost voices too: Mary Mann's impoverished villagers, Doreen Wallace's farming communities, Amelia Opie's social entanglements, Christopher Woodforde's eerie stories, Anthony C Wilson's boy detectives. And now the voices of a new generation demand to be heard: D J Taylor, Henry Sutton, Katherine Pierpoint, Andrew Cowan, Lynne Bryan... Norfolk permeates the work of all.

This companion is a representation of a unique corner of Britain, a distillation of the essence of Norfolk through its writers and writings. You don't have to visit Norfolk to enjoy it – one of the pleasures of reading is travelling without ever having to leave the page. But if you can, take a pilgrimage across an unspoilt landscape of immense character and experience the spirit of literary Norfolk.

> 'The Norfolk landscape sends a shiver through my soul.'
>
> Raffaella Barker, *Come and Tell Me Some Lies*, 1994

HOW TO USE THIS GUIDE

The chapters of this guide represent broad geographical areas of Norfolk (Fens, Broads, Breckland etc.). Within each chapter, locations are arranged in alphabetical order. All Norfolk place names are detailed in **bold**. Locations with references elsewhere in the guide are additionally marked by an asterisk*. There is a map at the front of this guide showing all primary and secondary locations.

Where more than one author is referenced under any single location, they are ordered chronologically. All writers are referenced in **bold**. Writers with references elsewhere in the guide are additionally marked by an asterisk*.

CHAPTER ONE

Across the Waveney

LITERARY LINKS

John Betjeman, Terence Blacker, Edwin Brock, Lindsay Clarke,
George Ewart Evans, H Rider Haggard, Lilias Rider Haggard,
Ruth Rendell, John Skelton, Anthony Thwaite, Ann Thwaite,
Doreen Wallace, Arnold Wesker, Dorothy Wordsworth,
William Wordsworth, Adrian Wright

Brooke

In 1968, one of the great oral historians of East Anglian life, **George
Ewart Evans** (1909–88), moved across the border from Suffolk to the
pretty village of Brooke. Although Evans found Brooke to be something
of a 'gentrified and dormitory suburb', he wrote seven books from his
snug, thatched cottage opposite the mere, sitting, as his friend and
illustrator David Gentleman records:

> … at a wooden desk surrounded by books, near a tall filing
> cabinet full of letters and tapes, with a bottle of sherry for visitors
> standing on the floor beside it. One window looked on to his
> hedge, the other on to a small lawn with a Portuguese laurel tree
> and the shallow Brooke mere beyond it: at the back of the cottage
> was a long garden shaded by apple trees.

George Ewart Evans

His oral histories provide a
voice for 'a class of people that
have had little opportunity to
speak for themselves'.

Born in Wales, into a family of eleven, Evans worked as a writer of
poetry, stories, film and radio scripts for children. It was not until he
reached his early fifties that he commenced work on his unique series
of East Anglian volumes. Through the pages of these books, Evans
explores the countryside and its traditions; its cycles of life and history.
He records the quiet 'revolution' – the transition of rural society from
a 'prior' (as opposed to a 'primitive') culture – to a mechanised,
machine-dependent one.

At a time when the relevance of oral history had yet to be fully
discovered, Evans pioneered an immediate and unashamedly subjective
way of viewing history. And as he writes in 1970, in *Where Beards Wag
All* (a quotation from sixteenth-century writer and poet **Thomas Tusser**,

whose agricultural writings Evans knew well), East Anglia holds its own special appeal for the purposes of recording an oral grassroots history, providing:

> …mainly the voice of a class of people that have had little opportunity to speak for themselves. They have left few letters, diaries or written accounts of any kind … in East Anglia the mass-education movement of the last century … made little impact on the rural population. There was no surge towards book-learning: on the contrary, there is strong evidence that there was a resistance towards it.

Evans' method of tapping directly into centuries of tradition involved interviewing a large number of 'informants': usually rural folk born in the latter part of the 1890s. His gentle and unassuming manner, his courtesy, respect and empathy with the individual enabled Evans to get close to the spirit of rural Norfolk.

His many interviews, conducted with tape-recorder and notebook – and always following the rural maxim of 'If you want to buy a pig, talk about the weather', yield an extraordinary insight into the lives of ordinary people. Retaining the Norfolk vernacular (though carefully annotated), the joy of Evans' writing is that it speaks authentically and directly from the mouths of many people.

Brooke Cottage – where George Ewart Evans spent the last twenty years of his life.

In their everyday language they used words like *mavis* (a thrush), *page* (an apprentice to a shepherd), *buskins* (leggings), *well-happed* (fortunate), *tempest* (a thunderstorm) – words I was familiar with in the early poets like Chaucer, Spenser, and Shakespeare, without ever expecting to hear them in ordinary discourse.

The Days That We Have Seen, 1975

Blacksmiths at work – one of many forgotten rural trades from the 'prior' culture recorded by George Ewart Evans' work.

Evans' approach is also reflected in the titles of his books: *Ask the Fellows Who Cut the Hay* (1956), *The Days That We Have Seen* (1975) and *The Crooked Scythe* (1993). Using the past to understand the present, linking rural nostalgia to ecological and environmental concerns, Evans' classics of oral history remain untainted by false romanticism or sentimentality, and are as readable today as ever.

Diss

The peaceful tree-fringed mere of this attractive market town offers fine views across to the grey flint church of St Mary the Virgin, which dates from 1290. Just inside the south entrance to this well-maintained and attractive church hangs a wooden plaque listing the rectors here since the thirteenth century. Included in this roll-call is the name of **John Skelton** (*c*.1460–1529), rector of St Mary's for twenty-five years and regarded as being the most notable English poet between **Chaucer*** and **Spenser**.

John Skelton

For though my ryme
          be ragged,
Tattered and jagged,
Rudely rayne-beaten,
Rusty and mothe-eaten,
Yf ye take well therwith,
It hath in it some pyth ...

from 'Collyn Clout' *c.* 1545

John Skelton distinguished himself in the Tudor Court with his early formal, rhetorical poetry and was appointed tutor to the young Henry VIII. Skelton was outspoken, far from modest and reputed to have had a sharp tongue and a bad temper – so his lessons and sermons must surely have been entertaining. More than once Skelton overstepped the mark, and one attack on Cardinal Wolsey (*Why come ye nat to Courte*, *c.*1522) resulted in the poet's imprisonment.

Skelton's original and hugely influential poetry, with its distinctive use of vernacular in short lines, includes numerous poems inspired by Norfolk life and his time in Diss. Poems such as 'The Epitaph of Adam

St Mary's church, Diss – a familiar sight to both John Skelton and John Betjeman; two poets laureate some five centuries apart.

Udershal' and 'A Devout Trental for Old John Clarke' (a set of thirty Requiem Masses) were certainly influenced by local characters, while Skelton's famous lament *Phyllyp Sparowe* (1505), tells of young Jane Scrope mourning the loss of her sparrow 'late slayn at Carowe' by a cat called Gyb. Skelton's infamous temper is exposed in his scathing 'Ware the Hawk' (*c*.1505) – aimed at a misguided neighbouring clergyman who had dared to exercise his hawks within St Mary's:

> This tretise devysed is
> Of two knaves somtyme
>   of Dis.
> Though this knaves be deade,
> Full of myschiefe and queed,
> Yet, where so ever they ly
> Theyr names shall never dye.
>
> John Skelton *c.* 1506

> I shall you make relacyon
> By way of apostrofacyon
> Under supportacyon
> Of your pacyent tolleracyon,
> How I, Skelton laureat,
> Devysed and also wrate
> Upon a lewde curate,
> A parson benefyced
> But nothynge well advysed.
> He shall be as now nameles,
> but he shall not be blameles,
> Nor he shall not be shameles;
> for sure he wrought amys
> To hawke in my church of Dys.

Skelton was created 'poet laureate' when it was still an academic distinction awarded by the universities of Oxford, Louvain and Cambridge, and the great Dutch humanist **Erasmus*** praises Skelton as 'a light of glory of English letters' for his erudition and style. More recently, poets such as **Robert Graves** ('Helter-skelter John / Rhymes serenely on /... / Old John, you do me good!') and **W H Auden*** have acknowledged their debt to a poet who is credited with the first use of hundreds of English words. The short rhythms and bunched rhymes – seemingly modelled around clerical verse, hymns and litanies – of 'Skeltonics' are familiar to much performance poetry today.

Over 300 years later, prolific novelist **Doreen Wallace** (1897–1989) came to teach in a Diss secondary school and lived in the town until her marriage in 1922, eventually moving to nearby Wortham Manor. Wallace, like **D L Sayers*** (whom she knew at Oxford), became one of the 'Somerville College novelists'. In 1931 she published her first novel, *A Little Learning*, which clearly foreshadows the two central concerns that were to guide her writing and her life: education and farming. In East Anglia, where she had been living since she was twenty-five, she had observed that there is 'something odd about land – it possesses its possessors, it grapples them to its soul with hooks of steel'.

During the agricultural depression of the 1930s, Wallace actively campaigned against the imposition of tithes, which were only finally abolished in 1977. This led to the impounding of the stock on her two farms in 1934, followed by a siege at Wortham Manor, a confrontation

Doreen Wallace

Prolific author, farmer and long-term campaigner in the 'tithe war'.

'How much, when winter is here, I love the winter! ... when you can really see the bone structure of the trees; winter, when a gleam of sun is worth a whole day of the expected and familiar sunshine of summer; ... in winter, expecting nothing, one is never disappointed.'

Doreen Wallace, *In a Green Shade*, 1950

with some local Blackshirts, and bankruptcy in 1939. During the years from 1934 to 1955 Doreen Wallace wrote her best work; observant accounts of personal and social relations in village life, farming and schooling – with a sharp eye for idiom.

Written as an exposé of conditions in certain private boys' schools, *Sons of Gentlemen* (1953) features Hereward and Kate Stringer, trying to run a school in a village modelled on **Baconsthorpe** near the north Norfolk coast. Despite grandiose intentions ('We prepare for Life!'), the school project is fraught with problems. While the insufferably patronising Hereward ('My good woman, this is Norfolk!'), son of a Norfolk Parson, complains that 'the standard of feeding is cheaper and worse in Norfolk than anywhere else in England', he is happy to recommend 'that sort of filthy boiled pudding ... (it's called a dumpling)' as a staple diet for the pupils to come.

The Millpond (1966) traces a year in the life of a rector's wife in Barnham, where Wallace lived for a while (explored earlier in *Barnham Rectory*, 1934), and *Ashbury People* (1968) is an absorbing account of farming life which enmeshes two families in a network of emotions. In 1978, two years after the publication of her last novel *Landscape with Figures*, Doreen Wallace came to live in Diss – at 2 Manor Gardens – where she stayed until her death.

Wallace's garden diary, *In a Green Shade* (1950), records a certain eclecticism in her choice of gardening tasks ('I refuse to grow vegetables. If I peel, scrape or wash them, cook them and eat them, that's more than enough for me'), and she expresses satisfaction at her continuing good health (helped by giving up smoking) and 'my fair-to-moderate literary success'. Now largely forgotten, Doreen Wallace died in 1989 with forty-eight novels to her name.

John Betjeman

The poet found Diss to be 'the perfect small English town'.

'Her books are all her own, and I like them very much', said **John Betjeman** (1906–84)*, of Doreen Wallace, forging his own connections with the town four and a half centuries after John Skelton. A poet laureate himself, Betjeman first visited in 1963 while working on a BBC series on English market towns. When he stepped off the train, Betjeman is said to have headed for the Jolly Porter – a small pub which was soon to be replaced by a cement works.

His concern for this kind of 'demolition by degrees' led to Betjeman's involvement in the preservation of Diss, which he described as 'the perfect small English town' and he later became the Patron of the Diss Society. Like his great friend **W H Auden***, Betjeman retained a lifelong passion for the English landscape and architecture, and vigorously opposed what he saw as smash-and-grab raids on ancient landscapes by modern planners.

In 1972 he accompanied Mary Wilson (who was herself born in the town), wife of the then Labour Prime Minister and both produced poems to commemorate the occasion.

'Dear Mary / Yes, it will be bliss / To go with you by train to Diss,'–
Betjeman's 'Mind's Journey to Diss' travels through Essex and Suffolk,
and across the 'widening fields' where there are 'Flint church-towers
sparkling in the light'. As they pass 'elmy hills with brooks between', their
destination comes into sight:

> Till in the dimmest place of all
> The train slows down into a crawl
> And stops in silence...Where is this?
> Dear Mary Wilson, this is Diss.

As the saying goes: 'When you cross the border the first town in Norfolk Diss appears' – though John Betjeman's fears that the medieval buildings and idiosyncratic town layout of Diss would be threatened by London overspill have not been realised.

More recently, **Ruth Rendell*** (1930–) sets her short story 'Weeds', from
The Copper Peacock (1991) collection, in an unnamed village close to
Diss. City dweller Jeremy Flintwine, a publisher, visits the Hithe family
for a weed-hunt in garden-proud Rodney Hithe's spotless garden. As
Hithe's daughter Emily explains: 'You have to see if you can find a weed
... If you find one all you have to do is show it to my father and he will
give you a pound for it.' As in her novel *The Brimstone Wedding* (1996),
Rendell uses her story to offer incisive and witty observations on urban
and rural realities. Flintwine, his mind already half-focused on the train
journey home to London, is the urban observer standing on the outside
of the gathering:

> People stood about on the lawn drinking tea and eating digestive
> biscuits which they had had to pay for. Jeremy always found
> country life amazing. The way everyone knew everyone else, for
> instance. The extreme eccentricity of almost everybody, so that
> you suspected people, wrongly, of putting it on. The clothes.
> Garments he had supposed obsolete, cotton frocks and sports
> jackets, were everywhere in evidence.

Already stifled by the 'oppressive' neatness of the gardens – 'some of the
flowers looking as if they had been washed and ironed and others as if
made of wax' – Jeremy Flintwine readily agrees to the 'weed' challenge.
But when he carelessly drops the poppy he has found, Flintwine
unwittingly triggers a disturbing chain of events.

In his third novel, *Revenance* (1996), novelist, journalist and children's
writer **Terence Blacker** (1948–) resurrects the memory of **John
Skelton***, whose mistress Margaret Cowper leaps forward 500 years to
grace the border village of 'Burthorpe' with her eerie presence.
Burthorpe, an amalgam of various border villages, though tentatively
locatable on the south-east fringes of Diss, has all the charm of the
eternal thoroughfare – impossibly criss-crossed as it is by the A140, the
railway, the river and the county border. Nothing much has ever
happened here, and in the arena of world history, Burthorpe is 'no more
than a spectator, in one of the cheaper seats, with an impeded view'.

Terence Blacker

'I love this particular area and its tension between past and present.'

But with the arrival of Margaret Cowper, events of unheard-of magnitude are about to take place.

By day, Margaret Cowper is a petite, dark-haired and slightly aloof young woman, graced with an unhealthy interest in matters of death and a total disregard for twentieth-century humour. But by night she assumes the menacing outline of a spectral dust-cloud, moving with impunity through the village, leaving only a mysterious trail of red blotches to mark her attendance at scenes of death.

Margaret's cathartic figure is placed in a village where sex seems to oil the wheels of community life, with wife-swapping ('doing bodies') occurring on an industrial scale. When Margaret – not quite the 'little popsy' she looks – takes up her position as the undertaker's secretary, things start to go seriously wrong and, as skeletons begin to emerge from local cupboards, her new employer soon finds business picking up. Meanwhile, Miles Larwood, a local academic and thanatologist, finds himself inexorably drawn towards this strangely different young woman.

The narrative of this intelligent contemporary ghost story is broken up by intertextual snippets of village life taken from the '*Diss Press*' and flashbacks of Margaret's dalliance with Skelton. This 'revenance' from the Middle Ages reveals Margaret as the young servant bedded and impregnated by John Skelton and subsequently dumped and abandoned in a lonely cottage. The existence of Skelton's common law wife is a historical fact, says Blacker, as is the scene of Skelton holding up his baby son to the congregation. Ironically, while Jane Scrope went down in the annals of literary history as the owner of a much lamented pet sparrow, 'Phyllyp Sparrowe', the real identity of 'Skelton's musket' is unknown to this day.

Hanging on Terence Blacker's study wall are two water-colours of his Wortham farmhouse executed by fellow novelist and amateur painter **Doreen Wallace***, farming and writing at neighbouring Wortham Manor earlier in the century.

Blacker's darkly comic blend of past and present, of fact and fiction, paints a very different view of Skelton's traditional image as the wise-cracking poet laureate, here depicted as a cruel, single-minded and blasphemous egotist. With the sideshow of the local squire's crumbling stiff-upper-lip existence at 'Garston Hall', confronted by his son's emancipation and the collapse of the genteel farmer image he treasures, *Revenance* is also a comment on stasis and change in rural life, without ever ceasing to be funny.

Ditchingham

It was Christmas time in 1882 when **Henry Rider Haggard*** (1856–1925) retreated to the Ditchingham estate of his Norfolk-born wife Louisa Margitson to rewrite his first novel, *Dawn*. Rider was then struggling to convince publishers of the merit of his work, and his future as a writer was far from certain. But the peaceful atmosphere of south Norfolk was certainly to his liking, and 'Mustard Pot Hall', as Ditchingham House was known locally (due to the yellow lichen

The Haggards at Ditchingham – Rider Haggard (standing centre right) with his wife Louie (standing second from left) and daughter Lilias (seated front left with dog).

covering its roof), was to remain an integral part of Rider's life for the next forty years.

The views here from the low escarpment above the Waveney valley remained for Haggard 'most quietly and consistently beautiful', as he notes in *A Farmer's Year* (1899):

> For the most part of the year, the plain below is golden with gorse, but it is not on this alone that the sight depends for beauty, or on the green of the meadows and the winding river edged with lush marshes that in spring are spotted by yellow marigolds and purple with myriads of cuckoo flowers. They all contribute to it, as do the grazing cattle, the gabled distant roofs and church spires but I think the prospect owes its peculiar charm to the constant changes of light which sweep across its depths. At every season of the year, at every hour of the day, it is beautiful but always with a different beauty.

Ditchingham Hall – 'Mustard Pot hall' to locals, the large bay window of Rider Haggard's former study is visible to the left.

Somehow finding the time to write a further novel, *The Witch's Head*, at the same time as successfully completing his law exams, Rider Haggard was disappointed to find that less than spectacular sales earned him just £50 for his efforts. Failure was something that he rarely encountered and never took easily, but Rider nevertheless prepared himself for a legal – rather than writing – career.

A bet with his brother – who had declared that Rider couldn't possibly write anything to match **Robert Louis Stevenson**'s recently published *Treasure Island* – spurred Haggard on to write *King Solomon's Mines* in just six weeks. Published in September 1885 to massive publicity, the book was an immediate success, and among the letters of praise was one from Robert Louis Stevenson himself. The 'white heat' of Rider's imagination produced two further novels, *Allan Quatermain* and *Jess*, in only ten and nine weeks respectively, while *She* – a powerfully charged adventure with mystical and sexual undertones completed the trilogy of novels released in 1887.

The settings for Rider Haggard's adventures are mainly exotic and far-flung; he perhaps preferred the intrusive literary light to shine away from the retreat of his beloved Norfolk walkways. But occasionally his heroes stray back into home territory – *Red Eve* (1911) and *Colonel*

Quaritch, A Tale of Country Life (1888) utilise East Anglian locales, while *Montezuma's Daughter* (1893) both opens and closes at Ditchingham Lodge.

Here, in 1588, Thomas Wingfield of Ditchingham Lodge listens to the news of the Spanish Armada's defeat with no small satisfaction – his past has been a series of battles with the Spanish, and with one man in particular: his 'devilish' cousin Juan de Garcia. After the murder of his mother by de Garcia, Thomas Wingfield swears to track down the villain and thus, heading first to Spain and then on to Mexico, begins a thrilling adventure of high passion and vengeance.

With his ferocious appetite for fiction, Rider Haggard forged a new trail for adventure romance, fleshing out the bones of historical fact – in this case the end of the Aztec empire – with the images of his own powerful imagination. As Thomas Wingfield sets down his adventures in *Montezuma's Daughter*, it could be Rider himself who writes: 'For the valley of the Waveney I see the vale of Tenoctitlan, for the slopes of Stowe the snowy shapes of the volcanoes Popo and Iztac, for the spire of **Earsham** and the towers of Ditchingham, of Bungay, and of Beccles, the soaring pyramids of sacrifice gleaming with the sacred fires, and for the cattle in the meadows the horsemen of Cortes sweeping to war.'

While Wingfield survives shipwrecking, escapes the sacrificial altar, eludes the dreaded Spanish Inquisition and marries the daughter of Montezuma, many autobiographical shards from Rider Haggard's own life gleam through the fabric of his tale. Thomas Wingfield, like Rider, falls in love with a local woman against the wishes of her father, but returns later to claim her hand. In 1892, Rider Haggard, like Wingfield, journeyed to Mexico in search of Aztec treasure, only to suffer the enduring pain of losing his nine-year-old son Jock after a bout of measles back home in England. Poor Thomas Wingfield meanwhile loses all four sons born to his two wives, and returns to Ditchingham Lodge with echoes of Rider's own mourning: 'Here in the happy valley of the Waveney, save for my bitter memories and that longing for the dead which no time can so much as dull.'

One of Rider's few close friends was fellow writer **Rudyard Kipling**, who was himself devastated by the loss of his son in the First World War. The two authors could often be found in Rider's study at Ditchingham exchanging ideas, developing plots and reviewing work in progress. But Rider Haggard was to be haunted for the rest of his life by the tragedy of his young son's death, and the event certainly led to a slowing down of his prolific fictional outflow. During the dark and introspective years that followed, Rider felt more than ever the 'desire to do something in my day more practical than the mere invention of romance upon romance'.

Meanwhile, the 240-acre Ditchingham estate remained a working farm, and every morning the 'long and loose-limbed' Rider would go out for his morning walk, his 'piercing blue eyes' missing nothing as he

Rider Haggard's *A Farmer's Year* (1899) correctly predicted terrible times ahead for British agriculture, illustrated by this cartoon from *The Landworker* twenty years later.

SEPTEMBER, 1922.   THE LAND WORKER   5

FOR EMIGRANTS

FARM LABOURER

NOT WANTED—IN ENGLAND.

completed a tour of inspection of his land and buildings. Rider was always a sensitive and spiritual person, and a nephew was later to note that 'he had a deep sense as he walked over his land of the generations that had walked it before him'.

Rider found himself drawn increasingly towards the workings of the rich Norfolk soil, strengthening his already active interest in agricultural affairs. Always a great campaigner, he combined his literary flair with a genuine feel for life off the land to produce *A Farmer's Year* in the midst of Britain's deep agricultural depression, to show the 'decrepit and even dangerous state of the farming industry in eastern England.' Keenly researched and lucidly argued, Kipling had hoped that Rider's work might become a second **Tusser***, but in reality the book was not a great success.

Two years later, in 1901 an undaunted Rider commenced a long and arduous tour of the country with visions of agricultural reform foremost in his mind. The result, *Rural England*, was published in November 1902 ('the heaviest labour of all my laborious life') but Rider's campaigning work and recommendations for reform were eventually frustrated by bureaucracy and political apathy. Nevertheless, both books reveal the depth of his love of the land, fostered by years of work at Ditchingham. Rider's devotion to a garden which he had tended for over twenty years, 'through summer's sun and winter's wild wet face', was later represented by *A Gardener's Year*, published as a diary of his work here throughout 1903.

In 1912, Rider was knighted, but his subsequent appointment to a Royal Commission to report on the health of the British Empire was interrupted by the declaration of war in August 1914. The Norfolk countryside was now teeming with soldiers, and zeppelin raids came close to the house at Ditchingham. But it was the 'continuous thudding roar of guns ... shaking the windows of this house' from across the sea which served as a constant reminder of the horrors of war.

This was also a terrible time for agriculture, and in 1916 Sir Rider reluctantly admitted defeat and abandoned farming. 'I have done my best, but the fact is that the adventure is scarcely possible for a gentleman in East Anglia', he wrote on 18 August 1916, and a year later the stock was sold and the land let. After thirty years of toil, such failure must have been heartbreaking, but like **Henry Williamson***, another writer-farmer some thirty years later, Rider remained pragmatic and stoical about his loss: 'I have made nothing ... but I have gained a vast amount of experience – perhaps I am well out of the business'.

That same year, Sir Rider donated his collection of bound manu-scripts to the Castle Museum, **Norwich*** – 'the gift of a Norfolk man to Norfolk.' For the remaining years of his life, he continued to write, but like many authors found it increasingly difficult to stay abreast of contemporary trends, his writing, in the face of emerging modernism, appearing rather dated and outmoded. Nevertheless, his adventures, many of which have been filmed, continue to inspire readers today.

Throughout his life, Henry Rider Haggard had been a regular at the church of St Mary's, Ditchingham, seated in the family pew at the

Bath House on the Ditchingham Estate – once home to Lilias Rider Haggard.

'Poacher with dog' by P H
Emerson, 1928

'I was Born in a small villige
in Historick Norfolk ... Abler
pens than mine have extolled
the County of Norfolk, but
like many Norfolk men, I
some times think that there is
no place like it.'

Fred Rolfe, *I Walked By Night,
Being the Life & History of the
King of the Norfolk Poachers*, ed.
Lilias Rider Haggard, 1935

front of the nave, and was noted for his memorable readings. His
mark is here today for all to see: the restoration of the south
porch was funded by him, and the clock, overlooking the fields of
Ditchingham from high up on the tower, was constructed as a memorial
to his son Jock. And it was to this church, after his death on 14 May
1925, that sixty-eight-year-old Sir Rider Haggard's ashes were carried
and laid in the family vault beneath a black marble slab in the chancel.
Having written fifty-eight novels and seven books on social, agricultural
and economic reform, Rider Haggard chose to be remembered as a
'Knight of the British Empire / Who with his humble heart strove to
serve his country'.

After his death, Rider's youngest daughter, **Lilias Rider Haggard**
(1892–1968), continued the family writing tradition. She had travelled

widely with her father in both Egypt and Africa and was awarded an MBE for her nursing duties during the First World War, but uses her deep knowledge of English country life throughout her writings. While her father's fiction is fired mainly by the scorching African sun, Lilias focuses her writing energy closer to home – on the wild and uniquely beautiful landscape around her native Norfolk.

Lilias uses this intimacy in her series of diary and notebook entries first published in the *Eastern Daily Press* and later providing the bulk of the material for her 'Norfolk trilogy': *Norfolk Life* (1943) – edited by **Henry Williamson**, *Norfolk Notebook* (1947) and *Country Scrapbook* (1950). Pieced together with consummate skill and no little literary talent, there can be few better representations of Norfolk country life during this troubled period of English history. Lilias also serves as her father's biographer in *The Cloak That I Left* (1951), a loving and intimate portrait of a complex and fascinating man.

Two of her lesser-known works demonstrate her eminent skills as a biographer and editor of country lore. The manuscript of *I Walked By Night* (1935) – the autobiography of 'local celebrity' Fred Rolfe – was passed on to Lilias by a farmer's wife, in the form of the 'dog-eared and grimy pages' of a 'penny exercise-book'. As Lilias writes in the introduction, working on this tale of the 'King of Norfolk Poachers' was a 'labour of love', partly because 'it is so essentially 'Norfolk' and partly because Rolfe bears a strong resemblance to a similar old poacher from Lilias' childhood.

Through Lilias' scrupulous ordering and sensitive arrangement of the material, *I Walked By Night* breathes life into the country poacher's original voice and touches too upon certain characteristics of ancient Norfolk: 'a breadth, a simplicity and an unhurried dignity about life in these remote villages'.

The second 'country' biography Lilias edited was *The Rabbit Skin Cap* (1939), which is the story of the harsh and sometimes violent life of George Baldry, son of a shoemaker, and his struggle to find steady paid work. Here Lilias continues her earlier themes of rural hardship and injustice and comes as close as any writer to entering the hearts and minds of country folk.

After her father's death, Lilias continued to live on the Ditchingham estate at 'Bath House' and took turns, along with her sister Angela, to stay with their mother at 'Mustard Pot Hall'. Like her father before her, Lilias loved the views out on to the Waveney Valley – her house lying 'in the cup of the wooded slopes' almost touching the banks of the river. Her house overlooked Outney Common, which, 'with its great expanse of marsh and heath, stretches out before my windows, and away into the distance towards Beccles and the sea'. In outward appearance, the house is little changed today, and the Ditchingham estate, woven into the landscape by the curves of the Waveney, still has a wonderfully wild remoteness.

Lilias Rider Haggard is buried alongside her young brother Jock in a grave at the south-east corner of St Mary's churchyard, Ditchingham.

The view across the Waveney towards Outney Common from Bath House, Ditchingham.

There is a great spirit of continuity in this part of Norfolk, and Sir Rider Haggard's 'dynastic sense' would undoubtedly be satisfied to find his estate lands now grown to some 400 acres and farmed by his grandson, Commander Mark Cheyne. Still remembering his grandfather's stern expression but 'heart of gold', Commander Cheyne now lives in the same lodge that is home to Thomas Wingfield in *Montezuma's Daughter*, while he has overseen the careful conversion of 'Mustard Pot Hall' (bearing less 'mustard' lichen today than in former years) into flats. As Bath House became too big for her, Lilias Rider Haggard moved back into one of these flats, and so it was that when she died here in 1968 she ended her life in the house in which she had begun it.

Forncett St Peter

William Wordsworth (1770–1850) suffered the cruel blow of losing his mother before he was eight years old, and his father when he was just thirteen. This left William and his sister **Dorothy Wordsworth** (1771–1855) strongly dependent upon each other. When William left the Lake District for St John's College, Cambridge, Dorothy jumped at the opportunity to move in with their uncle, the Reverend William Cookson, and she arrived at the relative calm and solitude of the rectory at Forncett St Peter in October 1788.

William Wordsworth

The young poet enjoyed extended stays at Forncett in 1789 and 1790.

The rectory still stands today, at the end of a long avenue of lime trees, close to the church with its pre-Conquest tower. The surrounding countryside has barely a roll in the land, but for Dorothy, writing to her friend Jane Pollard that Christmas, it was blissful:

> We are now happily settled at Forncett, and upon a nearer view my prospects appear even more delightful than they did ... we have walked every morning but the two last when it snowed so violently it was impossible to get out ... I often wish for you to walk with me in the garden; my room is one of the pleasantest in the house ... some of the views are very beautiful.

Dorothy Wordsworth

She found herself 'happily settled' at her uncle's rectory here for over five years.

Dorothy lived here for over five years, entering fully into country life, and writing often of her contentment at Forncett. Her brothers Richard, John, and Christopher (who later settled in **Oby***), all visited her at the Cooksons' and she was finally able to meet with her beloved William, who came for extended visits during the summer of 1789 and winter of 1790.

It is unlikely that William, who graduated in 1791, found much at Forncett to rival the scenic splendour of his adored Lake District, but he still felt inspired to write the little-known sonnet 'Sweet was the walk' after his visits to Norfolk:

> Sweet was the walk along the narrow lane
> At noon, the bank and hedge-rows all the way
> Shagged with wild pale green tufts of fragrant hay,
> Caught by the hawthorns from the loaded wain,
> Which Age with many a slow stoop strove to gain;
> And childhood, seeming still most busy, took
> His little rake; with cunning side-long look,
> Sauntering to pluck the strawberries wild, unseen.
> Now, too, on melancholy's idle dreams
> Musing, the lone spot with my soul agrees,
> Quiet and dark; for through the thick wove trees
> Scarce peeps the curious star till solemn gleams
> The clouded moon, and calls me forth to stray
> Thro' tall, green, silent woods and ruins gray.

William had received an offer from his uncle to follow him into a church career, and had certainly considered accepting. Dorothy writes of her anxieties for her twenty-year-old brother in a further letter to Jane Pollard in April 1790: '... he must, when he is three and twenty either go into orders or take pupils ...'

Even contemplating one of England's finest poets becoming another **Parson Woodforde*** is as bizarre as it always was unlikely. However, William's affair with Marie-Anne Vallon in 1792, and the subsequent birth of their daughter brought an abrupt end to these prospects. William never married Annette, and they were soon separated by the

'Sweet was the walk along the narrow lane' – Forncett St Peter, looking towards the old rectory that was once home to Dorothy Wordsworth.

Lindsay Clarke

'The landscape is not only a principal character in the kind of novel I write, it's also the authorising spirit.'

war between England and France. Such was the disapproval of his uncle, that William made no further visits to Forncett thereafter.

Despite the homely convenience of life with the Cooksons, Dorothy continued to miss William dearly, and writing in August 1793, speaks plainly of her '... Impatience to see this dear Brother. It is nearly three years since we parted. It will be exactly three years when we meet again.' It was her love for William and her desire that they be together, as much as her need for independence, that finally led to her departure from Forncett soon after – to make the long journey back to the spiritual home of Romantic poetry.

Gissing

When **Lindsay Clarke** (1939–) came to write his second novel, *The Chymical Wedding* (1989), he found himself drawn back towards this small south Norfolk village, some four miles north of **Diss**, where he had lived during the 1960s. The result is 600 beautifully-crafted pages of a 'grateful tribute to the county where twenty formative years of my adult life were lived'.

So it is that the young poet Alex Darken, self-confessed 'escape-artist of the moral universe', arrives at the fictional village of 'Munding' (a composite portrait of Gissing and **Tuttington**) in the early 1980s – hoping to escape from emotional deception. 'The Pightle' (an obsolete term for enclosure or croft), his publisher's wattle-and-daub cottage in Munding, is where Darken intends to achieve this aim:

> From my bedroom window I could count the towers of four churches. Only they and the scattered spinneys were vertical. All else lay supine – acre after acre of barley and wheat, patched here and there with the yellow dazzle of the mustard fields. Outside The Pightle one was as exposed as the rat flattened to the narrow road by a passing car.

However, when he starts researching into the forebears of the local squire, Ralph Agnew, Alex Darken finds himself drawn inexorably into the past and, 'dropped like a leveret on the run in the middle of the Norfolk deeps', forced to reconsider his own life in the light of what he finds here.

The Chymical Wedding won the 1989 Whitbread Prize for Fiction and is entrenched in the land and lore of Norfolk. When Clarke first came to Norfolk, after teaching for three years in the rain forests of Ghana (a 'landscape without horizons'), the contrast was immediate: 'the air, space and light of Norfolk soared through my senses like an elating gale'. But it was only after Clarke left Norfolk again for Somerset, in 1984, that he was able to 'get enough distance and perspective on the many ways its landscape had illuminated my imagination to write coherently about it'. These qualities of 'air, space and light' are reflected in the interaction of the Norfolk landscape and the characters who inhabit it:

> There has always been something reclusive in the way Munding St Mary's clasps the Norfolk light, and in that it perfectly matched the temperament of Sir Henry Agnew, and the undemanding taste of his daughter, Louisa Anne. For a long time that young woman had been at her window watching the clouds ferry the October light across the sky as though they were the carriers of urgent news ... For three days, since the month had changed, an easterly had fretted among the trees and would not back, but now she sensed a veering in the air, a softness where things had been gritty and bitter before.

More than a century before Alex arrives in Munding, Louisa Agnew and her father are dedicating their lives to solving the mystery of alchemy. 'Easterness', their ancestral home, with its 300-year-old beech trees, crunching beech-mast underfoot and whirring pheasants, is a liberal combination of the Halls at **Blickling, Felbrigg*** and **Mannington**. At the centre of their alchemic endeavours is the thatched 'Decoy Lodge' across the lake, 'sequestered a good half-mile down a gated but unsigned, and unmade-up, woody lane', which Clarke transposes here from **Fritton Lake** on the Somerleyton Estate.

Telling tales – a fifteenth-century pew carving, from St Peter & St Paul, Tuttington. Depicting a griffin killing a local man, this begins a story involving some ten other bench ends: 'The stories were repeated to every generation of Tuttington children until books took their place' (Church Guide).

The 'Chymical' of the title is an obsolete term for 'chemical', with its range of meaning extending to 'wild' and 'fanciful'. *The Chymical Wedding*, a fictional introduction to the Hermetic Art of Alchemy, is all about confusion and doubt, disappointment and madness in the quest for truth and self-knowledge:

> For the Christians the only answer to the human plight was trust in the redemptive love of Christ. For the alchemists such passive dependence was not enough. In every human body, they insisted, there remains a spark of the Divine Principle which once irradiated its entire being. Cased in the base metal of our fallen state, this 'star-fire' yearns to return whence it came. It longs to be golden again. The alchemists maintained that through the correct disciplines such a return might be made. If one knew how to go about it the Fall was reversible. The transmutation of base metal to gold was the paradigm of this sacred task.

When Alex meets the poet hero of his youth, Edward Nesbit – whose character, admits Clarke, 'owes much to **George Barker**'s* manner' – and the equally charismatic potter Laura, his own alchemic quest begins to take shape. Clarke's poetic and compelling novel juxtaposes and 'weds', the present and the mid-nineteenth century past, where the sophisticated Emilia Frere, wife of the newly appointed parson, finds the isolation of Munding a disaster waiting to happen.

The Old Rectory where the Freres live ('a yew-shaded Georgian manse of rosy brick') is based on Gissing's rectory, while the 'Feathers' pub was a 'quiet spit-and-sawdust local' when Lindsay Clarke was here. As the structure of twentieth-century village life in *The Chymical Wedding* changes visibly around him, St Mary's church, with its Saxon round flint tower, represents an 'awesome sense of continuity' to Alex Darken.

The Chymical Wedding – A Romance is indebted, says Clarke, to 'the luminous and airy spirit of a county that I love'. As for Gissing itself, Clarke confesses that it lies 'so deeply sequestered that I had a hard time finding it again when I last went back ... For a while, I wondered whether it was an otherworld place that only appeared periodically like Brigadoon!'

Low Tharston

This tiny hamlet lies just below the main village of Tharston, close to the River Tas which, meandering towards Norwich, splits here into a number of tributaries. One of these cuts would once have driven the wheels of Tharston Mill, which was a working mill making biscuit flour until 1970. The miller lived in The Mill House, the adjacent snug cottage, which is now home to poet, academic and editor **Anthony Thwaite*** (1930–) and his wife, the biographer and children's writer **Ann Thwaite** (1932–).

The Mill House was used part-time in 1972, when Anthony Thwaite was working as Writing Fellow at the **University of East Anglia*** but the couple really planted their Norfolk roots here the following year. One early poetic offering to his new working base was 'The Mill House' and Thwaite readily admits, 'I love the place, and never want to move'. Curiously, Thwaite's writing rarely focuses upon the lush landscape here in the Tas Valley, relying instead on the transience of international travel (British Council work, and regular trips to Japan) and the feelings of being 'an outsider, apart from it all … the slight tension when you know

'… for me the making of poems is both a commemoration (a moment captured) and an excavation (the archaeologist *manqué* side of me digging into something buried and bringing it to light).'

Anthony Thwaite

Anthony and Ann Thwaite outside the door to The Mill House.

Down in the dark water
Where the quick mill-race
　　　　flows,
Something hidden rises,
Something secret goes.

Rising, it flashes whitely.
Going, it sinks below.
You cannot recognise it.
You see the water flow

Quickly under the mill-race,
Race down and reach the
　　　　pond.
Whatever you have seen there
Goes on and out, beyond

Your vision or your
　　　　knowledge,
Untethered to one place.
It glints, and hints, and teases,
And shows you your own face

Peering below the sluice-gate,
Watching the mill-race fall
Forever and forever,
With not a word at all

Of what you saw – or fancied
You saw – rise up and sink
One moment in the water,
The next over the brink.

Anthony Thwaite, 'Gone', from
Selected Poems 1956–1996, 1997

you don't belong' to trigger his poems. 'It's too comfortable here', he says, 'but a marvellous base, a good place to work.'

Nevertheless, there is compelling evidence of the poetic sway of his Norfolk surroundings in such works as 'By the Sluice' from *A Portion for Foxes* (1977). Here, tapping out its rhythms of loss and gain, is the 'morse of water' speaking of memories swept away as everything, metaphorically, becomes water under the bridge: 'What have I hidden here, or let go, lost, / With less to come than's gone, and so much gone? / Under the gate the river slams its door.' These themes of movement and reflection, and Thwaite's flickering visions of something lurking beneath the surface shimmer of life are explored further in 'Gone'.

History is an ongoing concern in Thwaite's work, driven by a lifelong interest in archaeology, and his collection of seventeenth- and eighteenth-century pottery provides tangible evidence of his passion for the past. Thwaite's fascination with these 'sherds' (pieces of common pots) is fuelled by the concept of 'pottery as a guide to human functions'. 'It is all to do with delving', he enthuses, fingering these slivers of history, evoking memories of 'Accumulations', from *The Dust Of The World* (1994): '... it is the accumulation of so many pasts, / So many things written, things made, each so different / They cover the universe with their quiddities.'

His landscapes may be varied, and his poetry thereby subject to a wide range of influences, but Anthony Thwaite still retains a sharp focus on community life here in south Norfolk, where he is strongly involved in parish church, council and charity work.

Literary 'sherds' – the letters, documents and ephemera that evidence people's lives are equally of interest to Thwaite's wife, **Ann Thwaite**, who, as an award-winning biographer, admits to being 'protective' about her subjects. Her studies of Winnie-the-Pooh creator **A A Milne**, **Frances Hodgson Burnett** and **Emily Tennyson**, among others, have all been acclaimed, while she has also published a number of children's books and for twenty years ran a lending library for local children here in Norfolk.

After learning from the Thwaites of the imminent sale of The Granary (the 1950s addition to Tharston Mill), fellow poet **Edwin Brock** (1927–97) and his wife Elizabeth soon found themselves bidding for a move into the neighbourhood. Moving here from nearby Brundall, London-born Brock discovered the existence of a thriving network of writers, as Elizabeth recalls: 'We thought everybody was related to each other when we first arrived!'

Edwin Brock started his career in the police force, but after he left, PC 258 (Brock's police number) moved into the world of advertising. This included a spell with Bensons – the former London employers of **Dorothy L Sayers*** and, like Sayers, Brock evidently found no conflict between his emerging career as a poet and his day job in advertising.

Edwin Brock

'I believe that most activity is an attempt to define oneself in one way or another: for me poetry, and only poetry, has provided this self-defining act.'

Poetry was crucial to the assertion of Brock's identity, as he himself declared and much of his work is autobiographical. Given his working-class background and fine grasp of the complexities of modern life, his confessional style overcomes many of the traditional barriers erected by poetry. 'He knew what appealed to the ordinary person,' says Elizabeth Brock.

With his ability to define the poetic through his everyday surroundings, it was inevitable that Brock would turn to the immediacy of life in the Tas Valley as a source of inspiration for his work. 'He possessed the Tas', laughs Anthony Thwaite, and certainly poems from Brock's *Five Ways To Kill A Man* (1990) collection, such as 'Tas in March' and 'At Home' ('Norfolk breathes and the summer's weed / weaves a green runner going nowhere') seem to confirm this. Whether watching a pair of swans 'taut with sexuality' on the dark river surface, or poking fun at the famed flatness of the landscape ('This is a used country kept flat / by God so that cows can eat it'), Brock revels in his Norfolk environment.

At the time of his death in September 1997, Edwin Brock was 'going through a prolific phase' of writing and his posthumously published collection *And Another Thing* (1998) contains many fine examples of Norfolk-inspired verse. Poems such as 'Convalescing in Cromer' ('You can come this close / to unhappiness and have the landscape / accommodate it'), 'October at Burnham Overy Staithe' ('It is now; the

'Under the gate the river slams its door' – The Mill House (left) a home beside the Tas for Anthony and Ann Thwaite.

By my left eye the landscape is at slack tide: trees and barns barely flowing in a thick swell; soon it will turn, carrying us south on a regular current.

Edwin Brock, from the title poem to *The River and the Train*, 1979.

lowest of low tides: / cabin cruisers capsize upon the ribbed land / and sailing boats in winter wrapping / rattle their chains') and 'Winterton' ('Beachcombing between the season's / limbs to discover / loneliness / or coming off the frost-crisp dunes / rejoicing in ownership') all display a joyous sense of the natural world and Norfolk's local history, coupled with inescapable reminders of the closeness of death and Brock's increasing awareness of his own flagging mortality.

In 'The ghost dancer', Brock aligns himself with his beloved Tas, which barely has the strength to drag itself along. But even though the body is weak, the spirit remains indefatigable:

It is surprising to be here, now,
among these people at the end.
Far away, or so it seems, from
anywhere where anything happened.
The tiny river Tas drags its heels
past our windows, barely able
to push aside the willowherb and reeds.
The swans have flown to deeper water
and one pike has cleared the pond.

Yet it has happened to someone,
as surely as the ghost we saw
that wild autumn evening
dancing downhill beside
my father's grave. It was more real
than any question or belief,
more substantial.
I can still feel the wind in the trees
and the unaccountable silence
waving us away.

None of us wants less than this:
looking over the strands
of history
to one moment of memory
recalled in love.

Poringland

Although 'not a passionate country person', writer and biographer **Adrian Wright** (1947–) has lived in the village of Poringland for twenty-five years. Norfolk 'is where I belong, I suppose', says Wright, a genial mine of information about the county's more obscure literary connections (he toyed briefly with the idea of writing a sequel to **Anthony C Wilson**'s* Norman and Henry Bones teenage detective stories, and still cherishes **Christopher Woodforde**'s* supernatural tales).

Born in **Thorpe St Andrew**, Wright started out in the theatre, mainly on the **Norwich*** circuit, and has worked as a boy actor and a writer for Anglia TV, as well as directing a Victorian musical and writing a set of theatre sketches for the Maddermarket Theatre, **Norwich***. Despite his affection for less mainstream ventures ('I have always loved flops', he laughs self-deprecatingly, 'and cast-iron flop writers'), Wright's real commercial success came with the biographies of American film stars such as Arnold Schwarzenegger and Kevin Costner, allowing him to leave his day-job at Norfolk County Library after twenty-nine years.

'Hugely interested in British writers' ('For two years I spoke like characters from **Ivy Compton-Burnett*** – which was probably why I never had any friends'), Wright's latest biography is *John Lehmann – A Pagan Adventure* (1998). It was watching a TV programme on **L P Hartley***, that 'started me off on a quest' and ended in his writing the acclaimed biography *Foreign Country* (1996). Hartley's **Hunstanton*** suited Wright's fascination with run-down seaside towns perfectly – 'I love **Cromer*** and **Yarmouth***', he says, humming a forgotten Edwardian song, 'When you come to the end of a perfect day', written on Cromer cliffs.

Adrian Wright

Biographer and chronicler of Norfolk's more obscure literary past.

Redenhall

For playwright **Arnold Wesker*** (1932–), the fields of Norfolk were a world apart from the East End of London where he had been raised: 'The land was flat flat flat. Huge skies lorded over the landscape dictating what would be seen and not seen.'

Having joined his sister Della and her husband at their farmhouse in nearby **Long Stratton**, Wesker worked at a variety of jobs before joining the Bell Hotel in **Norwich***. It was here that he met his future wife, Dusty, whose family lived at Beck Farm, Redenhall. Experiencing work as a farm labourer – bending in the sugar beet fields beside seasoned farm-hands, hauling heavy sacks of seeds – presented Wesker with a different perspective, a different pace of life and the possibilities of entirely new dramatic material.

Arnold Wesker

His plays capture the 'slow pace of pause and silence in Norfolk rural life'.

Freed from much of the tension that strangled his earlier writing, and fired up by the success of *Chicken Soup with Barley* (1958), Wesker settled down here in 1958 to write his 'Norfolk play'. Based in the familiar territory of his future in-laws' family home, *Roots* not only has settings in Norfolk rural locales, but also uses the Bicker family and their friends as models for the stage characters.

Roots, successfully taken to the stage in May 1959, draws upon the 'expansive landscape ... the craggy personalities of the farm labourers, and the gorgeous Norfolk dialect with which I fell in love and was to use in four plays.' It also tackles the destructive powers and dilemmas of relationships and a fundamental inability to communicate, wrapped within the hardship, tedium and indifference of rural family life.

'But don't you come pushin' ideas across at us – we're all right as we are.'

Arnold Wesker, *Roots*, 1959

When 'Beatie' (inspired by Dusty) returns home from London, she realises what it is she lacks: 'I come from a family o' farm labourers yet I ent got no roots'. Yet it is Beatie whose vitality, spirit and desire to learn eventually enable her to break through the barriers of mundanity so firmly erected in the 'Bryant' family home. Her anger is directed at her mother in particular: 'You live in the country but you got no – no – no majesty'. Despite her rejection by 'Ronnie Khan' (based upon Wesker himself), Beatie becomes a stronger person by surviving her family's prejudices and by confronting the 'roots' of her own problems.

Wesker admits that 'what I was as excitedly eager to capture as much as anything was the slow pace of pause and silence in Norfolk rural life'. For a stage drama, it was a risky venture and needed careful rehearsing and co-ordination, while the Norfolk dialect presented genuine difficulties for the cast. Although *Roots* had been commissioned by the Royal Court theatre in London, they initially turned down the material which Wesker then took to Coventry, the scene of his first stage success with *Chicken Soup with Barley*. The play received some excellent reviews and went on to play in London later that year, while *I'm Talking about Jerusalem*, also with a Norfolk setting and Norfolk influences, appeared in 1960.

The Wesker Trilogy combines *Chicken Soup with Barley* with the two 'Norfolk' plays in a powerfully autobiographical portrayal of Wesker's own life and love. His relationship with his own family, and his feelings for Dusty were as complex and tortuous as his stage dramas, while Wesker was to share in his sister's sense of 'cultural isolation' in the beautiful but often difficult location of rural south Norfolk.

Cathedral City

Norwich

For centuries, Norwich has served as a spiritual and artistic capital for Norfolk, a major centre of commerce, and a market place for the county's agricultural produce. Norwich's early trading links were firmly focused on the fluctuating fortunes of the illustrious wool, weaving and silk trades, and the influx of the 'Strangers' (largely refugee Dutch and French weavers) in the sixteenth century helped to forge a reputation for religious tolerance, dissent and independence maintained to this day.

An exact contemporary of **Geoffrey Chaucer***, at a time when the gulf between the Church's preaching and practice was gaping wide, **Julian** or **Juliana** (*c*.1342–1413) was a mystic recluse whose anchorite's cell could be found at the small church of **St Julian's**, in what is today **St Julian's Alley** (between King Street and Rouen Road). In Julian's day the city was benefiting from a brisk wool trade with the Continent, but this was also the time of the Hundred Years War, the Black Death and the Peasants' Revolt.

Not much is known of Julian's life, certainly not her real name or family history, though she was probably educated by Benedictine nuns at Carrow Abbey (whose ruins and the rebuilt Prioress' house are in

Julian of Norwich

'He said not "Thou shalt not be tempested, thou shalt not be travailed, thou shalt not be distressed", but he said: "Thou shalt not be overcome."'

XVI Revelations of Divine Love – the first book known to be written by a woman in English.

The tiny anchorite's cell in St Julian's Church (rebuilt), off Rouen Road – Julian of Norwich spent the last forty years of her life here.

Bracondale Road). However, during a period of severe illness Julian's life was transformed by the divine 'revelations' she experienced on Sunday, 8 March 1373, witnessed by both her mother and a curate. Three years later, Julian retreated to her cell, adopted the name of the chapel in which she was to spend the rest of her life and settled down to a life of contemplation and worship.

Writing in her *XVI Revelations of Divine Love* (first published 1670), Julian describes what she was 'shown' in the sixteen revelations, followed by a summary of her thoughts and feelings, her responses to God, and her conclusions on the meaning of each revelation. Through a sometimes cryptic text requiring patience and close study, Julian's *Revelations* depict an image of a 'courteous' and 'homely' God of love quite unusual for the time, and also offer tangible images – such as that of the bleeding of Christ crucified:

> Those three images came to me at that time. The drops were round like pellets in coming out of the head, and like herring scales in spreading out on the forehead; in their unnumerable plenty, they were like raindrops falling from the eaves.

Julian's chapel survived the centuries, but couldn't survive the bombs of the Second World War and subsequently had to be rebuilt, incorporating the original roughcast stones. It is assumed that she would have participated in the liturgy through a small 'squint' in the wall and given counsel and received alms through another window, though neither of them was preserved by the reconstruction. The only visitor here to have left a written account is fellow 'mystic' **Margery Kempe*** whose *The Book of Margery Kempe* (c.1436) relates how 'Dame Jelyan' preaches patience and calm, counselling Margery to 'fear not the language of the world, for the more despite, shame and reproof that ye have in the world, the more is your merit in the sight of God'.

John Skelton* (?1460–1529) mourns the destructive work of two terrible fires in *Lament for the City of Norwich* (1507): 'All life is brief, and frail all man's estate. / City, farewell: I mourn thy cruel fate.' Almost 500 years later, on the morning of 1 August 1994, another fire dealt a cruel blow to the city's literary heritage when the County Library was gutted and many valuable documents went up in smoke.

The site of the old Carmelite Friary is now occupied by Jarrold's printing museum near **Whitefriars Bridge** and it was here that playwright **John Bale** (1495–1563) was educated. Bale went on to become an avowed Protestant and a vigorous supporter of the English Reformation. Enjoying the patronage of Thomas Cromwell, Bale wrote several anti-Catholic plays for Cromwell's troupe of itinerant players between 1537 and the Lord Protector's fall in 1540. In the writing of *King John*, Bale is credited with directing the morality play towards the historical play. King John (unlike **Shakespeare**'s*) is portrayed as an idealised Christian hero battling with the Pope and the whole 'heap of adders of Antichrist's generation'.

Although **Thomas Deloney** (?1560–1600) is remembered chiefly as a writer of broadside ballads, it was his prose works that contributed much to the development of the English novel. Working and travelling as a silk-weaver (**Thomas Nashe*** called him the 'balletting silk-weaver of Norwich'), Deloney depicted the ordinary lives of those working in the trades and crafts of middle-class Elizabethan England. The realism of his work – in contrast to the gallant romances and classic legends so popular at that time – is evidenced in *Jack of Newberie*, *Thomas of Reading*, and *The Gentle Craft*, published between 1597 and 1600, which deal with weaving, clothing and shoemaking respectively.

As a craftsman and an artisan, writing for other artisans, Deloney succeeded primarily because he wrote of what he knew. By flavouring such 'ordinariness' with local tradition and history, effective dialogue and occasionally a touch of adventure and romance, Deloney's works found immediate success though he is said to have 'died poorly'.

Writing in his autobiographical *The Life of Tusser* (1573), the influential agricultural writer and poet **Thomas Tusser** (?1524–80) reaches a city which has survived a recession and re-established its reputation as the weaving and cloth capital of Britain – and seen off Robert Kett's rebellion in 1549. Arriving 'At Norwich fine, for me and mine, / a citie trim', Tusser finds Norwich well suited for the rich: 'Where strangers wel may seeme to dwel / That pitch and pay, or keepe their day'. But Tusser also warns: 'But who that want, shall find it scant / so good for him.' With poverty still a major problem, and embarrassment (beggars were banned in Norwich between 1570 and 1580), Tusser seems relieved when finally departing the city:

> From Norwich aire, in great despaire,
> Away to flie, or else to die,
> To seeke more heelth, to seeke more welth, then was I glad.

Four years later, Tusser's seminal work *Hundreth good pointes of husbandrie* (1577) was published, containing versified advice on farming, housekeeping, gardening, and on general conduct, gleaned from years of work on his farm.

The dramatist, poet and pamphleteer **Robert Greene** (*c*.1558–92) condemned Deloney for being 'popular' and for producing 'trivial trinkets and threadbare trash'. However, Greene, who was born in the city and attended the **Grammar School** (founded in 1250 and later re-founded by Edward VI), rarely had a kind word for anyone. After completing his education and travels abroad, Greene returned to

'There's an upstart crow, beautified with our feathers, that, with his tyger's heart wrapt in a player's hide, supposes that he is as well able to trumpet out blank verse as the best of you ... in his owne conceit, the only Shake-scene in a countrey.'

Robert Greene on the up-and-coming Shakespeare in *Greene's Groat's-Worth of Witte*, 1592

England to marry and settle in Norwich. Witty, vain and briefly brilliant, Greene's notoriety is largely of his own making; his 'repentance' pamphlets setting out the failings of his character and indicative of his need to be acknowledged.

Despite being a voluminous writer, Greene's work is today almost forgotten. At the time, his avalanche of romances, tracts and dialogues were at the forefront of a revolution in theatre-going and delighted the literary public. However, Greene is perhaps best remembered for his audacious attack on Shakespeare in his autobiographical prose tract *Greene's Groat's-Worth of Witte* (1592), the first known reference to Shakespeare as a – non-graduate – London dramatist.

'I, otherwise called Caulaliero Kemp, head-master of Morrice-dancers, high Head-borough of heighs, and onely tricker of your Trill-lilles and best belshangles between Sin and mount Surrey, began frolickly to foot it from the right honourable the Lord Mayors of London towards the right worshipfull (and truely bountifull) Master Mayors of Norwich.'

William Kemp, *Kemps Nine Daies Wonder*, 1600

A few years after Greene's death, Norwich became the finishing point for the legendary exploits of comic actor and dancer **William Kemp** (*c*.1549-*c*.1603), whose nine-day morris-dance had begun in London. One of Shakespeare's leading clowns, Kemp seems to have been persuaded by the closing of the theatres in the capital and his altercation with Shakespeare to take on this Lent-time bet, recorded in *Kemps Nine Daies Wonder* (1600).

After morris-dancing for 125 miles, Kemp arrives in Norwich: 'Passing by the Market place, the presse still increasing by the number of boyes, girles, men and women, thronging more and more before me to see the end ...' Eventually, the pressure of the crowd in Holter Lane (**Dove Street**) becomes so great that Kemp leaps over the churchyard wall of **St John Maddermarket** and takes a short cut to the mayor's house, where he is received with due ceremony and awarded a reception in the **Guild Hall**. Predictably, Kemp encounters difficulties trying to collect his winnings on his way back to London.

> **Richard Corbet(t)** (1582–1635), Bishop of Norwich in 1632, was noted for his verse and ballads and in particular for 'A Proper New Ballad, entitled The Fairies Farewell', beginning 'Farewell, rewards and fairies' and lamenting the decline of folk-mythology under Puritanism. The seventeenth-century biographer and antiquary **John Aubrey** describes him as a lively character, who used to take off his episcopal hat ('There lies the Dr') and gown ('There lyes the bishop') in preparation for drinking sessions with his chaplain. While in office, Corbet quarrelled with the 'strangers' of Norwich and banned them from his chapel in 1634.

The author of the first record of Norfolk dialect and of the first treatise on archaeology in English, Thomas Browne was also Norfolk's first scientific ornithologist. Browne kept a pet eagle for two years, feeding him 'whelpes cattes ratts', while he noted that bustards – now extinct – were 'not unfrequent in the champain and feildie part of this country a large Bird accounted a dayntie dish'.

The physician, philosopher, antiquarian and naturalist **Sir Thomas Browne** (1605–82) set up his medical practice here in 1636. Marrying a girl from **North Burlingham**, Browne made Norwich his home until his death on his seventy-seventh birthday. If the bronze statue of Browne (1905) on the **Hay Hill** side of St Peter Mancroft could raise its head, it would be looking at the site of the **Haymarket** house where Browne lived for thirty-two years. The house was demolished in 1842, and all that remains of it is the ornately carved oak overmantel from its drawing-room now displayed in the **Castle Museum**.

It may be hard for modern readers to comprehend why Browne has often headed the county's literary roll of honour. Called 'obscure but gorgeous' by **Charles Lamb**, 'a crack'd Archangel' by **Herman Melville** and 'one of our greatest stylists' by **John Cowper Powys***, Browne's science, even in his own day, was charming but outdated; had he come across a dragon breathing fire through the streets of Norwich, he would no doubt have remained unsurprised. Nevertheless, his unique and humorous writing style, combining pertinent observation of the natural with an imaginative vision of the supernatural, is endowed with an unquenchable thirst for knowledge.

Sir Thomas Browne

'But who knows the fate of his bones, or how often he is to be buried?' In 1840, Browne's coffin, buried close to his marble memorial in the chancel of St Peter Mancroft was accidentally disturbed and his skull and coffin plate removed. After an intermezzo at the Norfolk and Norwich Hospital Museum and the taking of a few plaster casts for study, the skull was finally reinterred in 1922.

> ... since the heaviest stone that melancholy can throw at a man is to tell him he is at the end of his nature, Browne scrutinizes that which escaped annihilation for any sign of the mysterious capacity for transmigration he has so often observed in caterpillars and moths.
>
> W G Sebald, *The Rings of Saturn*, 1998

A fervent Royalist in the staunchly Parliamentarian environment of Norwich, Browne was knighted by Charles II during a visit to the city in 1671. Even the Civil War made little impact on Browne's work from his Norwich retreat; busying himself in his garden, tending to his patients in all four corners of the county, researching and writing his books. In his spare time, Browne – said to be of a kindly disposition, modest and blushing easily – collected nettles in **Gorleston***, hunted fossils at **Winterton***, and counted herrings at **Yarmouth*** ('an herring for every man in England').

Thomas Browne paired a love of science and archaeology with a writer's eye for detail and a poet's touch. *Vulgar Errors* (1646) is a fascinating and, with the benefit of hindsight, often hilarious collection of obscure legend and learning. *Religio Medici* (1643) is a philosophical and, for the time, unusually tolerant study of religion in which Browne reconciles the seemingly diametrically opposed elements of religion and science. However, it is *Urn Burial* (1658), a meditation on funeral procedures displaying rhythmical prose and rich diction, which remains perhaps his best-loved work. Here we see Browne standing in a field in **Walsingham*** looking past the recently ruined priory as his diggers unearth the 'sad sepulchral pitchers'.

John Evelyn

The diarist visited Thomas Browne in 1671 and delighted in 'this antient Citty'.

Browne corresponded with another Royalist – traveller, writer and diarist **John Evelyn** (1620–1706), who visited Norwich in 1671 and delighted in 'this antient Citty, being one of the largest, and certainly (after London) one of the noblest of England, for its venerable Cathedrall, number of Stateley Churches, Cleanesse of the streetes; and

Sir Thomas Browne's statue on Hay Hill, close to St Peter Mancroft, where he is buried.

buildings of flint, so exquisitely headed and Squared, as I was much astonish'd at'. Evelyn had overnighted in the Ducal Palace (once the largest house outside London, but in semi-ruins by the time Celia Fiennes saw it in 1698, and eventually demolished in 1711) and arrived exhausted after listening to the Duke of Norfolk argue all night with his carpenter about the dimensions of a room!

Evelyn notes with interest his host's 'whole house and Garden being a Paradise and Cabinet of rarities, and that of the best collection, especially medals, books, plants and natural things'. A great friend of **Samuel Pepys** and a close adviser to King Charles II ('An excellent Prince doubtlesse had he been lesse addicted to women'), Evelyn's six-volume *Diary* (only published in full in 1955) chronicles the remarkable events of a century that saw England transform itself into a major world power, with Norwich sharing in this growing economic prosperity.

An admirer of Norwich's architecture, especially the Ducal Palace and the Cathedral, was **Thomas Fuller** (1608–61), author of several deeply researched, well-structured and entertaining historical and biographical works. *The Holy and Profane State* (1642) had already confirmed Fuller's reputation as a leading literary light before the Civil War interrupted his work. Despite his popularity and moderate views, his challenging sermons and chaplaincy with Royalist forces inevitably led to difficulties. Unable to preach, and with his property confiscated, Fuller turned his energies towards his writing and among other works produced the immense and much-celebrated *Church History* (1656), as well as the equally famous *The Worthies of England* (1662) in which he speaks highly of Norwich. Noting the city's flourishing flower trade – 'a flower is the best-complexioned grass, as a pearl is the best-coloured clay' – Fuller goes on to describe Norwich as:

> ... either a city in an orchard, or an orchard in a city, so equally are houses and trees blended in it, so that the pleasure of the country and the populousness of the city meet here together. Yet in this mixture, the inhabitants participate nothing of the rusticalness of the one, but altogether of the urbanity and civility of the other.

The Worthies, an early form of travel guide to England, was published just a few months after Fuller's death in 1661. Although he died one of the most popular writers of his time, his reputation waned, and **Coleridge** later remarked that: 'wit was the stuff and substance of Fuller's intellect'.

Norwich's reputation for liberal ideas and dissent was already established by the time **Celia Fiennes** (1662–1741) visited in 1698. Perhaps confusing the downward walk from the castle hill with the city's proud tradition of Non-conformism, Fiennes records in her journal that 'a great many Descenters are in this Citty'. The daughter of a Cromwellian colonel and herself an ardent Non-conformist, Celia Fiennes travelled throughout England between 1685 and 1710, and her travel journals, which were only much later published in full as *The Journeys of Celia Fiennes* (1947), provide a remarkable picture of seventeenth-century Britain. Her accounts remain, however, strictly observational and provide little insight into the character of a woman who, often accompanied only by servants, made difficult and strenuous journeys.

Fiennes' visit to Norfolk was part of her 'Great Journey' of 1698, which took her as far north as Carlisle and as far south as Penzance. She

'The suburbs are large, the prospecte sweete, and other amenities, not omiting the flower-gardens, which all the Inhabitants excell in of this Citty, the fabric of stuffs, which affords the Merchants, and brings a vast trade to this populous Towne.'

John Evelyn, *Diary*, 1641–97 – first published 1818.

Little is known of Celia Fiennes, but a Norwich Lieutenant describes her as 'a light and sprightly Mademoiselle' who, 'fear'd not to ride in the darke' but who 'would be sure to be always on the front and a file leader, and to leave a whole cloud of choking dust behind her ...'

' ... the inhabitants being all busie at their manufactures, dwell in their garrets at their looms, and in their combing-shops, so they call them, twisting-mills, and other work-houses; almost all the works they are employ'd in, being done within doors.'

Daniel Defoe, *Tour of the Whole Island of Great Britain*, 1724

was impressed by the size of the city, noting: 'On the Castle hill you see the whole Citty at once, being built round it, its a vast place and takes up a large tract of ground ... 6 miles in compass.' Fiennes describes a city 'walled full round of towers, except on the river side which serves for the wall; they seeme the best in repair of any walled citty I know'. She notes the thirty-six churches, 'to be seen in a clear day altogether', herself counting thirty visible from the castle walls, though nothing remains of the castle except 'a green space', 'built all of flints ... which makes them look blackish and shineing'.

Fiennes travels through 'very clean and many very broad streetes' (no battle with the one-way systems and traffic congestion in those days) and records that three times a year were the 'great faires ... to which resort a vast concourse of people and wares a full trade'. Norwich, says Fiennes, looks exactly what it is, 'a rich thriveing industrious place', full of weaving, spinning, knitting and dyeing.

> Among the 'Descenters' of Georgian times, and a member of the 'Norwich coterie', was the writer and translator **William Taylor** (1765–1836), son of a Norwich manufacturer, whose revolutionary fervour was matched only by his capacity for drink. One of the few German scholars of his time, Taylor translated **Lessing**'s *Nathan the Wise* and wrote the influential *Historic Survey of German Poetry* (1828–30), as well as teaching **George Borrow*** the language. Taylor lies buried in the churchyard behind the **Octagon Chapel** in **Colegate**.

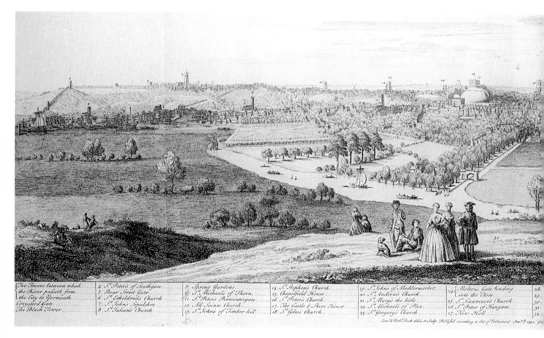

Two Towers between which the River passeth from the City to Yarmouth. | 4. St Peter's of Southgate. | 9. Spring Gardens. | 14. St Stephens Church. | 19. St John's of Maddermarket. | 24. Metcus Gate leading | 28.
Conesford Gate. | 5. Bear Street Gate. | 10. St Michaels of Thorn. | 15. Chapelfield House. | 20. St Andrews Church. | into the Close. | 29.
The Black Tower. | 6. St Etheldreds Church. | 11. St Peters Permontergate. | 16. St Peters Church. | 21. St Marys the late. | 25. St Lawrences Church. | 30.
 | 7. St Johns Sepulchre. | 12. All Saints Church. | 17. The Castle & Shire House. | 22. St Michaels of Plea. | 26. St Peter of Hungate. | 31.
 | 8. St Julians Church. | 13. St Johns of Timber-hill. | 18. St Giles Church. | 23. St Gregory's Church. | 27. New Hall. |

Robert Southey (1774–1843) once described Taylor as 'a young man of fortune, much diffidence, much genius, & very uncommon acquirements'. Although he later revised this to a rather less favourable assessment, Southey's visits to Taylor's home in **21 Upper King St** (rebuilt) and later **Surrey Street** marked the beginning of a real friendship. Taylor also provided Southey with an introduction to Norwich's radical set, which included **Dr Frank Sayers** (the author of poetical works on Northern mythologies), and Southey noted: 'Sedition there is in plenty in the circle to which I have been introduced.'

Poet laureate in 1813, Southey maintained his Norfolk connections with his *Life and Works of William Cowper* (1835–37) and *The Life of Nelson* (1813). Southey showed tacit approval of Norfolkman **Thomas Paine**'s* revolutionary views, but later withdrew his support of radical **William Cobbett**, describing him as 'poison'. Cobbett's response, at the time of the French Revolution, and hoping for similar reform in Britain, was to recommend that Southey be executed 'as one of the first acts of Radical Government'. Southey survived, but today is a much-neglected figure, to the extent that even his name (pronounced, as **Byron** joked, to rhyme with 'mouthey') is mispronounced.

Robert Southey

A regular visitor to Norwich, he wrote of a Norfolk countryside 'I connect with all those associations that soften & amend & elevate the heart'.

One of Southey's Norwich friends was the socialite, novelist and inexhaustible letter-writer **Amelia Opie** (1769–1853), whose birthplace stands opposite St George's Church in Colegate. Born Amelia Alderson, Opie was an unusual child who developed into a most unusual woman, a skilled conversationalist and sentimental novelist. Opie's life was also inextricably linked with the Gurney family at **Earlham**, to whom she

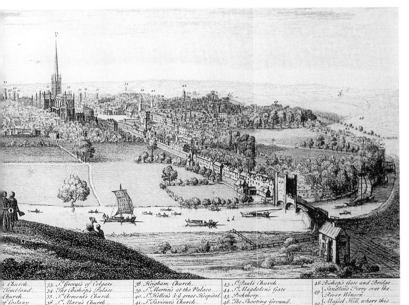

Prospect of Norwich from the south-east, 1741

'... either a city in an orchard or an orchard in a city, so equally are houses and trees blended in it, so that the pleasure of the country and the populousness of the city meet here together. Yet in this mixture, the inhabitants participate nothing of the rusticalness of the one, but altogether of the urbanity and civility of the other.'

Thomas Fuller, *The Worthies of England*, 1662

The Octagon Chapel in Colegate Street – This was the meeting house visited by Amelia Opie, Harriet Martineau and the Norwich coterie. A century later, when young Ralph Mottram attended, locals still referred to it as 'The Devil's Cucumber Frame'.

was close from childhood, while her love of her home city 'grew with her growth and developed with her strength'. Her literary career started young – with a couple of plays and a novel, *The Dangers of Coquetry*, written when she was eighteen. After her marriage in 1798 to John Opie, a Cornish painter (sometimes called 'the English Rembrandt'), the couple moved into a house on the corner of Devil's Alley (now **Opie Street**) and **Castle Meadow**.

It was here that Amelia took up her pen again to write the touching *Father and Daughter* (1801), a tale about virtue led astray and familial reconciliation and *Poems* (1802). More significant is *Adeline Mowbray* (1804), a fascinating exploration of a mother-daughter relationship (prompted by the tragic story of her feminist friend **Mary Wollstonecraft**) which remains just as relevant today as it was at the time. 'What is interesting about this novel, is that it makes no moral

Editha Woodville 'had a decided passion for literature, ... acquired from a sister of Mr Woodville, who had been brought up amongst literary characters of various pursuits and opinions; and this lady had imbibed from them a love of free inquiry, which she had little difficulty in imparting to her young and enthusiastic relation'.

Amelia Opie,
Adeline Mowbray, 1804

judgements', writes **Jeanette Winterson** in her introduction to the 1985 edition; '*Adeline Mowbray* deals with sex in a frank and unself-conscious manner, assuming that desire causes women as well as men to jeopardise their futures and override their families' wishes.'

After her husband's death in 1807, Amelia Opie returned to live in her father's house in Colegate. Her romantic novels continued to be very successful, and soon Opie, with her auburn hair and sparkling grey eyes, was not only a queen of provincial Norwich society, but also of the capital. Most of her life Opie divided her time between those two cities; breakfasting with **Sir Walter Scott** (her first novel moved him to tears), meeting **William Wordsworth*** (whom she found disappointing) and becoming friends with **Richard Brinsley Sheridan** and **Madame de Staël**.

Amelia Opie

The novelist and letter-writer moved freely between the quiet religiosity of Norwich's Quaker community and the social whirl of the capital.

Opie became a traveller oscillating between the world of dinner parties and dancing soirées and the Quaker world of introspection and quiet religiosity. Her inherent kindness, loyalty and upright spirit enabled her to walk freely between the two worlds, her prolific letters ensuring that she never lost touch with either of them. Although Opie herself admits to being a 'Strange, inconsistent being ... now walking along the Streets on the arm of a plain Quaker, now leaning on that of a volatile Viscount', her family loyalty remained strong and she never abandoned the bond of friendship that linked her to the Gurneys, especially to Joseph John, 'My dear Monitor', nineteen years her junior. Her novels, however, came to suffer from a certain predictability and the author herself was satirized by **Thomas Love Peacock** in *Headlong Hall* (1816) as 'Miss Poppyseed ... an indefatigable compounder of novels'.

Peacock was probably as surprised as anyone when Mrs Opie took the decision in 1825, after much soul-searching, to become a 'Plain' Friend and to adhere to the strict code of Quaker conduct. Grey gowns and a Quaker bonnet tied under the chin replaced her colourful dresses and with novel-writing now out of the question, all that the admirer of Scott and **Dickens*** produced for publication were dull and didactic works of tract literature.

In 1847, after living in **Lady Lane** for a while, Amelia moved into a Georgian mansion in Castle Meadow. Apart from the fact that the Castle contained the new prison, her view was a pleasant one of 'my noble trees and my castle turrets rising above them', and it was here that she received her fellow Norfolk author **George Borrow***.

About a year before she died, Opie, an inveterate traveller, went for one last visit to her favourite seaside and holiday resort of **Cromer**. When she returned, with a cold but 'more enamoured of Cromer than ever', she was carried upstairs, never to come downstairs again. At the age of eighty-five, Amelia Opie, possibly the most vivid Quaker ever to have walked the streets of Norwich, was laid to rest in the burial ground alongside the Friends' Meeting House in **Quakers Lane**.

At the age of nearly eighty, Amelia Opie, still composing at least six letters every morning, considered 'dead of letter-writing. A. Opie' as a suitable epitaph for herself.

George Borrow

Standing outside of the Victorian Establishment, Norfolk's 'Romany Rye' was an inveterate traveller with a working knowledge of at least sixteen different languages.

Writing in 1900, the Rev. Augustus Jessopp, later headmaster at the same Norwich Grammar School that Borrow so loathed, criticises Borrow for his lack of imagination: 'The fact is that Borrow, if he set himself to write any story for love or money, could only draw upon his memory, and only did so.'

'Borrow House' in Willow Lane – the home from which young George Borrow was able to explore the city.

At different times of his life, Norwich was home to **George Borrow*** (1803–81) – the 'Romany Rye' (meaning 'Gypsy Gentleman' or more specifically 'One, not a Gypsy, who loves the race and has mastered the tongue'). *The Romany Rye* (1857) was Borrow's second autobiographical work and formed the sequel to *Lavengro* (1851), which praises Norwich as:

> ... a fine old city, perhaps the most curious specimen at present extant of the genuine old English Town ... There it spreads from north to south, with its venerable houses, its numerous gardens, its thrice twelve churches, its mighty mound, which, if tradition speaks true, was raised by human hands to serve as the grave heap of an old heathen king, who sits deep within it, with his sword in his hand and his gold and silver treasures about him. There is an old grey castle on top of that mighty mound; and yonder, rising three hundred feet above the soil, from among those noble forest trees, behold that old Norman master-work, that cloud-enriched cathedral spire around which a garrulous army of rooks and choughs continually wheel their flight. Now, who can wonder that the children of that fine old city are proud of her, and offer up prayers for her prosperity?

Borrow's father was an army man, and it is possible that Borrow may have been born in his temporary quarters in the city (at a house in Pound Street – now the Co-op store in **Norwich Street**). More certain is that in 1816, the family returned to Norwich and rented a house in **Willow Lane**, and the two-storey 'Borrow House', still stands peacefully, if unspectacularly, today.

For three years, the young George Borrow enjoyed the relative luxury of unchanging surroundings, sharing an attic room with his brother John and attending **Norwich Grammar School**, then called King Edward VI Grammar School, in **Cathedral Close**. Its harsh discipline was not to the moody, dreamy Borrow's liking, and his great appetite for learning was equalled by his loathing for the school regime. He left in 1819, at his father's suggestion, to become articled to Simpson & Rackham, a law firm whose offices were in nearby Tuck's Court, off **St Giles Street**.

Though lodging with the Simpsons in a house in **Upper Close**, near **Tombland**, Borrow's infamous waywardness soon saw him spending more time learning foreign languages than studying law. He was taught German by **William Taylor***, whose anti-establishment attitudes and radical politics appealed to a young George Borrow now burning with a desire to travel. This desire was further fuelled by a meeting with travelling folk during one of his many long walks on the heathland and countryside surrounding the city.

At the Romany encampment in 'a small valley between two hills or downs, the sides of which were covered with furze', Borrow's quick-wittedness and desire to learn the Romany language impresses his new friends and even earns Borrow – the 'Lavengro', the 'Word-master' – his own song. Borrow's fascination with Romany life and his great respect for gypsy heritage and tradition was to be no passing phase. After completing his legal apprenticeship, Borrow left Norwich in 1824 and remained a 'wanderer' for much of his life, sharing the gypsy ability to disappear and reappear and at will.

Harriet Martineau

Although she once sat in the Octagon Chapel 'looking for angels', the novelist and social reformer later repudiated all religious belief.

Charles Dickens* visited the city early in 1849, no doubt lured by the recent 'Rush' murders at nearby **Stanfield Hall**. Twelve years later, Dickens rather unsuccessfully commenced his British reading tour here, feeling that the Norwich spectators 'were not magnetic'.

Following in his footsteps was **Anthony Trollope***, who sets parts of his 'Norfolk' novel *Can You Forgive Her?* (1864–5) in **The Close**, where the widowed Mrs Greenow is lodging. Hovering outside are her two suitors, Cheesacre and Bellfield, who both hope to obtain her hand in marriage – and the substantial fortune that goes with it.

When Borrow found employment with the Bible Society, nobody was more amused than social campaigner and writer **Harriet Martineau** (1802–76) who had known him 'in his Norwich days.' Martineau was the daughter of a Norwich manufacturer of Huguenot descent. She was born at **Gurney Court**, and, plagued by ill health and deafness nearly all her life, grew up in the large 'prosaic' Georgian house opposite at

Mousehold Heath *c.*1810 by John Sell Cotman – of the vast sixteenth-century common explored by George Borrow, once reaching as far as the Norfolk Broads, only some 180 acres of wood and heathland remain today.

31 Gurney Court – birthplace of Harriet Martineau and prison reformer Elizabeth Fry – a 'perfect example of a Norwich back court' (**Pevsner**).

Norwich School, 1819 – Horatio Nelson, John Sell Cotman, **George Borrow***, **James Blyth***, and, more recently, **D J Taylor*** were all pupils here.

24 Magdalen Street. In her *Autobiographical Memoir* (1877) Martineau recalls the 'little garden under the North wall', from which she and the other children tried to dig a hole big enough to get through to the other side of the globe:

> When we found our little spades would not dig through the globe, nor even through the brickbats, we altered our schemes. We lengthened the hole to our own length, having an extreme desire to know what dying was like. We lay down alternately in this grave, and shut our eyes, and fancied ourselves dead, and told one another our feelings when we came out again. As far as I can remember, we fully believed that we now knew all about it.

A devout Unitarian in her youth, Martineau commenced her writing career in Norwich with moral tales for children (*Devotional Exercises* was her first published work in 1823) after which she progressed to a political study, *Illustrations of Political Economy* (1832–4), and moved to London. Martineau's subsequent abolitionist campaign in America sparked *Society in America* (1837), after which she published her first novel, *Deerbrook* (1839) in which she compares town life with the joys of country living (fishing, walking and gathering cowslips) in the pretty village of Deerbrook. Her writing continued to be varied, with adventure stories sitting alongside translations of **Auguste Comte**'s work and, as she became a radical critic of religion, the anti-theological *Laws of Man's Social Nature* (1851). Her *Biographical Sketches* (1869) and the

posthumously published *Autobiographical Memoir* contain perspicacious and illuminating essays on her fellow Norwich writers such as **Amelia Opie*** and **William Taylor***.

> Noted for his studies of East Anglian history, **Augustus Jessopp** (1824–1914) was Head of Norwich School for twenty years between 1859 and 1879 before moving to **Scarning*** as rector. Under his direction, Norwich School flourished and increased in numbers from a mere thirty to 120 pupils. It was here that Jessopp spent fifteen years researching and writing *One Generation of a Norfolk House* about the Jesuit Father Henry Walpole, a member of the famous local family.

The now-forgotten author of popular poems for children, **Mary Sewell** (1797–1884), lived from 1867 up to her death at **125 Spixworth Road, Old Catton**. In the 'White House' (actually built in red brick), Mary Sewell wrote poems for children and ballads, her sympathies always lying with the poor working woman. Her *Mother's Last Words* sold over a million copies, and her attitude to language reflects the simplicity to which the Quaker family aspired in all walks of life: when an acquaintance of the Sewells once dared to refer to their bark-covered bee-hive as an 'apiary', Mary sharply retorted, 'It's a bee-hut.'

The L-shaped house flanking the main road from Norwich to **Aylsham** still stands, with a plaque commemorating Mary's famous daughter **Anna Sewell*** (1820–78). It was here that Anna wrote *Black Beauty* (1877), dictating scenes to her mother, as illness had left her unable to read or write. An early Sewell biographer, **Mrs Bayly**, describes the drawing room where *Black Beauty* was written as looking out 'over the garden and the fields beyond it to the village church and trees – in front across the high road to a grove of beech trees in Mr Buxton's park, where the deer would come to lie in the cool shade.' The copyright of *Black Beauty* was sold to Jarrolds for just twenty pounds, and, dying soon afterwards, Anna Sewell never lived to see the book go on to be translated into twenty languages and sell over 30 million copies.

There are few authors who can claim to have written their first story at the age of four, and six publishable books by the age of fourteen, but **Daisy Ashford** (1881–1972) managed precisely that. Born late in life to creative and often indulgent parents, Daisy grew up in a cultivated Victorian atmosphere and quickly learned to read and write. Perspicacious rather than precocious, four-year-old Daisy's imagination fuelled *The Life of Father McSwiney*, an entirely fictitious 4,000-word biography of a Jesuit priest visitor, for the dictation of which her parents acted as willing secretaries. But it was *The Young Visiters*, written in her own hand in 1890 when she was nine years old that proved to be the jewel in the crown of Daisy's youthful output.

Mary Mann* (1848–1929) was born in Norwich, and although moving to **Shropham** after her marriage, continued to use the city in her writing: *Grandma's Jane*, which gives a vivid insight into Victorian Norwich, opens outside the Castle as a crowd gathers for a public hanging.

Anna Sewell

The author of *Black Beauty* is commemorated by a stone horse-trough, erected by her niece, at the junction of **Constitution Hill** and **St Clement's Hill**.

Daisy Ashford

The author at home with her grandchildren – 'I can never feel all the nice things that have been said about *The Young Visiters* are really due to me at all, but to a Daisy Ashford of so long ago that she seems almost another person.'

Peter Pan creator **J M Barrie** thought Daisy Ashford's *The Young Visiters* 'a scrumptious affair and fit to make the right people jump for joy ... the thing as a whole is too masterly to have come from any brain but a child's'.

This perceptive and hilarious tale, following Mr Salteena's attempts to enter 'society' and his romancing of young Ethel, soon joined young Daisy's works in a box her mother kept of her children's drawings and papers. The books were only discovered after her mother's death in 1917, when the family began clearing her papers. In over twenty years, the stories had lost none of their entertainment value and were apparently read to howls of laughter.

The Young Visiters was released in 1919 and became an enormous commercial success on both sides of the Atlantic. A stage play and the publication of her other stories followed in 1920, a few months after Daisy's marriage to James Devlin. The couple settled in Norwich in the 1950s, living in **Woodland Road, Hellesdon**. Far from being inspired by the success of her books, Daisy Ashford was always bewildered by it, and, seemingly content to leave her writing career firmly in the past, died in 1972 without having written another line.

'A small portion flows in my veins he said but it does not worry me at all and after all he added piously at the Day of Judgement what will be the odds. Mr Salteena heaved a sigh. I was thinking of this world he said.'
Mr Salteena enquires after the Earl of Clincham's royal blood in Daisy Ashford's *The Young Visiters*, 1919

> **Henry Rider Haggard*** was adopted as Conservative candidate for East Norfolk in 1895 at Norwich. A tempestuous (and narrowly lost) campaign was typified by the 'Battle of Stalham Bridge, where an angry mob attacked Haggard and his party, forcing him to shelter in the nearby Swan Hotel until police reinforcements arrived!

Norwich is the birthplace of novelist **Ralph Hale Mottram*** (1883–1971) who went on to become the city's mayor in 1953. Mottram's father was chief clerk of Gurney's Bank, and the Mottrams lived above the bank itself in 'Bank House' on **Bank Plain** – a 'magnificent George the Second mansion', with servants and 'mountainous' stairs. No wonder that Mottram describes his early years as an 'exceptionally happy and fortunate childhood'.

The family followed a Nonconformist religion, 'not quite Quakerism', and from their home walked to the same meeting house frequented by the Norwich coterie almost a century earlier – the **Octagon Chapel** in **Colegate** (dubbed by older citizens 'The Devil's Cucumber Frame'). Mottram followed his father into banking before turning to writing, and quickly found fame with his prize-winning trilogy *The Spanish Farm* (1927). But the spirit of Mottram's work remains in the 'enclosed homely beauty' of East Anglia where so much of his later work is set.

It was a trip to the country to visit the family cook, Mrs Bumphrey, that formed the basis for Mottram's cleverly worked *Autobiography with a Difference* (1938). Here, in a house under 'an enormous open and empty sky' which he finds quite intimidating, young Ralph Mottram reads through a picture book, the images of which he then weaves into each individual chapter of his autobiography some forty years later.

Ralph Hale Mottram

The author of the acclaimed Spanish Farm Trilogy (1927) was mayor of Norwich in 1953

Autobiography evokes the tall trees and spires of Norwich, Mottram's childhood walks to **Cathedral Close** and along the banks of the Wensum to see the brightly painted wherries, and the intricacies of Norwich's social fabric. Characters such as the one-legged soldier who is regularly drunk and resists arrest by the local police to the cheers of a watching crowd, the young 'Travellers' who steal Ralph's sandwiches, the 'peculiar pungent odour' of a visiting circus on the **Cattle Market**, all bring to life late Victorian Norwich, in Mottram's good-humoured, humane, and quaint style.

The Twentieth Century – A Personal Record (1969), while lacking the childhood innocence of *Autobiography*, still presents a solidly Norwich-based view of a century pierced by two world wars. Mottram participates fully in this century's upheavals: enlisting for active service in **Eaton Park** in 1914, returning to a worn-out Norwich five years later, chairing meetings in the Carlton Cinema (turned into a bingo hall in 1973) and assisting at Royal coronations. In the Second World War, Mottram is 'posted on the top of **Norwich Castle** keep, with a field telephone and glasses', takes some of the **Norwich Library** books to safety in the cellar below, and records the Baedeker raid on the city in April 1941. After the war, aged seventy, Mottram became Mayor, and throughout this period continued to write a wide range of biography, autobiography, poetry and novels.

As a young child, Ralph Mottram used to walk the 'gentle slopes' of **The Rosary** – the beautiful former Unitarian cemetery overlooking the junction of the Yare and the Wensum. In *Autobiography*, Mottram recalls that 'I knew, when I was four years old, exactly where I could be buried', and true to his wish, after his death in 1971, he was lain under the trees

In his *Autobiography* (1938), R H Mottram recalls playing with his brother, on **Mousehold Heath** ('Mussel' in local dialect) 'knee deep in heather, waist deep in gorse and bracken and pitted with little circular holes a few feet across, which had been explained to us, to our utter boredom, as the results of glacial action'.

The magnificent mansion on Bank Plain (rebuilt) – once the Gurney's 'Bank House', this was where Ralph Mottram was raised and started his working life.

Ralph Mottram's grave in the beautiful Rosary Cemetery – 'I knew, when I was four years old, exactly where I could be buried.'

planted by his forefathers. The grave stone is a simple stone slab, close to a giant copper beech, alongside other Mottram family graves in the western part of the rambling and tree-studded cemetery.

In the autumn of 1933, **J B Priestley** (1894–1984), who through his huge output of fictional and dramatic works became one of the most popular writers of the time, undertook to travel around England. Norwich was the Bradford-born writer's last stop on the *English Journey* (1934), a surprisingly modern and readable narrative; warm, personal and humorous in tone. After attending a performance at the **Maddermarket Theatre** where he meets its charismatic impresario Nugent Monck (immortalised by **David Holbrook**'s* *A Play of Passion* some fifty years later), Priestley wanders the stage-set world of the city at night:

> … with century after century caught and held, in a gable, a bit of heavily shadowed timbering, a fat bulging bay window, a fanlight all Georgian elegance, in tiny spaces of yellow light and with a frosty glitter of stars above the sleeping city.

Priestley's precise descriptions and quick drawings of the local characters are interspersed with reflections on concerns as various as the wool trade (Priestley held a clerical job in a Bradford wool firm for years), buying antiques, city planning and the organisation of state. Soaking up the city's independent spirit, Priestley muses on the possible federalisation and decentralisation of England ('Home Rule for East Anglia'), imagining the noble senators of the 'Eastern Province ... stout men who take mustard with their beef and beer with their mustard, march through Tombland to assemble in their capital'.

Priestley, eager to learn of Norwich's literary heritage, even discovers that seventeenth-century **Sir Thomas Browne*** is still listed in the 1929 local directory as a medical practitioner! Later, he meets a 'Dissenter type' nursery gardener sporting 'cropped whiskers, shaven chin, and a mouth that turned down at each end' together with 'a wooden look that suddenly twinkled; a passion for imparting information'. Priestley chats to conservative farmers and to local shopkeepers 'given to rubbing their long chins', and a drink at the **Maid's Head** in **Wensum Street** ends a long but fruitful day spent breathing in the 'most Dickensian atmosphere of any city I know'.

J B Priestley

One of the most popular writers of his time, he stopped off here in 1933 as part of his *English Journey* and liked what he saw of the 'grand, higgledy-piggledy, sensible old place ... not a place to make money in and then to plan a sudden exit'.

'The expedition to Norwich was the turning-point: it changed everything,' says Leo Colston in **L P Hartley**'s* (1895–1972) classic *The Go-Between* (1953). Falling for upper class Marian, four years his senior, twelve-year-old Leo recognises only that a 'spiritual transformation took place in Norwich' and fails to see that her attention is already firmly focused on the farmer Ted Burgess. After lunching with Marian in the Maid's Head, an overwhelmed Leo contemplates the day in the sanctity of **Norwich Cathedral**:

> Never had I felt such harmony with my surroundings. It was as though the whole building, striving upwards to its famous vaulted roof, expressed what I was feeling, and later when I left the cool gloom of the interior for the heat and sunshine outside, the domain of Tombland whose name fascinated me, I kept craning my neck to try to fix the point, the exact point, at which the summit of the spire pierced the sky.

The Maid's Head Hotel in Wensum Street – dating from Norman times and a watering-place for writers through the centuries. In 1472, **John Paston*** advises the visitor: 'if he tery at norwyche ..., it were best to sette hys horse at the Maydes Hedde'. Now much enlarged, in a pseudo-Tudor style with an eighteenth-century façade, this is where **J B Priestley** stops for a pint on his travels through England in 1932, and **L P Hartley**'s Leo lunches in *The Go-Between* (1953).

It was only in her mid-sixties, after a career in journalism, that **Sylvia Haymon*** (1915–95) (writing as **S T Haymon**) produced the detective novels which would secure her wide critical acclaim and a Crime Writers' Association Silver Dagger Award. Norfolk is very much present in most of the detective fiction of this quintessentially Norwich author. Her tall, authoritative and darkly handsome Detective Inspector Ben 'Valentino' Jurnet – taking his name from the medieval Norwich Jew, Isaac de Jurnet – is first introduced in the **Walsingham*** mystery *Death and the Pregnant Virgin* (1980), but his investigations centre mainly on 'Angleby', a thinly disguised Norwich. Jurnet's difficult religiosity and the expulsion of the Jewish community from the city in the Middle Ages are persistent themes with Haymon, who herself was born Sylvia Theresa Rosen into a non-orthodox Jewish family.

Sylvia Haymon

In her history of the city, *Norwich* (1973), she revels in Norwich's 'completeness' and independence, the tangibility of its history and its 'genius for the visual'.

Death of a god (1987) draws heavily upon the life of another historical figure: rebel leader Robert Kett, who was hanged outside **Norwich Castle** in 1549, 'like a ham hung up for winter store'. Haymon's novel parallels the life (and decidedly unpleasant death) of 'Loy Tanner', the Messianic singer of 'The Second Coming' pop group with that of his sixteenth-century ancestor. The historical focus of this suspenseful mystery of adulation and deception is taken up again in Haymon's eighth and final detective novel *Death of a hero* (1996), published a year after her death. Once more we follow her familiar landmarks of the Castle, 'crouched like a brooding monster' and the city's one-way system blocking streets 'designed for the passage of ox-carts'. And once more here is Norwich's history of dissent, knocking on the city's door in the guise of 10,000 men assembling on 'Monkenheath' (**Mousehold Heath**).

In scenes reminiscent of Kett's march against overstocking and land enclosure some 450 years earlier, the charismatic figurehead of Charlie Appleyard leads his men in a twentieth-century protest against soaring unemployment. But, much as in real history, the hero is heading towards a painful end, and when news of his downfall in Norwich's red-light district ('Bergate') starts to spread, Appleyard's followers move menacingly towards the **Market Place**. Meanwhile, as the tale moves steadily towards its climax, Jurnet has his own emotional turmoil to resolve.

Considerably less gruesome, but perhaps even more engaging are Haymon's two volumes of frank and witty autobiography: *Opposite the Cross Keys* (1988) and *The Quivering Tree* (1990). *Opposite the Cross Keys* covers her childhood years from seven to ten – a time when Sylvia's Saturday afternoons are often spent on the same Market Place she later uses in her fiction. Haymon recalls autumn days in Norwich 'mellow as honey ... the memory of which keeps you going through the months when Arctic gales sweep down from the North Pole, and the damp of the Broads corrodes your very soul'.

Much of Haymon's memoirs focuses on the very different environment at nearby 'Salham St Awdry' (**Horsham St Faith**), to where

Opposite: Norwich Cathedral – it leaves **L P Hartley**'s Leo spellbound, but to **David Holbrook**'s Paul Grimmer appears only 'bleak and ridiculous in its aspirations'.

Robert Kett holding forth under the Oak of Reformation on Mousehold Heath in 1549 – he is the inspiration for S T Haymon's crime novels *Death of a god* (1987) and *Death of a hero* (1996).

seven-year-old Sylvia rides out one summer on her rather oversized bike. Passing Hellesdon Pond she respectfully bows at the old wooden sign at **Horsford Point** on the **Aylsham Road**, reciting the strange mantra of 'Ma gerto o ca!' to get past safely. The fact that 'one part of me knew quite well that the legend on the signboard, long abandoned and uncared for, had once read MANN EGERTON FOR CARS in no way lessened the dread and doom of Horsford Point'.

When the Haymons move to London, away from the 'vegetable existence' here, a stubborn and independent young Sylvia determines to stay instead with the working-class Fenner family in 'Salham'. The Fenners' small and impoverished cottage stands in a terrace of four opposite the Cross Keys pub. Here, camped on a horsehair sofa listening to the rats at night ('What could they find to eat in that empty house ... what if not me so conveniently at hand?'), Sylvia acquaints herself with the local gypsy culture, befriends her eccentric, foul-mouthed but charming neighbour, 'Chicken', and reads gruesome newspaper stories to the illiterate Mrs Fenner. Despite some disappointments and obvious differences in background between Sylvia and her adopted neighbourhood, she enjoys herself thoroughly, something Haymon conveys convincingly in this charming account of childhood. The Cross Keys pub itself burned down in the 1960s, though the cottages Haymon knew in *Opposite the Cross Keys*, now much altered, still stand.

'Read that one again,' Mrs Fenner would demand admiringly of the young Sylvia Haymon in 'Opposite the Cross Keys' at Horsham St Faith, ''bout the feller what chopped up them women an' buried the bits under the hen run. You read it so lovely...'

The second volume, *The Quivering Tree*, sees twelve-year-old Sylvia arriving, in 1930, at her home for the next two years: the solidly

Edwardian 'Chandos House', on the outskirts of the city, up the 'interminable gradient of Sprowston Road'. Already a self-confessed 'architectural snob', young Sylvia is less than impressed by the appearance of the house, 'a foolish irrelevance of pseudo-Tudor held up by outsize skittles painted a turgid green'. Lodging in a tiny room, fed hopelessly inadequate food, and overseen by an eccentric pair of teachers and a tyrannical housekeeper is quite an experience for the maturing Sylvia. Saving for whipped walnut creams to supplement her meagre diet and going on seaside trips with her formidable co-lodgers, Sylvia generally makes the best of life at Chandos House. But soon, she knows, she will be leaving the city of which she is so fond, 'that centre which, for all of my life up till then, had enfolded and defended me the way its ancient walls had once enfolded and defended the entire city'.

Novelist, poet and Cambridge don **David Holbrook** (1923–) was born 'not far from Mann Egerton's factory' on the **Eversley Road**, **Hellesdon** at around the same time that young Sylvia Haymon was on her way to Horsham St Faith. Holbrook remembers his first school well; now a garage, it used to take some very poor children from cottages on Cromer Road. The traumatic experience of one fellow pupil who trying to hang himself in a lavatory surfaces in the story 'I Can't Understand the Damn Boy' from *Lights in the Sky Country* (1962), Holbrook's first work of fiction.

In *The Gold in Father's Heart* (1992), fictionalising Holbrook's childhood experiences, we meet the author's alter ego, Paul Grimmer,

Horsham St Faith was not only the childhood home to Henry VIII's fifth queen Catherine Howard, but also that of Elizabethan poet and martyr **St Robert Southwell** (?1561–95). Southwell's works ('The Burning Babe', *St Peters Complaint*) were mainly written in prison, after the Jesuit priest was captured for celebrating Mass in 1592.

The cottages (now converted), standing opposite Cross Keys Close at Horsham St Faith – where a young Sylvia Haymon stepped into another world.

David Holbrook

Novelist, poet and follower of the critic F R Leavis, most of his fiction focuses on Norwich and Norfolk. His latest novel, *Getting it Wrong with Uncle Tom* (1998), even includes a glossary of Norfolk dialect.

for the first time and see him as a young boy, struggling to understand the changes in the family fabric when Paul's parents take in a lodger: 'Mademoiselle', a silk-weaver from the local factory. When Mademoiselle produces 'a strip of woven stuff, in the beautiful pattern known as Norwich silk' the effect of her work is stunning: 'It was a crowded pattern of twirls, full of golden and red colours, like a brilliant firework display with shapes like meteors or comets, all woven together with leaf shapes and winding tendrils'.

Later, Holbrook went on to the **City of Norwich School** on **Eaton Road**, whose headmaster Geoffrey Thorp, dedicated to the arts and an influential pacifist, is immortalised in *A Little Athens* (1990). In the **Central Library** on the corner below the Maddermarket, the schoolboy David Holbrook read **T S Eliot** and the Faber poets of the thirties, and managed to obtain **James Joyce**'s *Ulysses* 'because I knew one of the librarian girls'. He read it 'on a farm holiday out at **Reepham**, mostly sitting on a two seater lavatory outside a farmhouse'!

A Play of Passion (1978), takes up the story of Paul Grimmer as a sixth-former and a young stage hand at the **Maddermarket Theatre**. The time is 1940, and through his transition from school to Cambridge – again drawing on Holbrook's own experiences – Paul finds himself drawn into the sophisticated world of the theatre, towards his first sexual experiences, and into the vortex of confusion that is adolescence. Paul Grimmer's hero is the immensely influential theatre producer **Nugent Monck**, who bought the old baking powder factory near the church of **St John's Maddermarket** in 1921 and converted it into an Elizabethan-style theatre for Monck's Norwich Players. In the thirties, a young and enthusiastic David Holbrook helped here – cleaning up bus-tickets and heaving heavy curtains about.

The most recent novel of the Emeritus Fellow, *Getting it Wrong with Uncle Tom* (1998), is the story of fourteen-year-old Duffy, set on a farm in **Glandford** on the marshy north Norfolk coast in 1936 and suffused with Norfolk locale and dialect. When he finds an ancient artefact under a hedge, the local lads' resentment at the intrusion of the 'city boy' proves to be just one of many challenges facing young Duffy.

Exploring the worlds of childhood, adolescence and marriage with sensitivity and nostalgic charm, Holbrook's novels are firmly anchored in the Norwich, and Norfolk, landscapes of his youth. 'I still write poems about Norwich,' says Holbrook, though nowadays he seldom visits: 'I can't bear what the 'City Fathers' have done to it, carving it up and driving roads through the city, and radically messing up the centre, by burrowing under the former cattle-market where I used to go to whop bullocks.'

David Holbrook's most famous novel, *Flesh Wounds* (1966), is the account of Paul Grimmer in the Normandy Invasion of 1944. Norwich is described as: 'gloriously teeming with rich, unhygienic character, violence and filth'.

In **Timberhill**, just south of the castle, its Georgian frame neatly decorated in black and white, stands the **Bell Hotel**, which, back in the fifties, was a thriving hotel with a large and busy kitchen. Working here at the time was playwright **Arnold Wesker*** (1932–), who had left his home in the East End of London with a pile of rejection slips and his writing career seemingly behind him. Having worked as a pipe-layer, seed-sorter and farm labourer, Wesker, in his own words, 'had retreated into the kitchen of the Bell Hotel in despair of ever becoming a successful writer'. Like **George Orwell** (1903–50) whose *Down and Out in Paris and London* (1933) launched a major literary career, Wesker used his menial labours to develop his undeniable talent.

'Kitchen life appealed to me', he writes in his autobiography *As Much As I Dare* (1994) – a brilliant and unflinchingly honest self-portrait of an energetic and passionate playwright. Nor was life in Norwich too lonely, as his sister Della and her husband lived near by 'in the middle of the fields' at Hill House Farm, **Wacton Common** near **Long Stratton** where Wesker frequently visited. Always more of a town animal, he admits to a certain nervousness when taking the darkened road 'lined with trees through which the wind howled'.

Arnold Wesker

As a young playwright he arrived in Norwich despondent but left inspired to find literary success.

Back in the urban surroundings of the Bell Hotel, Wesker met his wife Dusty – the high-spirited 'simple country girl' who became the 'Beatie' of his plays and whose Norfolk family lived at Beck Farm, **Redenhall***. In his diary notes, Wesker recalls devouring books at a prodigious rate in the shelter of his small attic room at the hotel, while below him shoppers crowded the narrow streets:

> Today, Saturday, I can look out of my little window and see masses of people and cars in the streets. Christmas shopping! ... Not far away on the left are neon lights that burn into the night and keep my room in shadowed colours. The room is small, but is queerly shaped and must date back a few hundred years ...

The characters that Wesker met and worked with here in Norwich, and their varied and often tragic lives, were to nourish his creative spirit and sharpen the intensity of his writing. Though his cousin wrote to him in early 1954 with the warning: 'What chance can you have stuck over a pile of vegetables in a hotel?', Wesker had already sensed that success might not elude him for much longer. In fact, the themes Arnold Wesker developed whilst working in Norwich would remain almost constant throughout his later writing: 'lives wasted accepting second best; lives vulnerable from inadequate nourishment – spiritual, emotional, intellectual; lives stultified from the wrong choice based on chimeric dreams, self-delusion. All began in the Bell Hotel.'

In what he describes as 'the writing behind my back', Wesker had begun work on the unpublished 'The Terrible Valley' trilogy which included 'The Diary of Jon Smith' – effectively Wesker's own diary interweaving observations of life around him. Writing some months later to his mother, Wesker knew he had something: 'I don't know, but I am beginning to feel that maybe I will get somewhere.' 'Somewhere' turned out to be the Royal Court theatre in London, rave reviews for a string of successful plays and a place in theatre history alongside the

The Bell Hotel on Timberhill, to which Arnold Wesker retreated in the 1950s 'in despair of ever becoming a successful writer'.

Angry Young Men of the 1950s headed by John Osborne, whose *Look Back in Anger* (1956) so inspired Wesker.

Wesker's Jewish roots, left-wing ideology and complex, often fractured family relations make for compulsive theatre. *Chicken Soup with Barley* (1958), *Roots* (1959) and *I'm Talking About Jerusalem* (1960) form the successful trilogy which mirror Wesker's own life through that of Ronnie Khan and his family, while *The Kitchen* (1957) specifically draws upon some of his experiences at the Bell Hotel. The opening scene is inspired by the routine established in Norwich:

> Up at 6.30 to make porridge, fry bacon, sausages, and bread – eggs were done upstairs on the spot – and boil kippers all ready to be served by 7.30 from the heated serving cabinets. An empty hotel greeted me, I like that. It was a simple routine which I carried out with sleepy eyes, but exhilarating, awake just as everything is about to be set in motion ... Light the hot plate, load the dumbwaiter, pull the rope, go up to unload, stack food to keep warm, feel the still room heat up, fry eggs in preparation for the rush. It became hotter as activity increased. The first orders came slowly – the cups and saucers could be washed at an even pace – then with greater speed, heightened intensity, hum building to roar. Breakfast was on! Rhythm! Swing! Sweat! Temperament!

Judith Saxton

'My personal favourite Norfolk book is *Chasing Rainbows*. Perhaps it's because all the settings, and a good few of the people ... are so much a part of me, so well-known to me, that I loved almost every character as soon as they appeared on the page.'

Novelist **Judith Saxton*** (1936–) was born 'in the now defunct Stork Nursing Home in **Thorpe Road** opposite the station' and attended **Norwich High School for Girls**, where she was 'extremely happy and extremely undistinguished'. Today, Saxton is a successful popular novelist whose many locally researched romances and family sagas are written under a variety of pseudonyms. In her work, Saxton returns to Norwich time and again – in particular for her series of historical novels chronicling the lives of her own ancestors.

While *The Pride* (1981) is 'the most thoroughly Norfolk novel of all', her 'personal favourite Norfolk book' is the popular romance *Chasing Rainbows* (1988), tracing the complexities of various romantic entanglements around the Norwich café where Clare Arnold is working alongside acne-plagued teenager Deirdre and Mavis, who 'used make-up like a chef uses icing'. Laced with a gentle humour, *Chasing Rainbows* depicts a 1980s Norwich still full of its heritage charm:

> Outside, the city seemed to slumber beneath the rain. From here you could see – just – Norwich Castle up on its mound, and if you went to the door and peered to the right you could also see what used to be the Cornhall and was now the Anglia TV studios. Once, long ago, the car-park had been a cattle market and perhaps because of the number of cattle trucks which parked here it had a country air still, as though you were likelier to meet a calf crossing the road than a Porsche. On the other hand, Clare

Summer fields at Redenhall – where playwright Arnold Wesker found that 'Huge skies lorded over the landscape dictating what would be seen and not seen'

St Mary the Virgin, Gissing – the 'hunch-backed' church and its pre-conquest tower embodying 'an awesome sense of continuity' in Lindsay Clarke's *The Chymical Wedding*.

Ranworth Broad – 'the water reflected probable and improbable colours and looked oily ... as the eddies rippled along the oozy banks' (Gladys Mitchell, *Wraiths and Changelings*, 1978)

Norwich by night – on his *English Journey* (1934), J B Priestley sees 'century after century caught and held ... in tiny spaces of yellow light and with a frosty glitter of stars above the sleeping city'

Horsey Mere – 'the delicious interflow of the soft purity of the sky and the bright tranquillity of the lake' (Wilkie Collins, *Armadale*, 1866)

Yarmouth Quay – 'the finest quay in England if not in Europe', declares Daniel Defoe in 1724, not long after his Robinson Crusoe set sail from here.

The view from Happisburgh Church – with the Hill House from Conan Doyle's 'Dancing Men' below left and 'the violet rim of the German Ocean appear[ing] over the green edge of the Norfolk coast'

reflected, it might be the trees. A great big one grew right opposite them, dripping on her Mini, parked beneath its sheltering boughs. Clare winked at the car, then felt a fool and hastily bent down and got a cloth from the bowl beneath the counter.

Judith Saxton spent her teenage years in the village of **Blofield**. Now, with more than fifty novels to her name, she lives mainly in North Wales, but continues to use Norfolk locales for many of her stories, trying 'to come back every six to eight weeks' to visit friends and relatives, and 'browse and research backgrounds'. As well as using settings in and around her home city – *Full Circle* (1984) closed her Norwich quartet – Saxton has developed her own fictional north Norfolk town 'Haisby', while her more recent love story, *Still Waters* (1996), draws upon the tranquillity and 'misty magic' of the Broadland region.

There is a lot less romance in the fiction of contemporary author and journalist **D J Taylor** (1960–), who was born in the **Christchurch Road** area, attended **Norwich School** and went on to study Modern History at Oxford before commencing a career in writing. History and his hometown remain major influences in Taylor's work and are already discernible in his first, partly autobiographical novel, *Great Eastern Land* (1986). Here, narrator David Castell tries to come to terms with a past that shelters, but also threatens to engulf him ('We are a God-fearing people and we have been here a long time').

This 'Great Eastern Land' of Castell's youth, 'where history stares you in the face', is mirrored by a second location somewhere in the Far East where he is assembling his life story – a 'story about history' in a somewhat threatening atmosphere. Castell's 'Notebooks' also allow glimpses of the protagonist's occasionally self-indulgent, pompous and lecturing voice. Meanwhile, Castell's father, an amateur historian 'immersed in his spider's web of ancestry and connection' is fighting his own battle against history, attracting a reputation for his 'unscholarly', unorthodox attempts at genealogy, for 'taking liberties with the past':

> There was, in fact, a great deal of the stage East Anglian about my father. Though he affected to deplore local radio programmes in which professional actors assumed garrulous yokel accents and made jokes about turnip-topping, it was obvious that he thought them a necessary prod to local patriotism and would rather have regretted it had they ceased to appear. He had a great fund of anecdotes on the subject of Norfolk eccentrics – 'characters' they were called – men who had not spoken to their wives for twenty years, or were found drunk in ditches or, carrying their enthusiasm for the local football team to fanatic lengths, dyed their hair yellow and green.

Meanwhile, Norwich plays a pivotal role in Taylor's unsettling second novel *Real Life* (1992), which sees ex-pornography script-writer Martin

'So many of the books include something of Norfolk': *Family Feeling* is partially set on the Acle marshes, while 'the other one with quite a lot of Norfolk in it is *Someone Special*, which deals with the lives of three girls, one of whom later becomes Queen Elizabeth II ...', says Judith Saxton.

D J Taylor

'Norfolk has always exercised a profound influence on the things I write about.'

In a roll-call of Norfolk history, D J Taylor's *Great Eastern Land* (1986) recalls **John Fastolf*** 'in his draughty halls at Caistor, watching the wind careering over the flats', and **Parson Woodforde*** 'marooned' in **Weston Longville** by the snow, 'reaching uneasy, unspoken compromises with his creator as he trawls back and forth under the wide East Anglian sky'.

The old city walls on Chapel Field Road – described by Sylvia Haymon as 'lumps of masonry sticking up through the pavement like dragons' teeth looking for a very clever dentist' the walls are also an obsession for David Castell's father in D J Taylor's *Real Life*, 1992.

Benson return to his home city to live in the house his father has left him. More developed in style and humour than Taylor's debut novel, *Real Life* allows Norwich to play a leading role as the plot winds from Benson's home in **Glebe Road** (a mix of Georgian and Victorian red-brick terraces in leafy surroundings) through the alleyways and into the open parks of the city. But Martin's vision of this ancient place, where his father had charted 'the antiquities of Norfolk, the route and dimensions of the old city wall', is now both disorienting and disenchanting:

> Past the dogleg alley that leads you back into a maze of side streets and lock-up garages where tethered Alsatians whine balefully at the sky. Past the hole in the road with its arc of winking lights. Past the City Gates on the corner, where the door swings open for an instant and there is a sudden confused impression of smoke, light shining off glass, mute, aquarium faces ... Up College Road. Left along the dense outline of the park. The spectral hand of a more personal heritage looms up here, the twitch upon the thread grows insistent.

Spellbound by his past and intoxicated by memories of the enigmatic and elusive Elaine, Benson finds himself unable to make any sense of his life. More worryingly, as he drinks and talks football with Fat Eric (a brutish neighbour and walking case book of the lore of local horror), and maintains contact with a cast of other equally unsavoury characters from his 'Leisurevision' past, Benson is unable to recognise the very real danger in which he has placed himself. The Norwich of *Real Life* is far from the ancient civic splendour portrayed by many authors – here it is coloured by the same tension and disquiet, the same violent urbanity, of the London Benson is unable to leave behind him. Its permutations of violence – a post-match punch-up with Manchester United hooligans, drunken brawls at the 'City Gates' pub of Taylor's invention, the blunt physicality of sex without passion – are focused on Fat Eric, but Benson himself appears far from immune to such influence.

'Each stroll through the back streets of Norwich has become a tightrope walk over a frothing cauldron of reminiscence.'

D J Taylor, *Real Life*, 1992

As with David Castell in *Great Eastern Land*, the city's past is a central issue and a metaphor for the sordid past lying beneath Martin Benson's unreliable existence, which will, when the surface erodes, inevitably lead to his own sinking:

> You can tarmac over the hills, you can turn a wilderness into an asphalt floor, but you cannot tame what lies beneath. Under the West Norwich streets there are old chalk workings, refuse pits full of vanished Saxon dung. They open up occasionally and a bus disappears, lists comfortably into a funnel of cascading earth, a tree totters inexorably to one side, a house is scythed neatly in two by the shifting void below. The past refuses to lie down here.

In *Real Life*, Taylor weaves in his first-hand experience of accountancy, his intimate knowledge of urban landscapes and Norwich's mysterious local characters – all touched by the uncaring attitude that so typifies the 1980s. In this distinctly filmic and surreal novel, awash with undercurrents of violence and black humour, it is sometimes hard to distinguish exactly what 'real life' is. 'Real life is for people with no imagination,' says Benson, who is unable, or unwilling, to unsnag himself from the past and to recognise the genuine menace he faces, constantly yearning for something just beyond his reach. Swept along in the wake of other people's lives, Benson replays the loops of his own life like the cheap porn flicks he used to write. But when his co-habitee Suzi moves

'Under the West Norwich streets there are old chalk workings ... They open up occasionally and a bus disappears ...'

D J Taylor, *Real Life*, 1992

'Looking back, it was as if a giant paperweight, composed of the West Earlham houses, my mother and her cronies, the obligation to "behave proper", lay across my shoulders, and that it was my duty immediately to grow up and start the work of prising it free.'

D J Taylor, *Trespass*, 1998

out and his 'contacts' abandon him one by one, it can only be a matter of time before the past he has betrayed comes knocking on his door.

D J Taylor's fourth novel, *Trespass* (1998), acclaimed by **Hilary Mantel*** as 'an exact memoir of time and place, of class and of individual temper', begins by tracing the childhood of its protagonist George Chell, raised on the West Earlham Estate in the 1960s:

> In those days the council houses stretched all over the western side of the city: row after row of huddled, dingy dwellings in orange half-brick or pale white stucco, exotic street names – Fairfax or George Borrow – that weren't at all suggestive of the peope who lived in them. In summer the chemicals from the May & Baker factory two miles away came and hung round the doors and gardens with an indescribable smell of sulphur ...

George's mother, with an 'encyclopaedic' knowledge of West Earlham lore', her cronies, and life on the estate are convincingly drawn. She never refers to George's father, although somewhere in the background there is a mysterious uncle, a self-made financial entrepreneur. Apart from conker-hunting in the woods or wandering round **Castle Museum** on a Sunday, life on the estate leaves George singularly unimpressed, and running into class barriers in **Unthank Road** leaves an indelible impression on the young boy. At eighteen, he prises himself free and leaves for London.

In *Trespass*, Taylor returns with an assured voice to his earlier themes of the indifferent, money-grabbing 1980s, as the collapse of Chell Holdings and his uncle's dreams finds the adult George Chell marooned in a hotel further down the coast in Southwold, grappling with an elusive past.

University of East Anglia

Percy Lubbock

In *Earlham* (1922) he explores every inch of the home he found to be 'the wonder of the world'.

Now the administrative building of the University of East Anglia (UEA), **Earlham Hall** was once the home of the **Gurney** family. It was here, beside the waters 'that glided past', that the young **George Borrow*** spent many a happy hour 'rod in hand' or plunging into the 'deep pool' for a swim. Although chided by 'The man of peace' – Quaker leader Joseph John Gurney – for his 'cruel fishing', Borrow was nevertheless granted permission to be here, something most unusual within the grounds of a Victorian country home.

The brother of the same Quaker leader whom Borrow met beside the river was the great-grandfather of **Percy Lubbock** (1879–1965), critic and biographer, whose *Earlham* (1922) is considered his masterpiece. Here he describes an Earlham, hidden away behind thickly massed trees, its gables of flint and brick and its plain buff-white north front, which, at first sight, appears deceptively distant and unwelcoming:

> Your eye follows the line of the cart-road, across the open park, till it disappears in the shadow of the lime-avenue, and between the trees you catch this single glimpse of the house – the front-door only, with its low pediment, and a window or two beside and above it. It is a sight that tells you nothing of the place; you might think it rather formal and forbidding.

But for Lubbock, there is nothing 'forbidding' about the house he describes in *Earlham* as 'the wonder of the world' and where he spent an idyllic childhood among eccentric relatives at the end of the nineteenth century. Lubbock's grandfather, 'tall and gaunt and benevolent', had been rector of St. Giles on the Earlham Road, but for the compassionate figure of his grandmother, only one place is truly home:

> ... she was very tender and affectionate with it, as though the house were a kind old nurse, faithful and worn, with whom we must be gentle. She would lay her hand on a wall, a panel, a window-sill, with a touch that seemed to stroke it softly; 'the poor old place,' she said, with a kind of bantering tenderness. She lived there for nearly fifty years, and her many children grew up there. Nothing was ever changed.

This sense of permanency is central to Lubbock's work, as he guides the reader on a sentimental room-by-room journey through the house – the Green Room, the Chintz Room, the North Room, the Great Room,

The south front of Earlham Hall *c.*1810, by Richenda Gurney

'The hill slopes gently down to the margin of the stream. On the right is a green level, a smiling meadow, grass of the richest decks the side of the slope, mighty trees also adorn it, giant elms, the nearest of which, when the sun is nigh in its meridian, fling a broad shadow upon the face of the pool, through yon vista you catch a glimpse of the ancient brick of an old English hall.'

George Borrow, *Lavengro*, 1851

Percy Lubbock takes the reader on a walk through the grounds of Earlham, to admire the lawn and the fancy flower-beds: 'Geraniums roasting-red, French marigolds orange and mahogany-coloured, the tomato-note of waxen begonias, exotic herbage all speckled and pied and ring-streaked, dahlias, calceolarias – they were marshalled and massed together, they fought it out as they would.'

and so on. Using a steady flow of rhetorical questions, Lubbock's gently archaic narrative engages the reader to follow his 'true story' into every nook and cranny of the house. *Earlham* is suffused with moments of childhood solitude and reverie; reflections on the nature of time and memory, with simple items of furniture sparking off his chains of thoughts.

> Somebody came into the room, common life shut down upon the child again – so it happened; but so it always happens, I have never discovered the secret of prolonging the few rare moments. Enough that in passing they bestow their imperishable gift; the time, the place, are marked for ever afterwards, plainly to be seen over lengthening years. I am sure it is impossible to forget them – even when at last there are some that shine at a very far distance, like this of the great cool ante-room at Earlham. The remembrance hangs there, beaconing clearly, a long way off by this time; it is safe from all chances, it will only quaver and sink when the child is extinguished too.

But *Earlham* is much more than a simple collection of childhood memoirs; Lubbock touches upon many aspects of Norfolk life and lore with great lucidity. There is the language, the bent poetry of Norfolk place-names ('**Wramplingham!**'), the 'clear and liquid syllables', the usage of which give the author 'a fine sense of community with an ancient province, the kingdom of the easterlings'.

For Lubbock, Earlham Hall is at the centre of an 'intricate system of relationship that spread over half the county and knitted it with Earlham; cross-ties, intermarriages, confused the web beyond unravelling by any but those who were born to it'. As such Earlham Hall has witnessed the perpetuity of families and the continuity of generations which still sustain much of Norfolk today.

Novelist and academic **Malcolm Bradbury** (1932–), Emeritus Professor of American Studies at UEA, has been living in his favourite city since 1966. Five years after his arrival, together with **Angus Wilson**, he founded the country's first Creative Writing MA course and saw a string of high-profile writers graduate, including **Kazuo Ishiguro**, **Clive Sinclair** and **Ian McEwan**. Bradbury himself is an extremely versatile and prolific writer of TV drama, political satires, film scripts, critical studies, and novels which he says 'treat the problems of liberalism, humanism, and moral responsibility in the later twentieth-century world'.

Malcolm Bradbury

Pioneer of the Creative Writing course at the University of East Anglia and now a literary institution in his own right.

As a means of portraying different decades in their attitudes and outlooks, Bradbury has used his various 'campus novels' – such as *Eating People is Wrong* (1959), set in a second-rate, red-brick provincial university and *Stepping Westward* (1965), set on an American Mid-western campus – to map out the fictional country of the academic world. *The History Man* (1975) features a plate-glass university very much like UEA, and in *Doctor Criminale* (1992), the narrator arrives at a major conference held here, giving expression to the mixed emotions aroused by the ultra-modern university buildings:

> In my opinion a university campus is a rather strange place, out of time, into space, away from the drab urban grey, in the lush urban green, caught in a separate world that seems to have little to do with everyday history ... But this one was a strange form of paradise. Not so long ago, in a lush river valley some pre-postmodern architect had started pouring concrete; great staggered residence blocks, huge teaching towers, rose from the grass, speaking of mass and monumentalism and eternity. Maybe it was home to some; it was not to me. It was already history, the white cement slowly pitting and greying with age – just like the hundreds of professors of English whom I found at the opening conference reception. There they were, pressed tightly together amid breeze-block walls, looking mystified at one another.

An immensely successful novelist and short-story writer, **Rose Tremain***(1943–), who later edited the 1992 *Leaves on the Line* anthology of UEA's prestigious MA course, first arrived in Norfolk as a student herself in the 'particularly beautiful autumn' of 1964. Moving here from her native London to study English Literature under **Angus Wilson**, Tremain found Norwich and its surroundings 'very appealing indeed'. Tremain worked in teaching and publishing and produced two non-fiction studies before completing her first novel *Sadler's Birthday* – an evocative portrayal of the life and service of an elderly butler – in 1976.

Rose Tremain

Five years later Tremain once again found herself living in Norwich, and in 1985 she settled into 'one part of a very large Georgian house ... on a marvellous wooded hill' in **Thorpe St Andrew**. She shares her home here with her partner, the biographer and journalist **Richard Holmes** (1945–), whose *Coleridge: early visions* won the Whitbread Book of the Year Prize in 1989.

Rose Tremain's work only occasionally employs Norfolk locales – the prize-winning *Restoration* (1989), set in the north-west close to **King's Lynn***, providing one rare example. Nevertheless, Tremain is 'extremely attached' to the 'peaceful setting' of her Norwich base and, beyond the city, the journey to the marram-spiked dunes and sandy coastline of **Winterton*** is a particular favourite.

Rose Tremain's long-term connections with UEA continue today with her work as an occasional lecturer in creative writing. Her other prize-winning works include *The Swimming Pool Season* (1985) and *Sacred Country* (1992).

Tremain's collection of short stories *The Garden of the Villa Mollini* (1987) references Norfolk in the tale of 'Tropical Fish': while his father

'My study looks out onto a wide, sloping garden down to a rhododendron grove. From here we have a favourite walk which takes us round a "square" of green lanes and quiet road, across fields and past isolated cottages and one very beautiful house with a marvellous garden and a paddock where horses always graze. We check two ponds for rain levels and bird activity – as if we were the guardians of these places.'

lies dying back home on his Norfolk farm, Bob Sparrow is journeying to London for the *Agripower '87* exhibition. Following in his father's footsteps, Sparrow is preparing for the future and investing in new machinery to maintain the family's 'flat, featureless land'. The transition of old John Sparrow's farm into 'Sparrow Holdings Ltd' is brilliantly concluded with Bob Sparrow's birds-eye view of the small patch of land that is his inheritance – seen from the cockpit of his newly acquired light aircraft. Tying together two major Norfolk themes – agriculture and continuity – 'Tropical Fish' provides an incisive, if rather bleak, snapshot of modern rural life.

Like Malcolm Bradbury before him, Professor of American Studies at UEA, **Christopher Bigsby** (1941–), has already enjoyed a wide and varied writing career, including short stories, radio and TV dramas and literary titles. His position at UEA brings Bigsby into regular contact with many top international writers, but it is to a long-dead American writer that he turns in his assured debut novel *Hester – A Romance* (1994).

In this evocative historical romance, Bigsby reworks **Nathaniel Hawthorne**'s nineteenth-century classic *The Scarlet Letter* (1850) and locates its heroine Hester and her mysterious husband Roger Chillingworth on his own doorstep 'up against the river Yare' in the tiny hamlet of **Colney**. Here, a stone's throw from UEA's green fields at Earlham Park, the Saxon-towered church of St Andrew overlooks the action as Hester grows to regret her impulsive marriage and plans her escape to New England. Set in the feverish time of the Civil War, in an England awash with rumours, dissenters and spies, *Hester* combines Bigsby's didactic narration, powerful story and sense of place to great effect.

Bigsby convincingly weaves Norwich's landscape and local history into the early part of his tale, which finds Chillingworth lying in a Norwich gaol while Hester, having already started upon a love affair with a minister, disembarks from the *Hope* on to a new continent and into the town of Boston. But as Hester discovers, even in a faraway land her bond with Chillingworth is not so easily broken. When she finds herself to be pregnant, and is condemned to wear the scarlet letter 'A' branding her an adulteress, the future seems clouded with a tragic inevitability.

The child that is the source of both joy and despair to Hester becomes the subject of Bigsby's sequel, *Pearl* (1995). When Pearl leaves her mother's side and the Puritan repression of New England and returns to Norfolk to claim her inheritance, she is shocked by the strength of the conspiracy against her. Moving from the taverns of Cheapside to Norwich and its lawyer's offices in **Opie Street** (which then, appropriately, was known as Devil's Alley), *Pearl* continues to 'steal from history' and adopts the comic touch of Hawthorne's *The House of the Seven Gables* (1851), whilst retaining something of the 'smell of brimstone in the air'.

Christopher Bigsby

His award-winning novel *Hester – A Romance* (1994) includes 'scenes which I can see out of my window'.

'If you do choose to go there, however, it is better to visit in the daylight hours for I am told that at night the street sign has been known to transmute and Opie Street become Devil's Alley once again.'

Christopher Bigsby, *Pearl*, 1995

In **Barbara Vine's*** chilling novel *No Night is Too Long* (1994), Tim Cornish takes part in 'England's most prestigious Creative Writing course' in the grey concrete university in the city of 'P.', which bears a close resemblance to Norwich. This 'memorial to the past ... may have been a nice city once', but now the twelfth-century cathedral and narrow streets are vying for space with 'mock-medieval multi-storey car parks with castellated ramparts' servicing the heavy London-like traffic. If that sounds familiar, there is worse still, as Tim's falling in love with a charismatic paleontologist in 'P.' sets him on a path of destruction...

Professor of German and founder of the British Centre for Literary Translation, **W G Sebald** (1944–) has been teaching at UEA since 1970 and has published two novels, both translated from the German by the poet **Michael Hulse**, to huge acclaim. While *The Emigrants* (1996) explores the fate of European Jewry in an unsettling and innovative blend of autobiography and fiction, Sebald's Norfolk and East Anglian experience has filtered through much more permanently into his second work of fiction *The Rings of Saturn* (1998).

Suffused with melancholia and images of death and destruction, Sebald's 'rings of Saturn', are created from the fragments of a writer's journey in a landscape as unlike the Bavarian Alps of his childhood as

W G Sebald

He contemplates landscapes both real and imaginary in his powerful and complex *The Rings of Saturn.*

possible. Sebald's narrative, relayed by a not-quite-the-author narrator, meanders along the East Anglian coast, flanked by reflections on **Thomas Browne***, whilst casting a nostalgic glance back at the demise of the Yarmouth herring industry, the spread of Dutch elm disease in Norfolk and **Edward FitzGerald**'s sudden death at **Merton**.

Sebald's mesmerising narrative flows uninterrupted by speech-marks and is strewn with an eclectic range of uncaptioned photographs, creating a persistent and deliberate cloud of uncertainty. It takes up strands of the narrator's life and the life of the landscape around him; exploring them lovingly and effortlessly in a philosophical reflection laced with the omnipresent imagery of death.

The Rings of Saturn was acclaimed by **Michael Ondaatje** as 'as strange a triumph' as Sebald's first novel, carried by 'the subtlest and seemingly most whimsical of structures ... a book shaped not by plot but by a thrilling meditation on the rhymes and recurrences, on the private obsessions and the great dénouements of history.' It was from his home in **Poringland***, a village he has lived in for over a quarter of a century, that Sebald witnessed the trail of destruction of the freak hurricane that shook the eastern counties on 16 October 1987:

> I stood at the window and looked through the glass, which was strained almost to breaking point, down towards the end of the garden, where the crowns of the large trees in the neighbouring bishop's park were bent and streaming like aquatic plants in a deep current. White clouds raced across in the darkness, and again and again the sky was lit up by a terrible flickering, which I later discovered was caused by power lines touching each other. At some point I must have turned away for a while. At all events, I still remember that I did not believe my eyes when I looked out again and saw that where the currents of air had shortly beforehand been poring through the black mass of trees, there was now just the paleness of the empty horizon. It seemed as if someone had pulled a curtain to one side to reveal a formless scene that bordered upon the underworld.

A native German like Sebald, **Sir Nikolaus Pevsner** (1902–83) was holder of an Honorary Doctorate of Letters from UEA and author of the mammoth *The Buildings of England* series. 'Norfolk is the kind of county it is especially nice to do', he said after touring it for four months ('the biggest county job I have had to do so far'). 'People are proud of it, they like it, and it is a county in which one feels at home.'

At the time the poet and novelist **Michèle Roberts** (1949–) was Visiting Writing Fellow at UEA in 1992, she revelled in long walks under the big Norfolk skies. This wasn't the first time the Anglo-French author had been to Norwich: in the 1970s, Roberts attended women's conferences on spirituality here 'because of the Julian of Norwich connection – I am very interested in women mystics'. Roberts, who specialised in medieval literature at Somerville College, Oxford, frequently addresses both religious and feminist issues in her writing. In the late seventies, a weekend spent at a farm on the Norfolk coast ('a very beautiful place') inspired the poem 'norfolk weekend', while a 'strange experience – sort of visionary' Roberts had in Norwich Cathedral many years later led to the writing of 'the return' from her 1995 collection *All the Selves I Was.*

It was on the 1984–85 MA in Creative Writing MA course that **Andrew Cowan** (1960–) and **Lynne Bryan** (1961–) first met. Since then, both have gone on to become successful writers, though freely admitting that they struggled in the early years following the course. After a long spell in Glasgow, Bryan and Cowan moved back to the 'child-friendly' environment of Norwich in 1994 to see their daughter grow up here.

Bryan wrote 'A Regular Thing', a pacy and unusual love story, on the MA, and this formed the starting point for her short story collection *Envy at the Cheese Handout* (1995) – tales about 'womanhood, urban experience and escape'. The title story is set in a town very unlike Norwich, but derives from Bryan's experiences here, queuing for free lumps of EEC butter and cheese handed out by the Salvation Army from their headquarters in **St Giles Street**, at a time when both Bryan and Cowan were unemployed.

Bryan's stories, praised as 'an imaginative and accomplished collection' by the *Times Literary Supplement*, reference both the vibrancy and bleakness of urban life. 'Better Than Beer and Skittles' fictionalises Bryan's involvement with the 'Norfolk Quilters' and her regular visits to 'The Blue Goose' (a quilting and patchwork shop on **Elm Hill**) and charts the weekly escapism of a small group of women – with a comic twist at the end. In 'Hair So Black', a typically windswept **Cromer*** is the setting for the pivotal episode in a relationship between two women. The fleeting glimpses of quiet desperation and fragments of ordinary urban life offered by Bryan's stories and her first novel, *Gorgeous* (1999) complement the continuity of the couple's Norwich base.

we swallow the air like earth
the sky is a delicate wall
on which we paint with clouds
the orchard stoops and drops
dark pink
apples in the long
grass, little
fallen sunsets in
green twilight

the land is pegged
with churches, five
on the horizon
but it still flaps brown
and stony

far across the field
the blackbirds chatter on
and red barns hug the earth
trees whistle for fled blue
blue tiles, blue roof, blue
dark sky

Michèle Roberts, 'norfolk
weekend' from *The Mirror of
the Mother – Selected Poems
1975–1985*, 1986

**Lynne Bryan &
Andrew Cowan**

The authors with their daughter Rose, forsaking their Norwich base for a trip to Yarmouth beach.

Andrew Cowan's work, while exploring the scarred urban landscapes found further north in Britain also bears witness to his early Norfolk days. Arriving at UEA as an undergraduate in 1980, Cowan soon moved into a cottage in **Windmill Road** (off **Sprowston Road**) where he remained for three years. This cottage, with its old sow squealing loudly in the garden, is used in Cowan's first novel *Pig* (1994) as an escape for his protagonist Danny. Once home to Danny's grandparents, the cottage is now a threatened environment, but still provides a useful hideaway for Danny's love affair with his Indian girlfriend Surinder.

The cottage is central to Danny's struggle to come to terms with his individuality and symbolises the difficulties of his various relationships; with his less-than-inspiring immediate family, his down-to-earth and affectionate grandparents, the enigmatic Surinder and, crucially, with his task of maintaining the cottage, garden and 'Agnes' – his dead grandmother's pig.

After completing his MA, Cowan worked as an oral historian, a job which took him into a number of old people's homes around the city, inspiring both the character of Danny's grandfather and the home he ends up in. *Pig*, begun in 1987 in Norwich and completed almost five years later in Glasgow, is a challenging novel exploring personal identity within the contexts of both family and cultural backgrounds. And Cowan's own background continues to emerge in his writing – his second novel, *Common Ground* (1996), though derived mainly from his Glasgow experiences, was completed in Norwich and uses **Mousehold Heath** for descriptions of the threatened woodland at 'Hogslea Common'. 'This is home,' says Cowan, whose latest novel – about the tragic death of a five-year-old boy – employs locales along the Norfolk coast stemming from Cowan's own holidays in **Overstrand*** and **Hunstanton***.

The Broads

LITERARY LINKS

John Betjeman, James Blyth, Wilkie Collins,
George Christopher Davies, Alan Hunter, George MacBeth,
Jan Mark, Gladys Mitchell, Arthur Ransome, Oliver G Ready,
Lisa St Aubin de Terán, Peter Scupham, C P Snow,
Sylvia Townsend Warner

The Broads are a unique geographical feature – a number of interconnected lakes and waterways assumed until recently to be the remains of an age-old estuary. Not until 1960 was it confirmed that the Broads are in fact man-made, formed in early medieval times by peat digging. Ecclesiastical records from these times confirm that vast quantities of peat fuel were once being shipped around Norfolk. When the sea flooded back into these man-made pits, they became a haven for wildlife, with fish and wild-fowl thriving among the shaded waterways. Reed and sedge-cutting for baskets, thatch and matting, wild-fowling, shooting and eel-fishing were a way of life for centuries in an area once isolated without proper roads or railways.

George Christopher Davies

His *Handbook* brought
tourists flocking to the Broads

George Christopher Davies (1849–1922) was a writer, lawyer and Broads enthusiast. *The Swan and her Crew; or the adventures of three young naturalists and sportsmen on the Broads and rivers of Norfolk* was his second book and hugely popular with Victorian and Edwardian boys of all ages. At this time the Broads was an area acknowledged by sailing enthusiasts but little known as a holiday resort. But Davies' hugely popular *The Handbook to the Rivers and Broads of Norfolk and Suffolk* published in 1882 soon changed that, doing for the Broads what **Clement Scott*** was about to do for Poppyland. As tourists flocked to the area, *The Handbook* became so successful that it ran to fifty editions over the following forty years!

Fritton

'The vast flat land stretched its marsh and dykes to the horizon. The spirits of the marsh were awakening, their influence was hovering in the reek and murk of the coming night. The cries of lapwings wailed aloft.'

James Blyth, *The Smallholder*, 1908

The village of Fritton (not to be confused with another village of the same name near **Tharston**) lies close to a wild, flat and desolate marshland, through which the reed-curtained Waveney winds its leisurely way. It was into this relentless expanse of boggy fields, dykes and wide open skies that prolific novelist **James Blyth** (1864–1933) moved in the early twentieth century.

Little is known of Blyth, except that he was educated at **Norwich Grammar School** under **Augustus Jessopp*** and after graduating from Cambridge, became articled to a law firm at Lincoln's Inn, before mysteriously fleeing London, changing his name, and retreating to the marshlands here. His recreations, listed in a copy of *Who Was Who 1929–40*, were apparently 'sailing, shooting, fishing and bacteriology', so he certainly seems to have found himself an appropriate environment.

Contemplating a career in either photography or writing, Blyth settled for the latter after becoming so impoverished that he was forced to sell his camera. He made the right decision – after the curiously titled *Juicy Joe: A Romance of the Norfolk Marshlands* (1903) he went on to publish an amazing twenty-two novels between 1906 and 1909. He maintained this pace for a further five years, though clearly his prolific output affected the quality of his work.

However, *Celibate Sarah* (1904), describing 'the success of a daughter of the marshes in rising above her native environment', and *Rubina* (1908), a romance across the classes and marshes, provide two examples of his stronger work and are powerful and original novels.

Blyth writes often of the harsh and gloomy lives of marshland folk, using local dialect to great effect. Always tending towards melodrama, his highly opinionated novels sometimes outraged Edwardian society by tackling social issues head-on. One review in the *Daily Chronicle* described his work as showing 'rural life in East Anglia in its most sordid, most bestial aspects'. Issues of socialism and feminism are interwoven by Blyth with superstition and sensuality, lust and brutality, within the confines of a mystical and primitive marshland:

Opposite: The 'vast flat land' of Fritton, where James Blyth wrote his marshland novels.

> The dam wound its silver way along the deep shadow of the pollard willows. Beyond this border of obscurity the mighty marsh stretched vast, brilliant, but whispering and mystic. The dykes shone beneath the moon, but under the cover of their walls lurked shadows where the spirits of the marsh might lay in wait for the unwary, and where hob-o'-lanterns might nestle till his time came to flash out in dancing radiance to the terror of the more superstitious countryfolk. A faint breeze was wafted from the nor'-west, and the new-born sallow leaves whispered of its refreshing nature. As the party walked along the dam they fell into silence. The hardiest marshman in Hockingham is not free from the eerie charm of the marsh.
>
> James Blyth, *Rubina*, 1908

Walking through Blyth's landscape today, with the wave-like roar of distant traffic fading behind, there is a feeling of being concealed and exposed in equal measure. This is the haunt of harriers and herons, coots and swans – the stillness and flatness of the pastures broken only by the strident calls of wild-fowl, the motor of an occasional river boat and the keening wind that cuts through the few stunted trees stranded in the open fields.

Hickling

When George Christopher Davies' *Handbook* was published, **Oliver G Ready** (1864–1940) was eighteen years old. Ready was born in **Waxham**, but his childhood was spent mainly on **Hickling Broad**, at his father's vicarage which lay along a narrow lane 'so deeply pitted with ruts that it had all the appearance of a choppy sea'. On either side of this lane, 'towering up some eight or nine feet from broad water ditches', was the natural foliage of the Broads: 'dense tangles of bulrushes, flowering blackthorn, willows and feathery-plumed reeds'.

Ready's nostalgic but unsentimental *Life and Sport on the Norfolk Broads* (1910) was inspired by his idyllic boyhood here and is a measure of life before the trauma of two world wars, recalling the old ways that are now lost: reed-cutting, loaded wherries, eel-fishing, and the hunting, shooting and fishing of plentiful game.

Many of Ready's childhood adventures could come straight off the pages of an **Arthur Ransome*** book, though Ransome would surely have been disturbed by the 'atmosphere of powder and shot' that accompanied a lifestyle totally interdependent with nature. Reed-cutting preserved the unspoilt waterways in which wildlife flourished, while hunting kept the numbers down and fed the local population.

Ready also provides the solution to the mystery of the untidy-looking coots' nests which, though positioned close to the water, remain safe and dry: 'Their nests were composed of dry reeds and leaves heaped

together in apparent confusion, but in reality placed with consummate skill, for, on close examination, the lower part of each structure was found to possess the qualities of a raft, rising and falling with high or low water, and yet held in position through having been carefully woven about several thick, straight-growing reeds.'

Snipe shooting on the Broads in 1886 – Oliver G Ready describes the reek of an 'atmosphere of powder and shot'.

Nevertheless, the white-shielded head of the coot – with what Ready describes as its 'quite clerical look' – was best kept firmly down while Ready and his chums blasted away with their guns.

Horsey

Although afforded some protection by the steep-banked sea dyke and sandy dunes, the land here is so flat and exposed, that it is not difficult to conjure up the grisly images of ancient rhymes:

> When the sea comes in at Horsey Gap
> Without any previous warning,
> A swan shall build its rushy nest
> On the roof of the Swan at Horning.
> And a bald headed crow, contented and merry,
> Shall feast on the corpses that float by the ferry.
>
> *Anon.*

Wilkie Collins

'The world and the world's turmoil seemed left behind forever on the land; the silence was the silence of enchantment – the delicious interflow of the soft purity of the sky and the bright tranquillity of the lake.'

Armadale, 1866

Wilkie Collins (1824–89) is renowned for his superb rendering of a sense of place and in the summer of 1864, Horsey Mere, with its distinctive 'mill' (actually a water pump), became the focus of his research into locales for his new novel *Armadale* (1866). This novel (in which Horsey Mere becomes 'Hurle Mere') has the guilty secrets, complex plot and melodramatic style of the popular Victorian 'novel of sensation' first explored by Collins in *The Woman in White* (1860).

As with his great friend **Dickens***, the 'strangeness' of the area appealed greatly to Collins, who describes the Broads as being 'one of the strangest and loveliest aspects of Nature, which the inland landscape, not of Norfolk only, but of all England, can show'. Unlike his colleague **Trollope***, whose Norfolk-based novels offer little sense of place, Wilkie Collins successfully captures the change in the landscape as the area is approached at the beginning of *Armadale*:

The unspoilt waters of Hickling Broad today – viewed from National Trust walkways

Horsey Mere and one of the 'invisible boats moving on invisible waters' noted by Wilkie Collins in *Armadale* (1866)

Little by little, the face of the country began to change as the carriage approached the remote and lonely district of the Broads. The wheat-fields and turnip-fields became perceptibly fewer; and the fat green grazing grounds on either side grew wider and wider in their smooth and sweeping range. Heaps of dry rushes and reeds, laid up for the basket-maker and the thatcher, began to appear at the roadside. The old gabled cottages of the early part of the drive dwindled and disappeared, and huts with mud walls rose in their place. With the ancient church towers and the wind and water mills, which had hitherto been the only lofty objects seen over the low marshy flat, there now rose all round the horizon, gliding slow and distant behind fringes of pollard willows, the sails of invisible boats moving on invisible waters.

The distinctive and less-than-melancholy voice of **John Betjeman*** (1906–84) places a different perspective on the area. Journeying from the family home in London, Betjeman enjoyed many trips to Norfolk and grew, like his father, to appreciate the harmony of the countryside. Betjeman's 'East Anglian Bathe' (*Collected Poems*, 1958) heads back to the Norfolk coast of the poet's childhood and to the 'soft swirling music' of the sea close by. So it is with 'Hurrying steps from Horsey Mere' that the young Betjeman approaches the 'tumbled breaker-line' across the 'table-land' of beach before diving into a cold and rough north sea which contrasts with the inland tranquillity:

> How cold the bathe, how chattering cold the drying,
> How welcoming the inland reeds appear,
> The wood-smoke and the breakfast and the frying,
> And your warm freshwater ripples, Horsey Mere.

Ingham

Jan Mark

The award-winning children's author who fills Norfolk skies in *Thunder and Lightnings* (1976).

The acclaimed children's writer **Janet Mark** (1943-) lived in Ingham (which she fictionalises as 'Pallingham') for fifteen years and sets three of her children's stories here alongside nearby 'Polthorpe' (**Stalham**). *Thunder and Lightnings* (1976) was written only a year after Mark exchanged her teaching career for full-time writing and immediately won her the Carnegie Medal. It tells of young Andrew and his Kentish family who move to Norfolk in the early 1970s. Andrew makes friends with Victor, a local lad whose chief passion is for aircraft, and the squadron of Lightnings (interceptor fighters based at **RAF Coltishall**) in particular – but plans are being made for all the Lightnings to be scrapped.

The inspiration for *Thunder and Lightnings* came from above, as Mark explains: 'After living all my life in downland I was particularly struck by the breadth of East Anglian skies.' This was the Cold War period, and Mark's attention became drawn to the fighter planes which frequently flew over her house, situated some 'eight miles from the end of the runway, and in a direct line with the flight path'.

Mark's second 'Norfolk' book, *Under the Autumn Garden* (1977), is the tale of a boy at a local village school who, for a history project, tries to excavate a medieval priory, which he knows lies somewhere close to where he lives. 'This time I went down instead of up', says Mark, 'drawing on local legends and history; the ruined priory at **Hickling*** and the still-detectable causeway between it and the great church at Ingham ... haunted by the ghost of Sir Oliver de Ingham whose tomb still stands in the chancel.'

'Where were you at college?' Erica said.

'UEA,' Elsie said. 'That's how I came to know Norfolk and love it' ...

'University? For being a mechanic?'

'No, for being a nutter,' Bunny said, from his communion with Freddie's Honda.

Janet Mark, *Handles*, 1983

Handles, published in 1983, is the witty and pertinent story of Erica, who had once dreamed of becoming a nurse (but 'all Erica wanted to be now was a motorcycle mechanic'), and is set mainly in 'Polthorpe' in 'the world's smallest industrial estate'. A family friend of the Marks' used to run a motorbike repair shop off Stalham Street on a very similar estate, which went on to become 'Mercury Motorcycles' in the book.

Oby

'In such an out-of-the-way place as this anything might happen,' said the first sacrist of Oby, staring at the listless horizon towards which the sun was descending like a lump of red-hot iron.

'Anything or nothing,' replied the first prioress.

Sylvia Townsend Warner, *The Corner that Held Them*, 1954

There is nothing much to indicate the existence of Oby; the tiny settlement doesn't even merit a mention on the OS map of the area. Reassurances from a local post office ('It's signposted from Thurne – I think ...') help point the way, and the road signs from Thurne or from the B1152 at Clippesby do indeed lead to the isolated cluster of houses, bordered by fields and the Bure marshes, that is Oby.

Sylvia Townsend Warner (1893–1978) sets her favourite novel, *The Corner that Held Them* (1954), in Oby and dedicates it to her lover, Valentine Ackland. Written between 1941 and 1947, through the terrible war years, the book is also one of Warner's most popular.

The 'action' takes place between 1345 and 1382, at the time of the Black Death and the Peasants' Revolt, and revolves around 'the epitome of humdrum' of a Benedictine nunnery. The convent, founded in the twelfth century in memory of the adulteress Alianor de Retteville, sits on a rise of ground that was once an island:

> Oby had been part of Alianor's dowry, and in the early days of their marriage they had often lived there, for it was good hawking country along the Waxle stream ... [which] flowed north-east through a poor country of marsh and moorland: a muddy reluctant stream, full of loops and turnings, and constantly revising its course, for the general lie of the land imposed no restraint on its vagaries. In some places it had hollowed for itself long pools where the current seemed to have ceased altogether, in others it skulked through acres of rushes and spongy moss.

When the first batch of nuns arrive from France in midsummer, they see their new home at its best, 'perched on the little rise of ground' and 'half-circled by a loop of the Waxle Stream', exposed 'under the enormous vault of sky'. With the blue of the river and the fields 'striped in the colours of cultivation and fallow', the area looks like 'one of those maps into which the draughtsman has put every detail and coloured the whole to resemble life'.

'Anything or nothing' happens at the Oby nunnery, depending on the definition of 'happens'. On one hand their holy order – or disorder – dedicated to Our Lady and Saint Leonard, patron of prisoners, has to

Sylvia Townsend Warner

She found a favourite 'corner' here in Oby.

St Benet's Abbey gateway, etched by John Sell Cotman in 1813 – of all the religious houses in England, it alone survived the Dissolution. Today, the Bishop of Norwich is still Abbot of St Benet's and returns each August to hold a service amongst the boggy ruins of the abbey church.

Almost certainly inspiring Sylvia Townsend Warner's Benedictine nunnery in *The Corner That Held Them*, are the ruins of **St Benet's Abbey** – still standing today in splendid isolation close to the River Bure. Warner would certainly have known the area well from her time spent with Valentine Ackland on a houseboat in nearby **Thurne**.

The abbey is located down a farm track off the side road close to **Ludham Hall** and was established in the early eleventh century, although tradition tells of a much earlier settlement here. Today the gatehouse, with its eighteenth-century mill planted awkwardly in the middle, together with a few low walls of the church, are all that remain of a once splendid abbey. With its wealth and power, the abbey was the target of many attacks over the years. One gruesome tale tells of Norman raiders taking the abbey through the treachery of a monk called Ethelwald, who assisted on the condition that he be made abbot. True to his wishes, the Normans dressed him in an abbot's robe and placed a mitre on his head – before hanging him from St Benet's gateway.

This episode is taken up by **Gladys Mitchell*** in her novel *Wraiths and Changelings* (1978), where her London ghost-hunting party visit the Broads and arrive at the abbey remains – the 'ugly erection that some insensitive soul put up among the ruins', as one of their number describes it. Hoping to catch a glimpse of Ethelwald's ghost, what they actually find hanging from the gateway is a little too true to life, or death, for their liking.

deal with the Black Death, carnal temptation, the sacrilegious 'priest' Ralph Ketto and the Bishop. On the other hand, the more tedious aspects, the ins and outs of convent life (and death), are described in detail. Here the cellaress counts the provisions, dill cordial is prescribed to combat weeping fits, and the various jealousies and squabbles among the dames and novices are revealed.

Religion was a source of some conflict between Warner and Valentine Ackland, and some readers felt the ironic portrayal of convent life in *The Corner That Held Them* to be wanting in reverence, but Warner defended herself, saying that '... the evidence of contemporary ecclesiastical records makes it inescapably plain that the monastic establishments ... displayed all the characteristic faults of community living – as well as grosser faults. On this evidence I could have made Oby a much worse place, and still have had the support of contemporary ecclesiastics.'

George MacBeth

The poet arrived at Oby looking for 'a piece of land to feel secure on'.

It was a return to the simplicity of living, and the 'fruit of a new involvement with the countryside' that drew **George MacBeth** (1932–92) to the Georgian rectory standing on the corner of the Oby and Thurne roads. MacBeth was an established poet and extrovert

The Old Rectory at Oby, with its 'white stockade' of snowdrops.

literary figure who had for some twenty years promoted poetry on BBC Radio. His first book of poetry was published in 1954 while he was still an undergraduate, and he went on to publish over thirty other works of poetry, fiction, memoirs and children's writing.

MacBeth moved into Oby Old Rectory in 1979 with his wife, the writer **Lisa St Aubin de Terán** (1953–) and her young daughter Iseult, feeling 'the luck of settlement, finding a piece of land to feel secure on'. It was therefore with 'more optimism than usual' that he worked on a poetry collection, *Poems from Oby* (1982), and a children's story, *The Rectory Mice* (1982) – dedicated to Iseult.

The Rectory Mice is a moral tale of a family of mice living in the rafters of Oby as the First World War breaks out. The mice are cleverly characterised, with the tragic hero Tamburlaine soon being led into danger, and the plot is both simple and exciting. By contrast, the *Oby* collection, though tinged with hope, seems dominated by guilt and insecurity. The poetry is strongly autobiographical, reflective, and unflinchingly honest. MacBeth displays great pride, but also an unhealthy possessiveness for 'my great house' and 'my land', and is aware of the constant struggle against his feelings of jealousy and sexual dependency in his marriage to a woman some twenty-one years his junior.

In addition, the couple's passion for collecting Victoriana (much of it purchased at the nearby **Aylsham** auctions) and MacBeth's obsession with memorabilia from the First World War must have made for a chaotic and cluttered household. Meanwhile, the upkeep and renovation of the huge rambling rectory, in its grounds of some two and a half acres, must have been as much of a challenge as the literary work. So much for simplicity.

Nevertheless, a genuine appreciation of the natural world of Norfolk is certainly apparent. In 'Somewhere', from the *Oby* collection, MacBeth writes of the 'great roots of beech' and the magnificent trees which dominate the garden: 'In all those rooms, no light / Unfiltered by the trees'. The (private) house is still noted for its seasonal blanketing of snowdrops, visible each spring. In 'Snowdrops', MacBeth describes their 'active spearheads' and 'white stockade' and how:

> They teem with loyalty, and fight
> For a place in the sun. Static in flight
> Their icy lances pierce with green
> Last year's drowned leaves. I touch one. Clean
> And moist upon my reaching palm,
> I feel its energy, its calm.

'I wanted the bare field out there to be mine' – the view from MacBeth's study window

Oby is some nine miles from the sea, yet this is an area of Norfolk so nearly encircled by water as to be known as the 'Isle of Flegg'. The

window of what was MacBeth's study looks out over the fields and marshes beyond, to the sails of yachts at Thurne Mouth, where the Bure meets the Thurne:

> I wanted the bare field out there to be mine.
> Each day, at my typing, I saw the smooth line
> Of the sycamores, breaking the sweep of grass
> To the farm and the river. I saw the sails pass
> Far away, white and simple, where yachts moved
>   at Thurne.
> And I looked down, in my pride, at my nearest stone urn.
> From that urn to the sycamores, this was my land,
> With the wide breadth of Norfolk stretched gold
>   on each hand.
>
> George MacBeth, from 'The Field, Tomorrow',
>   *Poems from Oby*, 1982

Sadly, MacBeth's greatest fears proved to be justified and his marriage ended when Lisa St Aubin eloped with the painter Robbie Duff-Scott, who had been employed to paint her portrait. MacBeth's literary response following the dissolution of his marriage was the painfully intimate and clumsily autobiographical novel *Another Love Story* (1991):

> There had been a dream, and you had been in the dream, and we had been happy, and then there were only reminders, material things with echoes in them.

Even by the time she married George MacBeth, Lisa St Aubin de Terán had lived a life as wild as any work of fiction. Married at sixteen to a Venezuelan exile, she returned with him to the family's vast feudal estate in his home country. St Aubin ended up running the estate more or less single-handedly after her husband suffered continuous bouts of depression. The collapse of their marriage was almost inevitable, but the escape from an area totally under the control of her husband's family was less straightforward. Only when she returned to England for treatment of a kidney infection was St Aubin finally able to find freedom for herself and her daughter Iseult.

The isolation of Norfolk was precisely what St Aubin needed at a time when she wanted to recover from the trauma of recent events and to avoid detection by her former husband's family. Oby must have been an exciting challenge for a self-confessed 'house-addict', though later St Aubin admitted, 'I fall in love with places readily. I have been in love with so many places, that, like old lovers, I can no longer remember their names.'

Encouraged by MacBeth, Lisa St Aubin began writing enthralling and stylised accounts of her life. The award-winning and auto-biographical *Keepers of the House* (1982) had originally been written in

Lisa St Aubin de Terán

By the time the novelist arrived at Oby, she had already lived a life stranger than fiction.

a curious hybrid of High Spanish and English, as her time in Venezuela had left little room for spoken English. As she remarked at the time: 'The actual events were too fantastic for anybody to be able to accept them. I had to tone down the truth to turn it into fiction!'

Courted by the press and publishers alike, St Aubin was earmarked for a great literary future, and it was unlikely that the rectory at Oby would ever have been sufficient to house her ambitions. The forty-two-room Umbrian 'palazzo' that St Aubin and Duff-Scott eventually bought together resulted in another book, *A Valley in Italy* (1994), and finally gave the writer the place of her dreams: 'a house so huge that I could move from room to room without disturbing anyone'. The unremarkable, flat and boggy marshlands of Norfolk suffer in comparison to the sun-drenched Umbrian scenery and despite, or because of, her time in Norfolk, nothing of the spirit of the county or countryside permeates her work.

The distant sails are still visible from MacBeth's study window, the fig tree from 'To preserve figs' is still standing, and high on the north wall of the building hangs the 'green bronze bell', whose iron clapper brings an untimely end to the heroic Tamburlaine in *The Rectory Mice*.

Living near Oby now is the creator of the Inspector Wang novels, **Christopher West** (1954–), whose travels in the Far East prompted the writing of *Journey to the Middle Kingdom* (1991). West continues to focus his energies a little further east than most Norfolk writers, producing intriguing mysteries such as *Death of a Red Mandarin* (1997).

Potter Heigham

C P Snow

The Broads provided the starting point for his writing career.

Wrapped around by the Weaver's Way, whose footpath leads up from **Oby** towards **Catfield**, the 'reedy wastes' of **Heigham Sound** and **Hickling Broad** are beautiful, unspoilt and tranquil, and a perfect setting for a murder mystery. *Death Under Sail* (1932) by **C P Snow** (1905–80) sees *The Siren*, a pleasure wherry, sailing down the Bure with its skipper, Roger, shot dead at the wheel.

As a boating holiday turns into a murder investigation, the remaining guests are confined to a riverside holiday bungalow most tourists today would kill for. But when the friends, all murder suspects, see the bungalow, it is without any prospect of pleasure:

We all felt a sinking melancholy at the sight of it. For it was quite alone, led up to on land by a narrow footpath through swampy fields; and in front of it there was an unkempt garden which ran down to the water. Set out there amid the deserted marshes, it seemed to my dejected eyes to represent the solitariness from which hope has fled – the solitariness into which a callous crime

The 'reedy wastes' of Heigham Sound

had thrown my friends, and from which one of them at least would not come back. As we entered it and saw through the back windows the reedy wastes of Heigham Sound, the atmosphere of gloom deepened amongst us all.

With accusations flying thick and fast, Snow provides genuine tension in a ripping yarn that is probably more of a parody than a genuine murder mystery. Indeed, he himself described *Death Under Sail* as 'a stylised, artificial detective story very much in the manner of the day'.

Snow employs the decidedly eccentric methods of enigmatic Norfolk detective Aloysius Birrell ('Don't you see that investigation of crime is one of the greatest romances in the world'), who quickly seizes upon chief protagonist and first-person narrator, Ian, as his main suspect. Luckily, Ian's friend and 'civil servant', Finbow, serves as the real detective alongside Birrell's sharp-minded buffoonery. Needless to say, the murderer gets his comeuppance, though not before a neat twist at the end of the tale.

Aged twenty-six and still working as a molecular physicist when he wrote *Death Under Sail*, Snow was certainly aware of the significance of the book, later stating: 'to myself, though not to many others, it was a signal that I proposed to give up the scientific career and take to writing novels'. Snow went on to create the hugely successful eleven-book sequence of 'Lewis Eliot' novels as well as a number of other works of fiction and biography before his death in 1980.

'His mouth was twisted and his eyes stern. The reeds waved desolately over his face, and above there was a grey and hopeless sky.'

C P Snow, *Death Under Sail*, 1932

Ranworth

Gladys Mitchell

She conjures apparitions at every corner in *Wraiths and Changelings.*

It is into the perpendicular glory of St Helen's Church, built in 1370, outside the village of Ranworth that **Gladys Mitchell**'s (1901–83) fifty-third novel *Wraiths and Changelings* (1978) moves towards its climax. Here, after a whole book full of fake ghosts, we finally witness the only 'real' one.

Mitchell, a prolific mystery writer, took up writing thrillers in the late 1920s and 'turned to detective fiction after seeing from **D L Sayers*** that you could write that sort of book in decent English'. Dubbed 'The Great Gladys' by **Philip Larkin**, Mitchell wrote over eighty books in her lifetime and is famous for the creation of her detective Dame Beatrice Adela Lestrange Bradley – a Home Office psychiatrist who appears in more than sixty novels, has herself once murdered, and is known as 'Mrs Croc' after her reptilian looks.

Dame Beatrice's help is definitely required in *Wraiths and Changelings*, which sees an unlikely party, pieced together by the Crieff-Tweedle couple and led by Dum Crieff-Tweedle, setting off for a week's ghost-hunting on the Broads. Dum's wife Dee finds the whole Norfolk experience incomprehensible, and especially the labyrinthine roads: 'Remember to sound your horn at all the bends. I don't know why some of these Norfolk roads need to wind the way they do. There are no hills to speak of,' she says, as they wind through the countryside. 'Norfolk roadmakers always worked with their backs to the wind,' declares her colleague Professor Byland solemnly. 'That accounts for the bends.'

Belatedly, Dee discovers that Norfolk also provides an ideal stage for a murder. Meanwhile, the ghost-hunting schedule of their party, well versed in books of the *Ghosts of the Broads* and *Haunted Britain* variety, is truly daunting:

> *Tuesday:* ... Salhouse Broad. Open-air Mass. Possibly ghostly monk in Salhouse church. *Wednesday:* ... Burgh Castle. Body (ghost) thrown over wall of Roman fort ... *Thursday:* Horning. Re-crowning of Saxon king. Possible ghost of suicide. Woman in white. ('Shades of Wilkie Collins', said Eiladh) ... *Friday:* Belaugh churchyard. Ghost of distraught young woman ... *Wednesday:* ... We wait outside the entrance to Blickling Hall to see Anne Boleyn's ghost-coach come through. Headless horses and coachman and Anne with her own head in her lap ...

The ghost-hunters, based in bungalows in **Wroxham***, have no shortage of spine-chilling experiences. But which of the ghosts they see are 'real' and which are cleverly staged (or even a cover for a sinister crime) is more difficult to determine. And as the holiday wears on, it dawns on more than one member of the party that something isn't quite right. Mitchell's quaintly ironic narrative finds an ideal backdrop in the quiet tension of the haunting Broads waterscape:

The westering sun was beginning to set, but there was still plenty of light. Undisturbed by passing boats at that time of the day, ... the water reflected probable and improbable colours and looked oily as the river made its leisurely progress towards Thurne Mouth, where it joined the Thurne, Breydon Water and the sea. The orange, gold and shadowy violet of the sunset were repeated in the water, and there were also deep green patches moving into luminous pewter which turned to silvery white as the ripples washed ashore. Here and there in the reflections were streaks of kingfisher blue. Reeds rustled and tree-roots sucked as the eddies rippled along the oozy banks. There was the occasional plop of a rising fish, a scurry as a dabchick made for home and other, less identifiable sounds. A bat missed – or seemed to miss – Eiladh's head by a fraction of an inch.

St Helen's Church, Ranworth – where Gladys Mitchell's ghostly Brother Pacificus is reputed to have helped paint the 15th-century rood screen.

As the action moves towards Ranworth Church, a mysterious figure is seen praying at the altar before moving off, dog at his side, towards the broad – where he simply disappears. Legend has it that the Benedictine monk 'Brother Pacificus' used to row over from **St Benet's Abbey*** to help paint the rood screen that still spans the width of this 'Cathedral of the Broads' today. While at work, Pacificus would entertain the villagers of 'Randworth' (meaning 'the village by the water's edge') with stories about the saint he was painting and with snippets of local history. In *Wraiths and Changelings*, Gladys Mitchell uses this legend, and Pacificus' unexpected showing, to unnerving effect.

St Helen's Church has its own literary treasure: the service book *Sarum Antiphoner*, whose 285 sheepskin leaves were written in medieval Latin and illuminated by the monks of Langley Abbey (near **Loddon**) in about 1400. Containing the alternating chants of medieval liturgy and bequeathed to the church in 1478, the *Antiphoner* was removed in the sixteenth century, and all trace of it lost until the middle of the nineteenth century.

Additionally, for fitter visitors, the effort of climbing the eighty-nine steps and two ladders to the top of the church tower is rewarded by a panoramic view of the watery expanses of Broadland.

Ranworth Broad from the tower of St Helen's

Sloley

In July 1933, **Sylvia Townsend Warner*** (1893–1978) continued her close association with Norfolk by taking a lease on the seventeenth-century Frankfort Manor with Valentine Ackland: ' … a most lovely, large and tranquil house, and our bedroom the fairest room in it, as it should be. And I should be very happy here; and am happy.'

The couple finally seemed to have found the country paradise they had sought, even though the upkeep of this elegant old house – with its Norfolk reed thatch and carved oak staircase, but no electricity – was a formidable task. Much of their time was spent tending the large, overgrown garden, while the many outbuildings, 'rustling with rats', continued to cause problems.

This was a time of great social and personal change (both Sylvia and Valentine were accepted as members of the Communist Party) and excitement. As well as coping with the property, Warner worked hard at her short stories, poems and reviews to earn sufficient money for their upkeep. Much later, Warner was to publish *The Cat's Cradle Book* (1960) – a cat's eye collection of short stories inspired by the farm cats Warner observed stalking the perennial rats in the Frankfurt Manor outbuildings.

In January, Sylvia had a 'Dream or vision, I don't know. But this morning I had a complete recall of the Frankfort meteor. It was a foggy

November night, we were walking back from **Scottow**, had passed our first gate when a brilliant light darted down on us. Our roadside trees were suddenly blackened, defined, like shaggy iron. There we stood. There we still stand.'

Unfortunately, Warner and Ackland did not 'stand' at Sloley much longer. The good nature of the two women involved them in a libel case which they lost, forcing them to give up their Sloley hideaway after sixteen hard but happy months. They left in November 1934 and Sylvia wrote: 'We were never again so unimpededly good as we were at Frankfort Manor.'

Sloley Old Hall – previously Frankfort Manor – where Sylvia Townsend Warner and Valentine Ackland enjoyed great happiness together. When they left in November 1934, Ackland wrote:

Lovely the house is, sheltering and kind,
Warm and faithful against besieging winter,
But we shut the door, and nothing remains behind.

South Burlingham

'I think our place in the county has been earned by spade, sweat, strimmer and screwdriver. Not to mention the mysteries of limewash and lime-mortar,' says poet **Peter Scupham** (1933–), whose small Elizabethan Manor here has surrendered many secrets during its renovation.

Scupham's collection of poetry *The Ark* (1994) takes his Norfolk home as its theme and in the sequence of poems 'A Habitat' offers 'a kind of exploration of its nature and mystery as we worked on it'. These poems, a rush of images and emotions as dense as the dust-clouds raised during the restoration work, examine the spirit of 'A cock-eyed house, beset by open fields / And too much wind.'

The parts of a whole – the lime mortar, the glass, the tie-beams and the brick on brick – are a physical manifestation of history itself, and the house becomes a part of the process of living and dying. In 'All Roads Lead to it', the joyous transformation of the Old Hall, from a state of 'Widespread infestation, structural distress' is sung by the 'long marriage of queen strut, king post', while still asking questions of the countless lives involved with it over the years: 'Who bewildered those floors to sand, / Tumbled the tumbled brickwork?'

'Painted hounds, leashed on a limed wall' in the gallery of the Old Hall

Sadness, too, writes white:
Skin upon skin of lime,
nine skins to the long
                unmaking
for hunters lost in the snow.
Hammocks of dirt and frost
rock from the ghosts of trees
in cold Broceliande.
The room is a dark lantern
and something bays at the
                moon.
Four hundred years
slip westward nightly
across the window square.
Over-wintering peacocks
wake up again to die
as glass claps at their wings
and these, too, ache for light,
poor disjecta membra:
through saws of bracken
a boar's raised fell,
the fury of small eyes,
Skin upon skin of sky
settles vaguely on this.
A hunter parts his curtain,
swings a half-sword
at nothing, afraid and
                crouching.

Peter Scupham, *The Gallery,*
Old Hall, South Burlingham,
The Hunt III, 1998

Cromer by James Stark *c.*1835 – largely unchanged from the 'ancient market town that stands/ Upon a lofty cliff of mouldring sands' witnessed by John Taylor the 'Water Poet' some two hundred years earlier.

'Where the regal red poppies are born' – Beeston Hill at Sheringham, at the heart of the 'Poppy-Land' discovered by Clement Scott in 1883

Overleaf: High tide on the North Norfolk coast – 'The sea was calm, and the wind so light it barely filled the sail ... only the stars traversing the gaps between the clouds seemed to move and have purpose' (Sylvia Townsend Warner, *The Flint Anchor*, 1954)

Itteringham Mill – where poet George Barker watched the 'shallows and shadows' of a River Bure that 'sidles and idles/ through weed isles and fallen willows'

Brancaster Beach – 'its ribbed distances scrunchy with shells, its wind-wrinkled pools blinking fast as troubled eyes' (Angela Huth, *Invitation To The Married Life*, 1991)

The work of restoring an ancient Norfolk house is as full of frustration as it is pleasure – 'Perhaps the house is full of awkward questions', suggests Scupham in 'Where is the Key?' Ultimately, in the 'thick air' of his complex and often dark poems, the Old Hall here at South Burlingham asks more questions than anyone can ever answer.

'I feel with **Auden*** that poetry is a game of knowledge, and I enjoy the complexity of rules that make the game worth playing', acknowledges Scupham, who started work as an English teacher in 1957. His educational work continues today, at the Norwich School of Art & Design, and in earlier years ran alongside the production of poetry collections such as *Prehistories* (1975), *Summer Palaces* (1980) and *Winter Quarters* (1983).

The move to Norfolk and the rescue launch for the Old Hall came in 1990 – the same year that Scupham's *Selected Poems* was published – and continues to inspire new work. Within the house, Scupham has discovered an impressive range of late sixteenth-/early seventeenth-century wallpaintings, including some vividly drawn images of hunting scenes. These are the subject of his trio of poems 'The Hunt', where: 'The hunt is on, the room / dazed by in-the-beginning: / walls white at the flood, / lime sharp in the nostrils, the ground prepared.'

Through Scupham's careful work – both physical renovation and poetic celebration – at South Burlingham, he comes close to the definition offered by **Anthony Thwaite*** of poetry being both a 'commemoration' and an 'excavation' and as Scupham writes in 'Where is the Key?': 'Living here will be enough and more'.

Peter Scupham

'Living here will be enough and more.'

Wroxham

Little remains of the tiny Broadland village with its medieval bridge that once stood here on the banks of the Bure (known as the 'North River'). Today's Wroxham is the 'Clapham Junction' of the Broads, its centre now a mass of boat-houses, commercial boat-hire, hotels and holiday bungalows. The medieval bridge still stands, but is besieged by a constant flow of traffic.

Heading a little further out of Wroxham along the river in either direction, there are still glimpses of the unspoilt beauty that was. The banks of the Broads rivers are home to innumerable wild-fowl, notably the nimble coot. These black-feathered birds with white faces wade deliberately and cautiously around the waters and build their haphazard-looking nests in the tall reeds.

Coots are the focus of **Arthur Ransome**'s (1884–1967) in his delightful *Coot Club* (1934) – a children's adventure story set in the Norfolk Broads. With Tom Dudgeon, the Horning doctor's son in lead role, and using the North river as the setting for the action, Ransome sees the children set sail from a busy Wroxham:

Arthur Ransome

He lovingly charts Broadland waterways in his enchanting children's tales.

The flatness of the land was astonishing – not because it was flat, but because it was not flatter, not caved in altogether beneath the weight of the enormous sky. The drainage mills which stood about the vast green expanse looked heroic but doomed for daring to be vertical in such a landscape. By the time we reached our destination and got down from the truck on to a small concrete standing heaped with poke nets and sacks, it seemed an impertinence not to go on all fours.

Sylvia Haymon,
Opposite the Cross Keys, 1988

Never in all their lives had Dick and Dorothea seen so many boats ... The huge flags of the boat-letters were flying from their tall flagstaffs. Little flags, copies of the big ones, were fluttering at the mastheads of the hired yachts. There were boats everywhere, and boats of all kinds, from the big black wherry with her gaily painted mast, loading at the old granary by Wroxham bridge, and meant for nothing but hard work, to the punts of the boatmen going to and fro, and the motor-cruisers filling up with petrol, and the hundreds of big and little sailing yachts tied to the quays, or moored in rows, two and three deep, in the dykes and artificial harbours beside the main river.

The children's quest is to save the coots' nests from egg-thieves and from the reckless washes of motor launches such as the *Margoletta* owned by the 'Hullabaloos'. Very much in the same vein as *Swallows and Amazons* (1930), which made Ransome's name as a children's writer, *Coot Club* is also symbolic of the struggle for the Broads at a time when increasing commercialism and pollution were wiping out a way of life.

As a sailing enthusiast, Ransome was a regular visitor to the Broads, exploring the waterways and renewing his family's links with the area: 'We came to know the Broads extremely well and to feel very much at home there. In the sixteenth century one of my ancestors was a miller at **North Walsham** and he may have helped me to feel no stranger.'

Ransome, as **Roger Wardale** notes in *Arthur Ransome's East Anglia* (1988): 'was always responsive to landscape and he was charmed by the slow-moving rivers and little dykes full of all sorts of hiding places'. Certainly, Ransome's settings for *Coot Club* are remarkably accurate, and in this tale at least, the 'Hullabaloos' – representing the brash, noisy commercialism of the modern world – get their comeuppance!

It was at the suggestion of a family friend that Ransome prepared a sequel to *Coot Club*. The setting for *The Big Six* (1940) is nearby **Horning*** with the wicked George Owden again wreaking havoc along the riverside. Staying at the White Gates Hotel (now a private house) in Horning, Ransome developed an exciting and enchanting detective story which further explores the Broadland area.

'Arthur Ransome would weep if he could visit the Broads today,' says crime writer **Alan Hunter** (1922–) who, together with his creation Chief Superintendent George Gently, has witnessed many changes in his home town over the years. Hunter was born and bred in **Hoveton St John** on the River Bure, on the outskirts of Wroxham and 'brought up with boats and sailing'. He is saddened to see such vast numbers of motor launches churning through the water today, believing that the Broads 'are essentially sailing-waters, and in my view should be preserved as such'.

Even as far back as 1944, in Hunter's first literary endeavour *The Norwich Poems* (1944), he sounds a warning: 'The River's packed from dusk till dawning / From Wroxham Bridge right down to Horning.'

After working in poultry farming and in the book trade, Hunter settled into a writing career; a short spell of playwrighting being followed by a successful move into the crime fiction genre and the creation of his popular 'Gently' series. Some forty novels later Chief Inspector Gently is still sagely puffing his pipe as he tracks down criminals around the country. The novels *Gently Down The Stream* (1960), *Gently Floating* (1964), *Gently French* (1973), *Gently To A Sleep* (1978) and *Amorous Leander* (1983) all enjoy Broads settings, while in *Gently Scandalous* (1990), with its 'locale ... sketched from life', a boat-owner makes a grisly discovery in the 'Wolmer' river at nearby 'Eastgate':

> The man quavered: 'He's under my boat ... just his hand sticking out of the water.'
> 'A hand?'
> 'That's all I could see. I – I was down there to pump the bilge. But first I eased the moorings because she was hard on the mud. And then – oh lord! – this hand came up. He must be down there under the boat. And the bank is all trampled. It looks as though there was a fight.'
> 'You mean some bugger shoved him in?'

'There were boats everywhere' – Wroxham today, with its medieval bridge in the background.

Alan Hunter

'In my youth I actually met Arthur Ransome. I was fishing with some other kids when he suddenly appeared, followed by a man carrying a box containing bottles of ginger beer and sticky buns ... with these Arthur plied us while he questioned us about ourselves and our activities. At about the time when he would have been planning *Coot Club*, which seemed strangely familiar when I first read it.'

Gently gets involved when he receives a poison-pen letter implicating a local man in the drowning, and soon his investigations lead him around familiar muddy backwaters and down into the murky depths of the 'Wolmer'. Gently's dedication and quiet determination see the crime solved in typically modest style, but not before a few false trails are followed.

Gently's cautious and painstaking probing, combined with his all-too successful hunches, frequently raises the hackles of the local police force, particularly those in the Norfolk capital of 'Norchester' (**Norwich***). In *Gently Does It* (1955), the murderer is identified at an early stage, but it takes many long hours of investigative toil to overcome the naive cynicism of his Norchester colleagues. Only flashes of Gently's understated inspiration, culminating in a fortuitous trip to the 'Railway Road' home of Norwich City Football Club, produce sufficient evidence to convict the guilty party.

Alan Hunter himself now lives south of Wroxham in the riverside village of **Brundall**, close to 'Norchester', and as his self-deprecating CID detective continues to sift through the flotsam and jetsam of criminal activity, discarding red herrings as he goes, few can fail to be impressed by such an amiable and imperturbable character.

CHAPTER FOUR

The King of Fishes

LITERARY LINKS

John Aikin, Brian Aldiss, George Borrow, Amanda Dalton,
Daniel Defoe, Charles Dickens, Michael Drayton, Edward FitzGerald,
H Rider Haggard, Thomas Nashe, Anna Sewell, William Shakespeare,
Henry Sutton, Paul Theroux, Anthony Trollope,
Sylvia Townsend Warner, Parson James Woodforde

Great Yarmouth

Prolific Elizabethan verse writer **Michael Drayton** (1563–1631), perhaps best known for his sonnet 'Since there's no help, come let us kiss and part', winds his way eventually towards Yarmouth in *Polyolbion* (1622) – the great topographical poem on England which took him over twenty years to complete:

> But now to nimble Yar, turn we our active song,
> Which in her winding course,
> > from Norwich to the mayne,
> By many a stately seate lasciviously doth straine,
> To Yarmouth ill she come, her onely christned towne,
> Whose fishing through the realme,
> > doth her so much renowne,
> Where those that with their nets
> > still haunt the boundless lake,
> Her such a sumptuous feast of salted herrings make,
> As they had rob'd the sea of all his former store,
> And past that very howre, it could produce no more.

By the time Drayton arrived here, Yarmouth's position as a major seaport, with important trade links to the Netherlands, the Rhineland and the Baltic, had already been severely undermined. However, in the Middle Ages, Yarmouth was an affluent and strategic settlement, and from its location at the mouths of the rivers Bure and Yare was able to service the whole of East Anglia, then one of the wealthiest regions in England.

> Yarmouth had first (O more
> > than happy port)
> The honour to receive the
> > King and Court,
> And entertain, season
> > providing dishes,
> The King of England with the
> > king of fishes.
>
> Anon. from *Upon His Majesties
> Progress Into Norfolk*, 1671

Thomas Nashe

'There may bee more resounding bel-mettal in my pen than I am aware, and if there bee, the first peale of it is Yarmouthes'

Lenten Stuffe, 1599

As Drayton's contemporary **Thomas Nashe*** (1567–1601) noted, Yarmouth was a town born 'out of an hill or heape of sande, reared and enforced from the sea most miraculously'. But the debilitating struggle against the same silting which had first given birth to the town, and the continual efforts to maintain a clear harbour occupied the town for centuries and cost many fortunes.

Nashe's own fortunes as the self-proclaimed 'Pierce Penniless' of London were also on the decline when he fled here in 1597 after feeling the full force of Elizabethan censorship. As a satirist and pamphleteer, Nashe was no stranger to controversy – indeed his reputation as a writer depended upon it. His vitriolic but witty exchanges with the scholar **Gabriel Harvey** became legendary, continuing over several years until culminating in Nashe's victorious *Have With You to Saffron Walden* (1596). But his satirical sideswipes also found Nashe many powerful enemies, and provoked the State on many an occasion.

Thomas Nashe was born further down the Waveney at Lowestoft, which was at that time still overshadowed by its industrious Norfolk neighbour and Yarmouth's busy fishing fleet. Though noted for his profound disrespect of those in positions of power and authority, Nashe always retained a fondness for the fishermen whose job it was to haul 'the treasure of fish out of the profundities'. The sea was an ever-present companion in the first four years of his life, and the 'rugged brine' of 'the roaring territory', as he termed it, remained a major influence in his work. Nashe quickly felt at home in Yarmouth, which combined the urban bustle of a major town with the sharp sea-air blowing off the 'churlish frampold waves'.

At the peak of his career, Nashe enjoyed more success than **William Shakespeare***, some three years his senior. But after the publication of *Isle of Dogs* in the spring of 1597, on which the young **Ben Jonson** collaborated, Nashe found his writing banned and himself a wanted man. This was the same year that all London theatres were closed on the pretence of the 'great disorders' caused by 'lewd matters' appearing on stage. It was also a time of economic crisis, social unrest, famine and food riots.

Whatever Nashe and Jonson wrote in the *Isle of Dogs* will never be known, because the manuscript has not survived. But it was sufficient for Jonson to spend time in prison and for Nashe to arrive in Yarmouth as a fugitive. By now, impoverished and harassed, his career was spiralling into terminal decline, but he produced one last masterpiece: *Nashe's Lenten Stuffe* (1599). The work was drafted during early spring 1598, hence the pun on the period of Lent in what was a lean time for Nashe and many others.

Lenten Stuffe opens with a grand tour of Yarmouth, past the massive fortified walls and into the main thoroughfares of the town 'as long as threescore streets in London', with some 140 smaller 'lans' (rows) weaving through the centre. Nashe is captivated by the sight of the huge

shipping fleet here which clouds 'the whole skie with canvas', but he soon develops *Lenten Stuffe* into a vigorous satire on the town and the smoked herrings for which it is famous. The red herring, or humble kipper, is the 'English marchandise' which ensures trade and foreign funds, employment, and, crucially for Nashe, plentiful and affordable nourishment:

> Of our appropriate glory of the red herring no region twixt the poles articke and antartik may, can or will rebate from us one scruple. On no coast like ours is it caught in such abundance, no where drest in his right cue but under our Horizon; hosted, rosted and tosted heere alone it is.

Nashe's 'prayse of the red herring' is not only a celebration of the town and its food that kept him alive throughout that lean Lent period of 1598; through his abundant wit and his fables, proverbs and legends, Nashe proves himself the master of satirical pamphleteering, whatever the subject.

When Nashe died in 1601, still in his early thirties, Shakespeare, the bright and more permanent star of Elizabethan theatre, was just completing *Hamlet*.

By the time **Daniel Defoe*** (1660–1731) visited this 'antient town' over a century later, in 1722, Yarmouth had successfully completed the construction of its seventh haven, contributing greatly to its new-found prosperity. Defoe was certainly impressed by the imposing dockland architecture and concludes that Yarmouth possesses 'the finest quay in England if not in Europe', while the surrounding merchants' houses 'look like palaces rather than the dwelling houses of private men'.

Defoe supports Nashe's view that Yarmouth is the 'locke and key of Norfolke' and declares that the town is 'better built; much more compleat ... and for wealth, trade, and advantage of its situation, infinitely superior to Norwich'. The ships' sails still filling the skies here had already been inspirational for Defoe's writing – providing the starting point for Robinson Crusoe's epic voyage some years earlier.

Scotch girls loading herring into barrels – for centuries the humble kipper was a major source of trade in Yarmouth: '... what the whale hath in bigness the herring hath in number', notes Thomas Fuller in his *Worthies* (1662) some two hundred years earlier.

Physician, author and Dissenter **John Aikin** (1747–1822) settled here in 1784 to practice medicine and to be near his sister, the writer and poet **Anna Barbauld**, at Palgrave. Together they published *Evenings at Home* (1792–6), six volumes of popular children's prose.

While in Yarmouth, Aikin wrote *England Delineated* on national character and worked on several biographies and memoirs. He also gave up eating sugar as a protest against the slave trade, but found Yarmouth folk to be against his liberal ideas and eventually left for London in 1792.

In his *Diary*, **Parson James Woodforde*** (1740–1803) mentions staying at the 'Wrestlers Inn' on **Church Plain** which, though much-altered, still stands today. Walking along the quay, 'as fine a one as ever was seen', he sees sailors from a Dutch ship wearing 'monstrous large trousers' and, on a windy day, witnesses equally monstrous waves 'like Mountains coming into the Shore'. On the opposite side of Church Plain stands the seventeenth-century timbered house, now a restaurant, where the author of *Black Beauty*, **Anna Sewell*** (1820–78), was born some seven years after Woodforde's death.

Sewell House on Church Plain, birthplace of Anna Sewell in 1820

Charles Dickens* (1812–1870) visited Yarmouth in the first week of January 1849. He only stayed for two days but was immediately struck by the eerie flatness of the surrounding countryside, declaring it to be 'the strangest place in the wide world'. Perfect, in other words, for a literary locale. Always a great walker, Dickens and his two colleagues spent a day walking from Yarmouth to Lowestoft and back – a distance of some twenty-three miles. En route, Dickens passed the village of Blundeston which would soon become 'Blunderstone', the birthplace of David Copperfield, the author's 'favourite child'.

Although initially wary of his new surroundings, young David Copperfield soon finds his time at Yarmouth a breath of fresh air after the barely repressed hostility of his new stepfather, Mr Murdstone, back home. Wandering the maze of narrow streets, past the busy docks and 'rope-walks, boat-builders' yards, ship-wrights' yards, ship-breakers' yards, caulkers' yards, riggers' lofts, smiths' forges', David finally catches a glimpse of the Peggottys' eccentric seashore home: 'a black barge, or some other kind of superannuated boat, ... high and dry on the ground, with an iron funnel sticking out of it for a chimney and smoking very cosily'.

Charles Dickens

The author pictured *c.*1852, not long after the two day visit here which left such a lasting impression and inspired the setting of *David Copperfield*.

David Copperfield's carriage leaving Peggotty's boathouse on the Denes

Breydon water just outside Yarmouth – 'It looked rather spongy and soppy, I thought, as I carried my eye over the great dull waste that lay across the river; and I could not help wondering, if the world were really as round as my geography-book said, how any part of it came to be so flat.' Young David Copperfield's first impressions of the area, in Charles Dickens' *David Copperfield*, 1850

'To hear the wind getting up out at sea, to know that the fog was creeping over the desolate flat outside, and to look at the fire and think that there was no house near but this one, and this one a boat, was like enchantment.' – David Copperfield enjoying his stay at the Peggotty's boathouse in Dickens' classic.

During his stay in Yarmouth, Dickens seems to have learned of the curiously roofed boathouse once standing close to the Nelson Column which surely formed the model for the Peggottys' home. Today the area is much changed by its transformation into the East Coast's busiest tourist resort. The Denes – the area close to the South Beach that was home to the Peggottys' – houses a large caravan park overlooking the sea, while Nelson's victory column, much in need of restoration, stands stranded in the middle of a vast industrial area. Instead of the smells of 'the fish, the pitch, and oakum, and tar' that assailed the nostrils of young David Copperfield it is the cloying aroma of chips, ice-cream and candyfloss which fills the seafront air today.

Nevertheless, throughout *David Copperfield*, the 'sharp bracing air' and the 'crisp and clear' sea of Yarmouth stand in stark contrast to the pollution-smudged grime and often claustrophobic chaos of London, while the simple and genuine friendship of Mr Peggotty, Ham, Em'ly and their friends represents the hospitality Dickens himself met with on his visit here.

Approaching the climax of his novel, Dickens transforms the previously peaceful image of the sea into a scene of howling winds and a violent and tragic storm – 'a rending and upheaving of all nature'. The dramatic shipwreck scene begins even as David Copperfield approaches Yarmouth: ' ... long before we saw the sea, its spray was on our lips'. Arriving here, David makes his way through streets 'strewn with sand and seaweed, and with flying blotches of sea-foam' to join the townsfolk on the shore, watching a schooner battling desperately through the 'rolling abyss' of the sea. When the ship eventually breaks up, Ham battles his way out through the waves, trying to rescue David's old friend Steerforth, with tragic consequences.

David Copperfield is a deeply personal novel through which Dickens revisits many of the scenes of his own anguished childhood. But the charm of Yarmouth and the memory of walks along the beach here lingered long after his visit, as they do for David Copperfield:

> I never hear the name, or read the name, of Yarmouth, but I am reminded of a certain Sunday morning on the beach, the bells ringing for church, little Em'ly leaning on my shoulder, Ham lazily dropping stones into the water, and the sun, away at sea, just breaking through the heavy mist, and showing us the ships, like their own shadows.

By his own admission, a man of 'rather a peculiar mind and system of nerves', **George Borrow*** (1803–1881) moved to Yarmouth in 1853, lodging at 37–39 Camperdown Place (now a hotel but unrecognisable from Borrow's day) and at 169 King Street, where he stayed for two years and completed *The Romany Rye* (1857). Here at Yarmouth he was able to enjoy one of his favourite pastimes: swimming. Rarely a day went by without an invigorating dip, whatever the weather, and *The Bury Post* of the time recalls a daring piece of life-saving by Borrow in high seas – a feat which testifies to his continuing physical fitness.

Anthony Trollope (1815–1882) held little affection for either Norfolk or its coast, though through his visits here while working as a Post Office Surveyor, he was surely more familiar with the area than Dickens. Trollope's most successful novel, *Can You Forgive Her?* (1864) – the first of his 'Palliser' series – features Mrs Greenow, a jolly widow and capable flirt, as the 'prize' awaiting one of her two nervous suitors.

Anthony Trollope

'Yarmouth is not a very prepossessing place to the eye ... There is an old town with which summer visitors have little or nothing to do; and there are the new houses down by the seaside, to which ... belongs the full advantage of sea air ... There is no beauty unless the yellow sandy sea can be called beautiful. The coast is low and straight, and the east wind blows full upon it.'

Can You Forgive Her?, 1864

As Trollope continues to subvert the images of *David Copperfield* in this enjoyable farce, there seems little left to recommend Yarmouth, except that 'the place is healthy'. But the sea air too has its hazards – soon Samuel Cheesacre, a podgy, foolish, but affluent farmer from the fictitious Norfolk village of 'Oileymead' is organising a beach picnic, following his unendearing motto: 'Do good and talk about it'. Cheesacre is one of Mrs Greenow's suitors, whilst also partaking of the picnic party is his friend and rival for the 'prize', the penniless but witty Captain Gustavus Bellfield.

It is finally decided to have the picnic on **Ormesby Sands**, north of Yarmouth. The scene here is an almost exact replica of David Copperfield's enjoyable times at Peggotty's boathouse a little further down the sandy seafront, but Mr Cheesacre's enthusiasm is not shared by all:

Yarmouth is not a happy place for a picnic. A picnic should be held among green things. Green turf is absolutely an essential. There should be trees, broken ground, small paths, thickets, and hidden recesses ... there should certainly be hills and dales, and, above all, there should be running water. There should be no expanse ... But the spot chosen for Mr Cheesacre's picnic at Yarmouth had none of the virtues above described. It was on the sea-shore. Nothing was visible from the site but sand and sea ... there was a long, dry, flat strand; there was an old boat half turned over, under which it was proposed to dine: and in addition to this, benches, boards, and some amount of canvas for shelter.

Immune to his guests' possible discomfort, Cheesacre is soon singing the praises of the county while denigrating Captain Bellfield as being someone 'better for eating and drinking with than he is for buying and selling with, as we say in Norfolk'. The plot moves on to **Norwich*** as Trollope keeps the reader guessing whether Cheesacre's loud Norfolk patriotism will be sufficient to win his 'prize'.

Henry Rider Haggard (1856–1925)*, visiting his daughters Angie and Dolly in Yarmouth in August 1915 recounts how First World War 'spy mania' has affected the town. In his *Private Diaries 1914–25* Haggard notes that the venetian blinds and curtains drawn at their lodgings are 'not of the newest or best' and goes on to tell what happens when a window behind them is opened:

Presently there arose murmurs from the esplanade without, which I should explain is plunged in the most intense darkness in these dark and moonless nights and yet seems to be the haunt of hundreds who wander about in the gloom, feeling their way from post to post. Next the landlady's daughter arrived saying that soldiers and police had called complaining that light was escaping from the window; that the esplanade was filled from side to side with a mob who swore that signalling to the Germans was going on from the house and that there was much excitement ... the whole thing is madness for how could anyone signal with a lamp or candle over the Yarmouth Roads filled with mine sweepers to the deep water miles away? In Yarmouth I am informed this spy hunting has become an absolute mania, so much so that the unfortunate landlady ... thinks she will have to leave the house.

'A harmony of slight noises rose everywhere, from farm and field, comprising the orchestral silence of a Norfolk night.'

Brian Aldiss,
Remembrance Day, 1993

In his 1993 novel *Remembrance Day*, **Brian Aldiss*** (1925–) introduces Hengist Morton Embry, an American professor of Stochastic Sociology on a sabbatical year at the **University of East Anglia***. Embry has relatives buried in Great Yarmouth cemetery and is drawn back to the town through his ambitious hypothesis of 'transpsychic reality'. He hopes to test his 'social causation' theory on the seaside resort where,

in the mid-eighties, four people were killed at a small hotel by an IRA bomb. What were these people doing here, and in what way did their tangled web of relationships contribute to their own deaths?

Yarmouth from the air – Breydon Water lies beyond and the Nelson monument is just visible on the South Denes to the top right.

In a tale weaving through north Norfolk, Aldiss references the history of the area from the fifteenth-century **Pastons***, through the denuding of extensive forest areas by the Enclosures of the nineteenth century, to the more recent CND campaigns at local airbases. In this carefully constructed, uneasy novel, any tranquillity offered by Yarmouth is soon shattered as the past is returned, in its full tragedy, to the present.

American writer **Paul Theroux*** (1941–) arrived at Yarmouth in 1982, as a part of his travels around the coastline of Britain forming the basis for *The Kingdom By The Sea* (1983). Still puzzling over the misleading nature of many of the East Anglian place-names he encountered on the way here, Theroux notes: 'Freshfields was always the semi-slum, and Messing, Turdley and Swines always the pretty villages'. In Yarmouth's miles of bustling seafront amusement, Theroux finds 'the English seaside characteristic of being self-destructive in its own way'.

Paul Theroux

The American writer follows in the footsteps of Henry James when he arrives at a 'self-destructive' Yarmouth during his 1982 tour of Britain's coastline.

Taking in the radically altered face of the town, Theroux is aware that he is following in the footsteps of fellow countryman **Henry James** (1843–1916) who had written that the town's 'mile of cockneyfied seafront ... now strikes the wrong note so continuously that I, for my part, became conscious on the spot, of a chill to the spirit of research'. But in *The Kingdom By The Sea*, Theroux is more realistic in his assessment of Yarmouth's transition from Dickensian hideaway to modern holiday resort and provides his own explanation for James' obvious disappointment:

He had hoped to sit on the front and sink into a reverie of David Copperfield and the Peggottys. But it was often a mistake in England to revisit fictional landscapes. Local people blamed the German bombing for Great Yarmouth's gappy, still-damaged look, but James's dismay was proof that the town had been just as raucous and profane a hundred years ago ... it had long ago stopped being Dickensian.

Caister

Standing just outside what was once a strategic Roman port, Caister Castle remains as a monument to one of **Shakespeare's** (1564–1616) most fascinating literary creations: Sir John Falstaff. Constructed between 1433 and 1448 by the real Sir John Fastolfe towards the end of his long and largely distinguished military career, Caister Castle was one of the first brick-built castles in Britain and resembles a moated Rhineland Schloss more than a traditional English castle.

William Shakespeare

The 'Norfolk Portrait' of the playwright which has been held in the care of Norfolk families for generations.

'Falstaff unimitated, unimitable Falstaff, how shall I describe thee?'

Samuel Johnson, notes to his Shakespeare edition, 1765

'The better part of valour is discretion; in which the much better part I have secured my life.'

Sir John Falstaff in Shakespeare's *Henry IV* Part I, V, i.

There is much debate as to whether Shakespeare's characterisation of Falstaff as a cowardly, bumbling, drunken 'fat-kidneyed rascal' can be the same man. Whatever literary licence was applied by Shakespeare, his creation of Falstaff was hugely successful. First appearing in *Henry IV* (1597), Falstaff was so popular with Elizabethan audiences that Shakespeare was compelled (some even say instructed by Queen Elizabeth I) to revive his comic character. Having reported Falstaff's death in *Henry V* (1599), Shakespeare subsequently shapes the farcical romp *The Merry Wives of Windsor* (1602) around a Falstaff who, as both lover and fool, is subjected to all sorts of humiliation.

The original Fastolfe was born at the manor of Caister in 1378 into a moderately wealthy Norfolk family. He began his military service in France during the Hundred Years' War and adopted the motto 'Me faut faire' ('I must be doing'). This inscription can still be seen, together with his coat of arms, on the carved stone chimney-piece in **Blickling Hall**. Blickling, acquired in 1432, was one of ninety-four manors owned by Fastolfe when he died!

Unlike his Shakespearian character, Fastolfe had a reputation for being not only brave, but also feisty, unforgiving, and unlikely to be fond of jests. So why the characterisation? Writing in 1625, **Richard James**, the famous Elizabethan scholar, explains: '... in Shakespeares first shew of Harrie the fift, the person with which he undertook to playe a buffone was not Falstaffe, but Sir John Oldcastle, and that offence beinge worthily taken by Personages descended from his title ... the poet was putt to make an ignorant shifte of abusing Sir John Falstophe, a man not inferior of Vertue'.

In 1429, at the Battle of Patay, the French army under Joan of Arc defeated the English in a battle that saw Fastolfe having to abandon the fight and withdraw from the field. Rumours of cowardice resulted in

his temporary disgrace and lent Fastolfe a reputation: 'He who fights and runs away / Lives to fight another day'. When eyewitness reports confirmed that he had deserted the battle only when the situation had become hopeless, his honour was restored – but the damage had been done.

After his death, Fastolfe was buried initially, in accordance with his wishes, in the grounds of **St Benet's Abbey***, but his tomb was later moved to St Nicholas' church in **Great Yarmouth** where it can be seen to this day on the north wall of the nave.

Caister Castle in the eighteenth-century – now housing a car museum, it was originally built by John Fastolfe, enemy of the Paston Family and, thanks to Shakespeare's character of Falstaff, the butt of many Elizabethan jokes.

Gorleston

Edward FitzGerald (1809–83), eccentric writer and translator of *The Rubáiyát of Omar Khayyám* (1859), was a keen sailor and once bought a boat here with his fisherman friend Joseph 'Posh' Fletcher. In 1857 FitzGerald and his wife Lucy (their marriage lasted but a few months) were in Gorleston, supposedly looking for a house in which to live. They received a surprise visit from **George Borrow***, then living near by in **Great Yarmouth***. Borrow had sent 'Old Fitz' a copy of his recently published *The Romany Rye* and as the pair started drinking, FitzGerald and Borrow argued about the book. Borrow, drinking strong port, voiced his 'contempt for anyone who could drink Sherry', so Fitz proceeded to down copious amounts of it. He then insisted on walking home with Borrow and on the return journey collapsed by the roadside and slept most of the night there.

Henry Sutton

The *enfant terrible* of this seaside town, on the lookout for scandal in his debut novel *Gorleston*.

The writer **Henry Sutton*** (1963–) was born in the village of **Hopton**, just south of Gorleston, and spent the first eight years of his life here before moving to **Norwich*** and later to London. After working in journalism, including a spell as travel editor of *The European*, Sutton opened his full-time career as a novelist with *Gorleston* (1995), in which he exorcises the memories of his home town and develops his concept of the way character and landscape 'might mirror each other'.

Sutton's controversial *roman à clef* draws much upon the history of this 'quintessential English seaside retirement town', from its beginnings as the Roman fort 'Garianonum' to the modern but dilapidated seaside resort he depicts. The overall impression Sutton gives of Gorleston – 'my idea of the town's long past and its short future' – seems to lean towards **Thomas Nashe**'s* description in *Lenten Stuffe*, some four hundred years earlier, of the town as a 'decrepite over-worne village'. A sense of decline and desolation, laced with claustrophobia, pervades Sutton's book and while pensioners line **Marine Parade**, staring out across the waves, the edges of Gorleston are slowly tumbling into the North Sea.

Sutton replaces the old adage 'Gorleston ere Yarmouth begun / And will be Gorleston when Yarmouth is gone' with a less complimentary one of his own: 'Sadly, Gorleston will not be Gorleston, when Yarmouth is gone, for Gorleston will be gone first.'

'Gorleston is all about waiting. Everyone is always waiting for something,' says Percy Lanchester, one of the Marine Parade pensioners, a man struggling to overcome the death of his wife. However, when he meets flame-haired Queenie, a widow and the scandal of the town, his life certainly changes. Sutton's descriptions of the social circuit of Gorleston, a town 'that from the exterior appears deathly quiet and depressing' but where 'behind the drab exterior lay outrageous goings on', are quite explicit and frequently utilise real place names. The character of Queenie, who refuses 'to slip away in the middle of the night', owes much to Sutton's 'pretty flamboyant relatives' living in the town.

Meanwhile, elsewhere in Sutton's Gorleston, people talk over each other's heads, American oil-rig workers fondle their wives' bottoms, small-talking women have impossible mauve hair-dos or crisp crumbs all over their faces, and the pensioners' haunt of 'The Breydon Suite' dining room smells of urine. Little wonder that after the publication of his first novel Sutton wasn't too popular in polite Gorleston society and was even threatened with a libel suit – though he claims that 'most people in the town seemed to enjoy the notoriety'.

Any reputation for strange goings-on that Gorleston might have had before Henry Sutton's novel was published, find full expression in **Amanda Dalton**'s (1957–) small cycle of poems *Room of Leaves* (1996). Dalton's poems are reportedly based on a real occurrence on the fringe of Gorleston in 1994, when a seventy-year-old woman was found dead, perched in the tree house she had been living in for years – unnoticed. Jilted at the altar, she had established her nest in the tree with the help of several umbrellas, and had kept herself alive by occasional shopping sprees into Gorleston. When her body was found, bruised, covered in dirt and malnourished, it emerged that her wedding presents were still hanging from the tree by pink ribbons.

Gorleston beach, close to the gateway of Yarmouth harbour – 'Gorleston is all about waiting. Everyone is always waiting for something.' (Henry Sutton, *Gorleston*, 1995)

Daniel Defoe

The creator of Robinson
Crusoe was well aware of the
dangers of shipping here, and
in *A Tour Through the Whole
Island of Great Britain*
(1724–6) observes: 'Country
people had scarce a barn, or
a shed, or a stable ... but what
was built of old planks, beams,
wales and timbers etc, the
wrecks of ships and ruins
of mariners and merchants'
fortunes.'

Dalton poetically charts the fall of 'Gracie' and recreates the events leading up to her wedding day, the insecurity paralysing her fiancé 'Frank' and Gracie's subsequent decline into a 'bird's existence', clutching at eggs, trying to 'breed'. *Room of Leaves* expresses sympathy with all sides of the tragedy – the helpless mother, kneeling in church, praying; 'Frank', unable to assume his bridegroom role ('Frank in a Fog'), and 'Gracie' lost in her barren disillusionment: 'There is a cave in me / and its voice reverberates / along my hollow bones.'

Winterton

Here at Winterton, signs warn of the dangers of swimming and, beyond the shelter of the dunes and the sparkling sands of an exposed and windswept shore, its flint lumps scattered like broken bones, swirls a churning, peat-coloured sea.

Daniel Defoe* (1660–1731) knew well the perils of this coastline for shipping, describing it as 'one of the most dangerous and most fatal to sailors in all England'. It is off these treacherous shores that the eponymous hero of his great novel *Robinson Crusoe* (1719) is ship-wrecked for the first time.

On the eighth day of waiting at anchor, Crusoe tells how there blows 'a terrible storm indeed' and as the seas rise and the weather worsens, the ship takes water and begins to sink. The passengers are taken off by a rescue boat, with Crusoe feeling that 'my heart was as if it were dead within me'. They are steered 'past the light-house at Winterton ... here we got in, and tho' not without much difficulty, got all safe on shore, and walk'd afterwards on foot to Yarmouth'. Leaving Yarmouth for London, Crusoe soon finds himself on board a ship bound for Guinea and adventures now immortalised in fiction.

The tombstone of Martha
Rudd's parents in Winterton
churchyard

In Winterton churchyard, close to the north porch, stands the gravestone of James and Mary Rudd, the parents of one of the less famous occupants of this 'bleak seaside hamlet'. Martha Rudd was one of eight children who lived with their parents in a tiny cottage in **Black Street**. Martha went to work in nearby **Runham**, now a district of **Yarmouth***, where **Wilkie Collins*** (1824–89) was staying in the summer of 1864. Writing in the 1886 *Arrowsmith's Christmas Annual*, Collins describes a less than fictional scenario in 'The Guilty River':

> I had met with a girl, possessed of remarkable personal attractions ... a girl at once simple and spirited; unspoilt by the world and the world's ways, and placed in a position of peril due to the power of her own beauty ... '

Collins, who through his fiction married prostitutes with clergymen and noblemen with country girls, and who wrote so passionately of the reintegration into society of 'fallen' women, never married Martha. But

she bore him three children and seemed content with the 'Mrs Dawson' alias he created for her.

Like Dickens, Wilkie Collins had seen for himself the urban poverty in London, but through Martha he witnessed first-hand the suffering possible in rural areas. Once more he incorporated these themes into his writing, this time through the clergyman in *The New Magdalen* (1873):

Saving the crew of the brig Providence, wrecked here in 1815 – almost a century earlier, Robinson Crusoe experienced 'a terrible storm indeed' and was himself shipwrecked off Winterton coast.

> I had no idea ... of what the life of a farm-labourer really was. Never before had I seen such dire wretchedness as I saw in the cottages ... I asked myself if they could endure, and *live*... week after week, month after month, year after year on the brink of starvation; live, and see their pining children growing up around them; live, with the poor man's parish-prison to look to as the end, when hunger and labour have done their worst!

When **Sylvia Townsend Warner*** (1893–1978) and Valentine Ackland first fell in love in 1930, the couple visited Winterton together. **The Hill House**, a Victorian villa close to the dunes and sea, was Valentine's family home and she had often wandered here with her poetry and books.

Warner had begun life as a composer and musicologist which had first brought her to Norfolk during her work with Tudor Church Music. But now she was making a name for herself as a distinguished and truly original writer of poetry, short stories and novels. Ackland, some twelve

The Hill House today – once home to the Ackland family and visited by Sylvia Townsend Warner, the house now forms part of a holiday complex.

years Warner's junior – a distinctive figure like a 'very handsome boy' in trousers, six foot tall, with Eton-cropped hair – also wrote poetry, but with less success than Warner. The lovers were to make many visits to 'The Flat' here over the years and, whether playing together on the beach or relaxing in the local inn, enjoyed provoking comments from the villagers. On 16 February 1932, Warner records in her *Diaries*:

> A ravishing morning. We went down to the beach. The waves were casting up a quantity of foam. I ate it, it tasted bitterly of iodine. Then I must needs paddle, and she did too. Then we played games – running a heart with our foot-tracks, and crashing together as we ran the arrows, morris-dancing like rabbits and grangles, lying together at the sea's edge, and playing at horses – she unseated me every time. We found a pure white pebble, very small and smooth. 'Sometimes I love you like this' she said – And threw it up against the blue, and caught it, like catching the moon.'

Sadly, Valentine Ackland died of cancer in 1969, leaving the lonely and inconsolable Sylvia Townsend Warner to write several years later: 'One cannot grow out of a loss; one cannot grow round it. The only expedient is to grow *with* it, for the loss persists, develops, amplifies.'

Opposite: The view from the Hill House, across Winterton dunes to the sea

CHAPTER FIVE

Poppyland

Jane Austen, George Barker, E F Benson, William Cowper,
Kevin Crossley-Holland, Arthur Conan Doyle, Elizabeth Gaskell,
Lilias Rider Haggard, Patrick Hamilton, P D James,
R W Ketton-Cremer, Compton Mackenzie, Ralph Mottram,
Paston family, William Rivière, Judith Saxton, Clement Scott,
Stephen Spender, Chris Sugden, A C Swinburne, John Taylor,
Paul Theroux, Anthony Thwaite, Theodore Watts-Dunton, Oscar Wilde

---

Cromer

John Taylor

The 'Water Poet' who arrived
in Cromer – 'half dry, half
wet' – to a hostile reception.

And much amaz'd ran crying
   up and down,
That enemies were come to
   take the town.
Some said that we were
   pirates, some said thieves,
And what the women says, the
   men believes.

   John Taylor, 'A Very Merry –
Wherry – Ferry Voyage', 1623

Today's Cromer still acts as the gateway to 'Poppyland', but in the
seventeenth century – long before the days of bathing machines, pier
entertainment and tourist-soaked promenades – it was a small fishing
town engaged in a daily battle against erosion and in real danger of
sliding into the sea.

Casting a wary eye over events at the time was one of Cromer's
earliest literary visitors, the 'Water Poet' **John Taylor** (?1578–1653), a
Thames waterman whose adventurous journeys around Britain were
captured in the pages of his lively verse and prose.

In 'A Very Merry – Wherry – Ferry Voyage' of 1623 Taylor tells how,
sailing from **Yarmouth** to York and carrying papers from King James I,
his boat is forced ashore by bad weather: 'And thus half soused, half
stewed, with sea and sweat / We land at Cromer Town half dry, half wet'.
Taylor was unlikely to forget his 'welcome' by the hostile townsfolk, and
turned the subsequent drama into a hilarious and lively poem. As the
women and children watch Taylor's unarmed party of five land, they
are 'possessed with fear' and alert the townsfolk to their presence.

An 'army' is quickly raised and Taylor's party finds itself threatened,
interrogated and held under armed guard while their boat is vandalised
by drunken louts. Only when two local dignitaries arrive can Taylor
once more breathe easily: 'And though they knew me not in prose and
looks, / They had read of me in my verse and books'. Duly rescued,
Taylor generously forgives the townsfolk, but before departing remarks
upon the perilous state of the settlement:

It is an ancient market town that stands
Upon a lofty cliff of mouldring sands;
The sea against the cliffs doth daily beat,
And every tide into the land doth eat.
The town is poor, unable by expense,
Against the raging sea to make defence;
And every day it eateth further in,
Still waiting, washing down the sand doth win,
That if some course be not ta'en speedily,
The town's in danger in the sea to lie.
A goodly church stands in these brittle grounds,
Not many fairer in Great Brittain's bounds;
And if the sea shall swallow it as some fear,
'Tis not ten thousand pounds the like could rear.
No Christian can behold it but with grief,
And with my heart I wish them quick relief.
So farewell, Cromer, I have spoke for thee,
Though you did'st much unkindly deal with me.

'...the best of all sea-bathing places' – Cromer's east beach in 1895, with the newly-opened Hotel de Paris at the rear.

Jane Austen

In *Emma* she acknowledges Cromer's reputation as a resort when the Woodhouses debate the virtues of sea-bathing

Two centuries later, **Jane Austen** (1775–1817) writing in *Emma* (1816) demonstrates that the town with its 'goodly' church has not only been saved from the sea, but is now enjoying a growing reputation as a fashionable seaside resort. Emma Woodhouse finds herself embroiled in a family debate about the virtues or otherwise of sea air and bathing. Her father scorns the supposed virtues of nearby Southend ('an unhealthy place') – preferring the lure of the more distant Norfolk coast: 'You should have gone to Cromer, my dear, if you went any where – Perry was a week at Cromer once, and he holds it to be the best of all the sea-bathing places. A fine open sea, he says, and very pure air.'

When his other daughter, Isabella, lends her support to the view that the additional sixty-mile journey may not really be worth the effort, Mr Woodhouse remains adamant: 'Ah! My dear … where health is at stake, nothing else should be considered; and if one is to travel, there is not much to chuse between forty miles and an hundred.' Which of course was not strictly true – in Austen's time there were no railways (the rail link to Cromer was not established until as late as 1877) and although regular, coaches to the town still involved a long and not inexpensive journey.

Although it is highly doubtful that she ever visited Cromer herself, Austen is clearly aware of the town's standing as a resort – something which must also have been known to **Elizabeth Gaskell** (1810–65) when writing her classic novel *North and South* (1855). Here, Gaskell's contemplative heroine Margaret Hale accompanies her Aunt Shaw and the Lennoxes to the coast for a rest-cure:

Elizabeth Gaskell

The author of *North and South* sends her heroine Margaret Hale to Cromer for a rest-cure: 'She was soothed without knowing how or why'.

> Cromer was, in one sense of the expression, the best for her. She needed bodily strengthening and bracing as well as rest … She used to sit long hours upon the beach, gazing intently on the waves as they chafed with perpetual motion against the pebbly shore – or she looked out upon the more distant heave and sparkle against the sky, and heard, without being conscious of hearing, the eternal psalm, which went up continually. She was soothed, without knowing how or why.

The coming of the railways really opened up the town to holidaying Edwardians, who were soon to flock here in their droves. Many arrived inspired by the pen of an early traveller on the Great Eastern Railway, **Clement Scott** (1841–1904). At the time, Scott was busy establishing himself a reputation as one of Britain's best-known drama critics and as a journalist also contributed regular travel accounts to the *Daily Telegraph* – the reason behind his visit here in 1883.

Arriving in Cromer on 'one of the most beautiful days of the lovely month of August', Scott sets out to explore 'perhaps the prettiest watering-place of the East Coast' and the nearby villages of **Sidestrand***** and **Overstrand*****. His highly sentimental articles, poetry and prose later published as *Poppy-Land – Papers Descriptive of Scenery on the East Coast* (1886), really struck a chord with a readership keen to discover for themselves this 'smiling' corner of Norfolk, where the 'regal red poppies are born'.

Hot on the heels of Scott came the much-mellowed poet **Algernon Charles Swinburne*** (1837–1909), who recalls his first visit to this 'seaside nest' in his collection *A Midsummer Holiday* (1884), describing Cromer in 'A Haven':

> East and north a waste of waters, south and west
> Lonelier lands than dreams in sleep would feign to be,
> When the soul goes forth on travel, and is prest
> Round and compassed in with clouds that flash and flee.
> Dells without a streamlet, downs without a tree,
> Cirques of hollow cliff that crumble, give their guest
> Little hope, till hard at hand he pause, to see
> Where the small town smiles, a warm still sea-side nest.

Clement Scott

Journalist, drama critic and 'Poet of the Seaside', his immortal 'Garden of Sleep' launched a whole Poppyland industry.

Swinburne's poetry has a much more assured feel to it than Scott's simplistic verse (which earned him the title 'Poet of the Seaside'), but many of Scott's travel observations remain true today. Cromer's slightly faded charm is best viewed from the tower of St Peter and St Paul's Church – at 160 feet by far the tallest in Norfolk. A steady climb to the top reveals a huddle of older dwellings and a maze of narrow, traffic-choked streets below, crowded with shops and holidaymakers, and the seafront hotels and amusements beyond. To the east, high on the 250-foot clifftops, the lighthouse blinks out a steady warning.

There was an old person
of Cromer
Who stood on one leg to
read Homer
When he found he grew stiff
He jumped over the cliff
Which concluded that person
of Cromer

Edward Lear (1812–88)

TO CLEMENT SCOTT.
WHO BY HIS PEN IMMORTALISED "POPPYLAND"
ERECTED BY MANY FRIENDS NOVEMBER 1909.

The 'fountain' commemorating Clement Scott at the junction of Northrepps Road and Overstrand Road

Arthur Conan Doyle

He came to Cromer for a golfing holiday and left with the plot for *The Hound of the Baskervilles.*

Good grounds for a story – Cromer Hall *c.*1900, pictured at the time Conan Doyle was transforming it into Baskerville Hall in *The Hound of the Baskervilles.*

Scott wrote: 'no-one thought of going beyond the lighthouse; that was the boundary of all investigation', and even today few visitors follow in his footsteps eastwards along the coast to find a tranquil escape from what Swinburne describes as the 'metropolitan splendours' of Cromer. Scott is remembered fondly by the town that he placed so firmly at the centre of Poppyland. Travelling out of town, the Overstrand Road meets the Northrepps Road close to the lighthouse. On this junction is the 'fountain' – actually a stone water trough – which commemorates Scott and opposite is a new development which also bears his name: Clement Scott Mews.

Another writer seeking fresh air and better health was Sherlock Holmes creator **Arthur Conan Doyle** (1859–1930). Returning from South Africa with enteric fever, Doyle headed for the Norfolk coast in March 1901, for rest and a golfing holiday with his companion Bertram Fletcher Robinson. What he learned here inspired Doyle to write his great mystery *The Hound of the Baskervilles* (1902).

There are many versions of the chilling ancient legend of Black Shuck – the giant spirit dog prowling the gathering darkness with eyes glowing like coals. Anyone unfortunate enough to meet his gaze, it is said, will not live to tell the tale. Conan Doyle was certainly captivated by his golfing companion's spine-chilling rendition of the old country tale, and in the comfort of the Royal Links Hotel the two men plotted the outline for a new book.

Local lore has it that one of Black Shuck's tracks runs through what today is Mill Lane – then a deep, narrow sandy track leading from the coastline past the Royal Links Hotel, over the hill and into the grounds

of Cromer Hall. The original hall was destroyed by fire and subsequently rebuilt in a modern Gothic style with the high-angled roofs, tall chimneys, heavily mullioned windows, towers and crenellations used by Conan Doyle in *The Hound of the Baskervilles*.

With his connections to Lord Cromer, and his insatiable curiosity, it seems unlikely that Conan Doyle would have missed an opportunity to explore such a powerful locale and the descriptions of the ivy-draped 'Baskerville Hall' match Cromer Hall almost to perfection. Sadly for Norfolk, Conan Doyle then moved on to Dartmoor to explore the book's eventual setting. Sadly for Robinson, his role was later downplayed by Conan Doyle, who acknowledged Robinson's contribution as a 'remark' and nothing more.

Prolific author and journalist (**Edward Morgan**) **Compton Mackenzie** (1883–1972) – famous for his novel *Whisky Galore* – published the ten 'Octaves' of his autobiography *My Life and Times* between 1963 and 1971. The Mackenzie family holidayed in Cromer on several occasions, first visiting in 1887 when young Compton was just four years old.

In *Octave One (1883–91)* Mackenzie admits that the 'first memory I have of that summer in Cromer is of the difficulty my mother had in persuading me to paddle'. Fortunately he was able to overcome his fear of the sea and on one occasion found himself seated on the beach next to a 'tall and beautiful lady' with heavily plaited dark hair and a notebook on her knee, who turned out to be the Empress of Austria. What impressed young Compton more than anything – having 'just smoked my first cigarette' – was the fact that the Empress herself also smoked.

Returning here four years later, Mackenzie notes that 'Cromer must have been one of the first seaside places in England that made golf an outstanding attraction' and clearly remembers the red jackets the golfers wore to make them easily visible around the course, leaving the green slopes of East Cliff 'dotted with scarlet figures'.

Mackenzie loved the surrounding countryside; its fields of poppies and ox-eyed daisies, which 'always seemed to be overflowing from behind into the little seaside town', and the smell of the honeysuckle in the July dusk 'mingling its sweetness with the salty air' made a lasting impression.

In 1982, American novelist and travel-writer **Paul Theroux*** (1941–) set out to travel clockwise around the British coast. As on most of his travels, Theroux relies largely upon public transport and his own two feet to complete the journey related in *The Kingdom by the Sea* (1983).

Braving the national rail strike at the time, Theroux arrives at Cromer where its 'atrophied charm' and 'high round-shouldered Edwardian look' greet him. It is summer, and even the 'loudest seagulls in Norfolk' can't deter him from buying a ticket for the 'Seaside Special '82' playing at Cromer Pier. Here, Theroux witnesses the 'decent vulgarity' of a

From saucer pulks
where pale light lingers longest
we made his eyes
In this seedbed only think:
Dead Hands wave,
        Things worm,
marsh lights flicker.
We made his blood
        from arteries
obsidian in the moonlight,
his hair from shaggy
        sea-purslane.
His chains are chains of
        marsh mist.
Striker, Hooter, Fenrir:
these are his blood-brothers.
We gave him the howl of wind
carried from Siberia
And witnesses?
With terror or with
        damp black
earth, one way or another
he stops every mouth.

Kevin Crossley-Holland,
'Shuck', 1986

Compton Mackenzie

The prolific writer recalls family holidays spent at Cromer in his autobiography *My Life and Times*.

Paul Theroux

Stopping off on his travels around the British coast in 1982, the writer enjoys Cromer's 'atrophied charm' and 'decent vulgarity'.

sparsely attended show and, while the surf sloshes against the iron legs of Cromer Pier beneath him, observes England's 'secret life – its anxiety in the dismal jokes, its sadness in the old songs'.

Performance over, Theroux's day closes within the distinctly more up-market surroundings of 'an enjoyable pile of brick and plaster splendour' – the Hotel de Paris. Theroux's travelogue, though witty and perspicacious, still lacks the genial warmth and expansiveness of **J B Priestley's*** *English Journey* (1934).

> In his memorable poem 'On a Friend's Escape from Drowning off the Norfolk Coast' (1954), **George Barker*** sounds a warning against the dangers of sea bathing, as 'Came up that cold sea at Cromer like a running grave' to sweep a swimmer under its 'blackcapped wave'. The swimmer's wife meanwhile, is dozing on the 'hourglass sand' while their son plays near by. Opening her eyes to the sight of her husband drowning, the woman rushes into the sea to rescue him, while on the shore 'their son / Stood laughing where / He was almost an orphan.' Exhausted by the drama, 'Then the three lay down / On that cold sand, / Each holding the other by a living hand.'

The 'atrophied charm' of Cromer is absorbed into the 'Haisby' novels of romance and family saga writer **Judith Saxton*** (1936–). Written under her most famous pseudonym, Judy Turner, the novels *The Arcade* (1990) and *Harbour Hill* (1991) focus on the thriving seaside town of 'Haisby' – an amalgam of Norfolk coastal resorts, but borrowing heavily from Cromer for its pier, promenades and amusements, its bustling High Street and shopping arcades. Haisby's forty-foot-high cliffs oversee a sandy beach strewn with pebbles and divided by wooden groynes 'shaggy with seaweed, thickly sown with mussels', next to a pier theatre (reminiscent of Cromer's own Pavilion Theatre) that is annually threatened with closure.

The Arcade centres on a range of shops and an up-market restaurant, 'Sam's Place', which, is apparently not dissimilar to a small restaurant owned by Judith Saxton herself. Sam's Place is peopled with engaging, if rather stereotypical, characters: old dears, a cockney dressmaker, the aristocratic M'Quennell family ('"I say!" Tufton exclaimed. "Oh, Di, I say!"') and on a more serious note, the abused daughter of a sadistic clergyman.

There is also plump Caresse, who sells beauty aids (when she is not consuming marshmallows or doughnuts), and Diane, trying to make a go of a fashion boutique with the assistance of her aunts. At a gathering to toast the success of Diane's venture, her Aunt Violet proves 'once and for all, that she was not really in the nineteen-nineties at all. Raising her glass, glancing coyly round, she echoed, "The boutique!" and then

Opposite: Cromer pier, overlooked by the massive church tower of St Peter and St Paul and the 'enjoyable pile of brick and plaster splendour' that is the Hotel de Paris.

Judith Saxton

Her 'Haisby' novels are brimful of Norfolk's coastal character.

added, "What's a boutique?"' The ups and downs of business life apart, there is plenty of human drama, with much matchmaking (and breaking) in these eventful days of the 'Haisby' shopping arcade.

In the sequel, *Harbour Hill*, Haisby presents a suitable backdrop for struggles with fatherhood, betrayal and gratuitous violence. Henry, a retired sailor and Keith, a chef, are starting up a residential sailing school at 'Ambleside Hotel', at the top of Harbour Hill in Upper Haisby. Further down the 'Hill', in her 'Lavengro' flat, **Acle**-born Nicola is trying to rebuild her life after the heart-breaking deception of her husband. Meanwhile Ceri, who shares Nicola's flat, is struggling both with the thwarting of her professional ambitions as a journalist at the *Haisby Chronicle*, and with the first stirrings of her heart.

As *Harbour Hill* – with its blend of affable characters, gentle humour and traditional values – draws to a close, Keith wrestles with a life-or-death decision:

> It was a long walk though, even with the wind on his side, now. It was six o'clock when he saw Haisby's dimming lights loom and looking east, he knew that dawn was not far distant. The stars were paling, the moon no longer looked like a big white penny and the wind, though it moaned around the eaves, was no longer a wild animal snatching the gulls from the sky. Walking cat-quiet through the deserted town he wondered where he should go, what he should do ... In the quiet night, he looked at the town and saw it was beautiful, loved it for the way it had accepted him. He did not hurry now, he strolled; along Lord Street, up Harbour Road, past the fish wharves where he saw a thin and solitary cat sitting on an empty fish box grooming herself. He crossed the swing bridge, seeing the yachts swinging at anchor in the marina, hearing the soft clunk of the rigging as it twanged to the wind's breath. He was on Harbour Hill now and it seemed that everyone slept. And at last he knew what he would do.

Eccles

In 1937 **Lilias Rider Haggard*** (1892–1968) writes a poignant entry in her *Norfolk Life* (1943) about the lost town (not to be confused with **Eccles** in Breckland) here on the exposed north-east coast. Constantly besieged by the 'roaring territory' of the German Ocean, this once substantial settlement was eventually engulfed in the early seventeenth century and as Haggard reminds us, the 'wide lands and manors, its farms and churches' now lie 'some miles out to sea'. Eccles is not without its legends, and Lilias Rider Haggard recollects that 'when I was a child the fishermen used to say if you heard those long drowned bells tolling through the sound of the surf breaking onto the beach, it was a warning of storm and death'.

Such a legend is adapted by poet **Kevin Crossley-Holland*** (1941–) in his mesmerising children's tale 'Sea Tongue', taken from his collected East Anglian stories *Long Tom And The Dead Hand* (1992). Here, while a church bell sounds to warn of the coming storm, the sea-god claps his 'luminous hands', intent upon luring passing fishermen into the 'foam-and-snarl' of his treacherous depths.

Through the haunting rhythm of the tale that follows, Crossley-Holland leads the reader safely into the clarity of the morning after the storm, where the fishermen reveal that the previous night they had all heard a bell, and dropped anchor for safety because of it. 'But there is no bell', they realise, looking around them, 'there's no belfry along this coast'. Meanwhile, 'far under the swinging water', the two-ton bronze bell that fell into the sea long ago continues to protect those who sail the storm-tossed waves above it.

Perhaps this very bell may have once rung out from the round tower of St Mary's church, whose crumbling remains were finally claimed by the sea when Lilias Rider Haggard was young, with 'scouring' tides revealing further evidence of the people who once populated the area:

> One September day years ago, when the tower of Eccles Church still stood on the dunes, there came a north-easterly gale and a 'scour' which swept the sand from the old graveyard, leaving the long outlines of the graves washed clean by the sea. In one lay an almost perfect skeleton embedded in the clay, the hollow-eyed skull gazing up at the limitless sweep of the sky. I remember standing there looking at it, feeling the sting and bite of the flying sand against the back of my bare legs, and wondering about the past of that strange coast. It is heavy with the memory of much that made history, now lying with the bones of the men who played their part in it, far out beneath the shifting sands and racing tides. The two thousand acres of land dwindled and dwindled to a mere three hundred, until one night in the reign of Charles I, the tide came up backed with a tearing north-easterly gale, broke through the sandhills and swept away sixty-eight houses and the Church, with the loss of nearly three hundred lives.

Since then, human bones have been found washed up on Eccles Beach in abundance, though today the area is eerily empty, except for a few flinty reminders of the washed-away buildings and a stretch of newly erected coastal defences. Nothing remains of the church tower, which lies buried under sand, some fifty metres distant from the shoreline at North Gap.

Squatting behind the high dyke that shuts out the pounding sea, **Eccles on Sea** now consists largely of the motley array of bungalows which form the Bush estate, and a Bed and Breakfast for those wishing to expose themselves to a sense of precarious proximity to the sea and to witness the transience of human settlement.

The relationship between the swallowed-up town that was Eccles Juxta Mare and the gnawing sea is a notion that was to prove irresistible to another poet, **Anthony Thwaite*** (1930–), for whom archaeology and history are long-standing themes. In 'Eccles', his haunting requiem for the long-drowned settlement, Thwaite explores not just the landscape, but also the identity borne by the very name of the town:

> Cliffs sifting down, stiff grassblades bent,
> Subdued, and shouldering off thick sand,
> Boulders – compacted grout and flint –
> Jut from a stranded beach, a land
> Adhering thickly to the sea.
> Tide-drenched, withdrawn, and drowned again,
> Capsized, these buttresses still strain
> Towards perpendicularity.
>
> The place-name mimes the fallen church,
> Abbreviated, shrunk to this
> Truncated word, echo of speech,
> A Latin ghost's thin obsequies
> Carried by wind, answered by sea –
> *Ecclesia*: the syllables
> Curtailed, half heard, like tongueless bells
> From empty steeples endlessly.

The remains of Eccles church tower after the great storm of 1862

Felbrigg

In his role as drama critic for the *Telegraph*, **Clement Scott***'s views could be as outspoken and vitriolic as his seaside verse was sentimental. He once described **Henrik Ibsen**'s *Ghosts* as an 'open drain' and 'a loathsome sore unbandaged' and found another victim for his prejudice in the flamboyant wit and playwright **Oscar Wilde** (1854–1900).

In August 1892, Wilde rented a farmhouse in the village here, where he rested, imbibed the pure Norfolk sea air (his doctors forbade him any other form of imbibing as he was attempting to improve his health at the time) and worked on his new play: *A Woman of No Importance* (1893).

Wilde's daring but ultimately tragic challenges to the Victorian Establishment incurred the displeasure of many conservative critics, including Clement Scott, who, writing for the *Telegraph*, celebrated the playwright's two-year jail sentence for indecency in 1895 with the declaration 'Open the windows! Let in the fresh air.'

Oscar Wilde

He came to Poppyland for a rest in 1892.

The distinguished Norfolk historian **Robert Wyndham Ketton-Cremer** (1906–69) bequeathed Felbrigg Hall to the National Trust on his death. Ketton-Cremer produced many fine studies of people and events across Norfolk, including *A Norfolk Gallery (1948)* and *Felbrigg, the story of a House* (1962) – a detailed record of Felbrigg ('a place of mystery') in which he pieces together his family history from the early seventeenth century.

Happisburgh

Built in 1791, Happisburgh lighthouse stands on a small hill on the outskirts of the village – a one-hundred-foot-high, red and white striped beacon. Scanning the horizon from here, at least ten church towers are visible around the headland, including the commanding tower of **St Mary's**, just half a mile away. From the top of this 'lofty' church tower (ten foot taller than the lighthouse) there is a stunning view of the erosion-threatened landscape used by two icons of crime fiction: **Arthur Conan Doyle** (1859–1930) and **P D James** (1920–).

In 1903, the **Hill House**, lying in the shadow of St Mary's, provided a welcome break for **Arthur Conan Doyle,** whose time here proved inspirational for *The Dancing Men* – published at the end of the year and one of Doyle's own favourite stories. The white painted brick building is today run as a pub and has one corner dedicated to the famous pipe-wielding detective, while a plaque on the outside of the building marks Conan Doyle's stay here. Inside, just above the entrance, is a photo depicting the twenty-five 'dancing men' cipher at the heart of the story. It has been suggested that this cipher was invented by the

'The Whistler's fourth victim was his youngest ... and she died because she missed the nine-forty bus from Easthaven to Cobb's Marsh.'

P D James, *Devices and Desires*, 1989

son of the then proprietor of the Hill House Hotel, called Cubitt, who lends his name to the main characters.

In *The Dancing Men*, Hilton Cubitt discovers a string of strangely coded messages around 'Ridling Thorpe Manor' (the nearby village of **Ridlington** probably providing this name) – the Norfolk home he shares with his American wife. Hilton rightly suspects that they have something to do with his wife's elusive past, and, breaking his promise to never probe into her former life, calls in the expert – Sherlock Holmes.

While Happisburgh is not mentioned by name in the story, Doyle's description of the Manor's location on the coast, seven miles from **North Walsham**, fits the bill perfectly. On the drive up here, Holmes is lost 'in a blank melancholy' while Watson gazes out at the sight of:

> ... as singular a countryside as any in England, where a few scattered cottages represented the population of to-day, while on every hand enormous square-towered churches bristled up from the flat, green landscape and told of the glory and prosperity of old East Anglia. At last the violet rim of the German Ocean appeared over the green edge of the Norfolk coast, and the driver pointed with his whip to two old brick-and-timber gables which projected from a grove of trees. 'That's Ridling Thorpe Manor,' said he.

Unfortunately, by the time Holmes and Watson arrive, the damage is already done: the client shot through the heart, his wife on the brink of death. Meanwhile, the villain of the piece – 'the most dangerous crook in Chicago' – is hiding on 'Elrige's Farm' not far off at **East Ruston**. From here, and to the amazement of Inspector Martin of the Norfolk Constabulary, Doyle's cunning detective must lure him back to the scene of the crime.

In the summer of 1798, two years before his death, **William Cowper*** (1731–1800) was coaxed into a boat by his kindly cousin, the Rev. John Johnson and rowed from **Mundesley*** to Happisburgh. Johnson notes in his diary that Cowper 'went with me to see the Light House and appeared to enjoy in some measure looking thro' a telescope from that very lofty building, at the ships in the offing.'

P D James

Her *Devices and Desires* lends the remote Happisburgh headland a sense of foreboding.

In *Devices and Desires* (1989), crime novelist **P D James'** (1920–) first and most famous detective, Commander Adam Dalgliesh is taking a short break from his Scotland Yard duties to enjoy his increasing reputation as a poet. Hoping to spend a peaceful two weeks' rest in the Norfolk mill his aunt has left him, Dalgliesh instead finds himself drawn into the hunt for a sinister and vicious murderer, the 'Norfolk Whistler'.

St Mary's Church – 'The tower must have been the last sight of land for hundreds of drowning mariners in peace and war'. In 1801, some 300 people lost their lives here when HMS Invincible was wrecked offshore. At the north-east end of the churchyard, there is a mound which is believed to be the unmarked mass grave of 119 victims whose bodies were recovered.

As well as dissuading anyone from taking a quiet evening bathe in the North Sea, P D James applies 'the power of a beautiful setting to heighten horror by contrast' as almost everything along this exposed stretch of coast becomes tainted with secrecy, guilt and murder. Approaching Larksoken, Dalgliesh himself is touched by this brooding atmosphere:

> The headland was empty and almost bare, the few straggling trees, distorted by the wind, struggled to keep their precarious hold in the uncompromising soil ... [it] had the desolate look of an old battlefield, the corpses long since carted away but the air vibrating still with the gunfire of long-lost battles, while the power station loomed over it like a grandiose modern monument to the unknown dead.

'The Whistler's fourth victim was his youngest ... and she died because she missed the nine-forty bus from Easthaven to Cobb's Marsh.'

P D James, *Devices and Desires*, 1989

Bromholm Priory – the twelfth-century ruins, sunk in a sea of weeds at the bottom of Abbey Street in **Bacton**, bear a strong resemblance to the ruined Benedictine abbey in *Devices and Desires*. This was once one of the most venerated shrines in England and the Holy Cross of Bromholm is referenced in **Chaucer**'s* 'The Reeve's Tale' and **William Langland**'s *Piers Plowman*.

In true P D James style, the locations of *Devices and Desires* are a fine blend of carefully researched fact and imaginatively detailed fiction, though the influence of the history-drenched coast around Happisburgh is undeniable:

> Even on the darkest night, by the light which the sea seemed mysteriously to absorb and reflect, he could make out the splendid fifteenth-century west-tower of Happisburgh Church, that embattled symbol of man's precarious defences against this most dangerous of seas. And it was a symbol of more than that. The tower must have been the last sight of land for hundreds of drowning mariners in peace and war ... Built in an age of faith, the tower had stood as a symbol, too, of that final unquenchable

hope that even the sea would yield up her dead and that their God was God of the waters as he was of the land. But now mariners could see, dwarfing the tower, the huge rectangular bulk of Larksoken Power Station.

These are the reflections of Dr Alex Mair, director of the controversial Larksoken nuclear power plant which finds itself at the centre of a copycat murder mystery. P D James was born close to the site of Sizewell nuclear power station and she exploits her familiarity with the area to the full, while the 'bulk' of the oil refinery at **Bacton** may well have provided further inspiration here.

In *Devices and Desires*, James contrasts the old-fashioned lifestyle on the remote headland with the modernity of nuclear power, while weaving environmental and metaphysical issues into her elaborate and compulsive plot. In this atmospheric and complex thriller, nothing is quite what it seems, not least the trail of the 'Whistler'.

Finally, Dalgliesh's return to Larksoken sees memories of the 'Whistler' banished, as, for the moment, past and present fuse and the worries of life 'with its trivial devices and desires' give way to a more peaceful reality evidenced by the sunlit Norfolk coast.

Mundesley

William Cowper* (1731–1800) arrived here in August 1795 and stayed for a few months at the home of his cousin John Johnson in the High Street before relocating to **East Dereham***. In a letter written shortly after his arrival, Cowper identifies himself with a 'solitary pillar of rock' he has seen close to the crumbling cliffs here: 'I have visted it twice and found it an emblem of myself. Torn from my natural connections, I stand alone and expect that the storm shall displace me.'

The doorway to Cowper House – William Cowper spent some of the last months of his life here, awaiting the final 'stifling wave'.

These words pre-empt Cowper's last major work, 'The Castaway' (1799), in which he depicts his own isolation and helplessness through the desperate image of a sailor who, having fallen overboard, can only watch in despair as his shipmates fade into the distance. Cowper continued to visit Mundesley throughout the last five years of his life, but like the drowning sailor of his poem, increasingly felt himself to be a 'castaway' from life. Ironically, Cowper's 'castaway' is a strong swimmer, which only serves to prolong his agony as he thrashes through the 'whelming brine'. Witnessing this almighty struggle with the forces of nature, the end brings only a sense of welcome relief:

> At length, his transient respite past,
>   His comrades, who before
> Had heard his voice in ev'ry blast,
>   Could catch the sound no more.
> For then, by toil subdued, he drank
>   The stifling wave, and then he sank.

Overstrand

E F Benson

Visits to his 'colony of friends' in the area resulted in the plotting of his spine-chilling 'spook' stories.

Waves breaking onto Overstrand shore.

During the Victorian building boom, this tiny sanctuary became both a Cromer overspill and a millionaire's paradise, with new homes being developed on every available acre. **Clement Scott*** (1841–1904) was later to lament the transformation of his beloved Poppyland into what he angrily dubbed 'Bungalow Land'.

One of the new dwellings here was The Pleasaunce of Lord and Lady Battersea, who regularly entertained a number of literary friends in their sumptuous and imaginatively designed seaside home. **E F 'Fred' Benson*** (1867–1940), creator of the 'Dodo' and 'Lucia' novels, was one visitor and in his informal autobiography *Final Edition* (1940) he recalls: 'I usually spent some portion of August in the houses of a colony of friends on the north coast of Norfolk'.

A prolific and popular writer and the fifth of six children from an eccentric literary family, Benson is probably best remembered for his collections of spine-chilling ghost stories – *Spook Stories* (1928) and *More Spook Stories* (1934) – inspired by his regular trips to various coastal resorts around Britain.

The crumbling cliffs of Overstrand play a crucial part in 'The Dance', set in a house within 'a hundred yards of the cliff-edge' where the sadistic and crippled Philip Hope watches his young wife Sybil fall in love with his secretary, Julian Weston. After toying with the couple, Hope then sacks the hapless Weston in a cliff-top confrontation – 'a hundred sheer feet above the sea' – only to find himself caught in a landslide which drags him to his death. Sybil and Julian then marry and, for reasons best known to themselves, for their honeymoon return to the house where the malevolent spirit of Philip Hope awaits them.

It was ghost story maestro **M R James** who really aroused Benson's 'latent interest in the supernatural', while both Fred's brothers also dabbled in the genre. James himself rated Benson's work very highly, but was critical of him for 'stepping over the line of legitimate horridness' and it is certainly hard to reconcile the menacing tone of Benson's 'Spook' stories with his lightly comic English village novels.

Limping ghouls in vast, creaking houses and benign 'middle-aged, unattached' narrators much preoccupied with golf are commonplace in Benson's tales, but despite these formulaic devices his sinister stories are often genuinely frightening. In *Final Edition* Benson recalls reading one of his tales to an ageing Lord Halifax: 'It's too frightful', said Halifax. 'Go on, go on. I can't bear it!'

The dreaded spectre of Black Shuck raises its ugly head again when **Ralph Hale Mottram*** (1883–1971) spends his childhood holidays here. In *Autobiography with a Difference* (1938), he recalls one of his many stays in the house of Mrs 'Now you be keerful, Master Ralph', Rogers. In the village, as on the whole of the north Norfolk coast, he finds that belief in the Devil and the awful Black Shuck ('a gre't ole dawg, wi' no head, but tew blazing eyes') is flourishing.

Ralph is housed in the Napoleonic extension to Mrs Rogers' ancient flint cottage, where one of the windows had once been bricked up to avoid window tax: 'The effect was exactly that of a seafaring man, retired ashore to respectability, but wearing still the patch over one eye which he had gained in some unspecified, probably unsavoury, escapade, far away, and long ago, of which he only gave highly romantic accounts to his present friends.'

One evening, young Ralph decides to take a walk down the deepening shadows of the 'lond' (lane between cottages) with the 'sea murmur, so vague, so vast, so belittling to any city-bred boy' in his ears. Suddenly there is a rustling from somewhere beside him. Bravely pushing back the thick hedgerow, he is faced with a terrifying sight: 'a dark shape, four-legged, and surely headless'. Fortunately, the 'beast' turns out to be a 'placid old donkey' feeding in the meadow. But for many locals, as Mottram discovers, the belief in the real Black Shuck remains unshakeable.

The words are always as
strange and dead as those
fragments and oddments that
the wave casts up on the shore:
I stand in the sea mist
gazing down at the white
words and old bits of wood
and wonder what they were for
...
I neither understand
nor know why I am moved
beyond these words by the
odd bits of bleached wood
cast up on Overstrand
or by the black and twisted
October evening tree
dying beside the road
...
I walk upon Overstrand shore
and the crab at my foot
inscribes praise in the sand.
The wave bursts with glory
because it rises up like
angels out of the sea,
and the dead starfish burns
on Overstrand promontory.

...
Why do I hear them cry
out from the far side of life,
those forms and impulses
unborn beyond the sky?
Why should they hope
                        and seek
above all else to be?
Tonight on Overstrand
I know for one moment why.

George Barker, from *In Memory of
David Archer*, 1973

Paston

From 1468, John Paston II ('Sir John') compiled the 'Great Book' – a bound collection of separate documents written by scrivener William Ebesham which survives to this day. Also in his library were works by **Chaucer*** and **John Lydgate** and *The Game and Play of Chess*, one of the first books to be translated and printed by Caxton in 1475.

A vast collection of over a thousand documents and letters, the **Paston Letters** provide a unique and intimate insight into family life in fifteenth-century Norfolk. Describing matters of land, law, religion, fashion, currency, marriage and social convention, the letters are mainly written during the Wars of the Roses and span the reigns of five English kings and three generations of a Paston family always on the fringes of great events.

The bulk of the collection is written by **Margaret Paston** (*c.*1420–84) and her husband **John** (1421–66) as the family battles for land, power and patronage during turbulent times. They are personal letters, never written with publication in mind, and the spelling and syntax are often as chaotic as the events they describe. With four sons and two daughters surviving to mature years, some confusion is also caused by the names of continuing generations: William I fathered John I and William II, while John I (husband of Margaret) fathered John II, John III and William III!

The effects of the Black Death and other diseases which followed in its wake were still visible in the Pastons' Norfolk. During this time the entire structure of the land had been altered, with wholesale depopulation, settlements deserted and churches left to crumble. In the early fifteenth century, the population of England was fewer than two million, and Norfolk, with a population of some 100,000, was one of the most isolated yet prosperous counties in the land. With a fertile and varied terrain sustaining rich arable farms, cloth-manufacturing and wool industries around them, **Norwich***, **Lynn*** and **Yarmouth*** were three of the wealthiest and most densely populated towns in England.

Fifteenth-century England is a place of rapidly shifting allegiances and the most important question always seems to be who you know (and sometimes, who you shouldn't know). At this time there was no central land registry and claims for ownership of land could often be quite arbitrary. Many of the letters deal with protracted property feuds which involve lengthy legal and, occasionally, rather more direct action.

Writing in the summer of 1449, John Paston petitions Parliament for the return of his manor at **Gresham**, 'peaceably possessed' by his family until January when 'Lord Moleyns sent to the said mansion a riotous people to the number of a thousand persons ... arrayed in manner of war, with cuirasses, briganders ... glaives [spears], bows ... guns, pans with fire, long crooks to drag down houses ... and long trees with which they broke up the gates and doors, and so came into the mansion, the wife of your beseecher at that time being therein, and twelve persons with her.' Margaret Paston and her servants were driven out of the manor, which was then ransacked and occupied by the 'misdoers'.

Opposite: Paston Barn – evidence of the passing of a powerful family.

More problems followed when John Paston was bequeathed **Caister Castle** by **Sir John Fastolfe*** in 1459. John was an executor to the will which was hotly disputed, especially by the Duke of Norfolk, resulting in long-running and violent conflicts.

Paston Church today, with its fourteenth-century flint tower and mural paintings, is a simple and well-proportioned example of a Norfolk parish church. Many members of the Paston family are buried here, but of the letter-writers of the fifteenth century the most significant is John Paston whose table tomb is reputed to have been moved from his burial place at nearby **Bromholm Priory***. Close to the church stands the huge (163-foot-long) flint barn built by Sir William III in 1581, which is all that remains of the many buildings once owned by this powerful family.

> The site of the Pastons' confrontation with Lord Moleyns' villains is 'Chaucer's Farm' in Gresham, said to have been known as such ever since it was owned by **Chaucer**'s* son, who sold it and the manor to Sir William Paston.

William Rivière

'There's quite a lot of my family's history buried in the deep structure of *Echoes of War.*'

Family unity and survival are crucial themes for **William Rivière*** (1954–), who returns to Norfolk for his most successful novel to date, *Echoes of War* (1997). Set in the turbulent period surrounding the Second World War, this epic novel is seeped in historical detail and the century's devastating war experience for an upper-middle-class Norfolk family. But first and foremost Rivière's best-seller is pervaded by the spirit of the north Norfolk coast so familiar to the author, who grew up at **Dilham Grange**, not far from **North Walsham**.

A wealth of localities (**Paston Hall, St Benet's Abbey***, **Morston*** **Manor**), with sail-less windmills holding out their 'bony arms' and 'snaking creeks' making for the shore, are offset against settings in Burma, Italy and France. In this ambitious and lyrical work, the two world wars of the twentieth century continue to reverberate, 'echoing' through the lives of the Lammas family. Other facets of the 'continuity' so often encountered in Norfolk fiction are also presented here; the tragic futility of wars that cannot secure a lasting peace, the nostalgia for innocent pleasures, and the enduring strength of family bonds in the face of tragedy and loss.

The village of **Ovington** was the only one in Norfolk to have all its men return safely from the Great War, but in *Echoes of War*, Blanche Lammas' brother Michael is one of those who do not return. Thus the novel opens in Paston Church with the family's annual laying down of a wreath to Michael's memory. Here the author interweaves his own family history – Rivière's grandmother lost both her favourite brother and her fiancé in the First World War and the intricate commemorative window at Paston depicts a lost great-uncle of the author's.

As the family's story progresses, a storm rages on the Norfolk coast, pounding the crumbling cliffs and moving inland where, 'the shifting of the balance of power of the waters could still be felt':

Detail from the memorial stained-glass window in Paston church, in memory of William Rivière's great-uncle R M Mack

> In Norfolk the freezing wind which roared in the trees around Paston church battered all the flint churches which stood parish after parish along that coast of muddy cliffs and salt marshes and shingle foreshores, frenzied to a St Vitus' dance the blizzard-stunted sycamores and oaks and thorns. In that region of windmills, the storm shrieked in their rusting turning-gears, shook their groaning spars ... All afternoon in the relative hush of low tide the men had checked their warps. They had over-hauled mooring-chains, they had laid out kedge-anchors. They had rowed ashore in their cockling scows. Now at high water their smacks were exposed to the undiminished force of the gale; they chucked their tethered heads like frightened horses; they shuddered under the blows of the breaking seas.

In *Echoes of War* we meet Morston Manor again – familiar to readers of Rivière's *Watercolour Sky* (1990) and, according to the author, 'exactly as I remember that house from childhood memories'. From here the Lammas family head to Morston Quay to sail their old crab-boat as the sun comes breaking through the 'harum-scarum clouds'. Their household at **Edingthorpe** is presided over by the charismatic painter Charles Lammas. With his 'sea-and-sky eyes', Charles is a survivor of the First World War (where his brother was killed) and thus considers himself to have had what he terms a 'good war':

> The simplest things triggered off his rejoicing. To walk the dogs along his wood-side with [his son] Jack on a late autumn afternoon, notice fieldfares pecking at the red berries of a mountain ash. Bitter wind soughing through the marshy, leafless wood, rustling a sere reed-bed. Lammas' survivor's joy in life would clog his throat, twist his lips. A son in muddy boots calling to a terrier. A gaunt heron standing immobile by a dyke, then

slowly rising behind a screen of willow and silver birch on tatterdemalion wings, alighting again beyond the next copse ... Survivor's rewards: simple, incomparable.

Echoes of War is scoured by the salt-rough of the marshes, painted with Rivière's sailing vocabulary and passion for wildlife and architecture, and tainted by the certain knowledge for these Norfolk families that a precarious peace is not to last. As the Second World War progresses, the bombing of **Norwich*** and the Ferry Inn at **Horning*** brings the war to their very doorstep and the first local war casualty is brought to rest in **Irstead** church.

As the Lammas family awaits news of their son Jack and their nephew Bobbie, fighting in the Mediterranean, Charles' feelings of utter powerlessness match the quiet desperation of his wife Blanche, part of this 'doubly tortured generation'. Blanche expresses the grief of 'her generation of European women', having seen their brothers, their lovers, or husbands go to war, and then seeing their sons, the next generation, go to fight in the next war: 'Versed in fear for their men, that generation of women. Versed in grief, and in stoicism.' They find relief in the quiet observation of nature's unchanging rituals, as 'even in war time, out there in the briny sunlight and the emptiness you could sense the peace lapping around you.'

Far from Norfolk, Burma is still at peace and Georgia Burney, the Lammas' Anglo-Burmese goddaughter is still unscarred by war. Remembering her godfather taking her to Norfolk churches, she reflects on the spirit of belief of a county with more churches per square mile than any other county in Britain, recalling what Charles Lammas:

... had said to her once or twice about how he was the kind of man who in any age and any land would have frequented the local temple. Would with a quiet mind have gone through the rituals of whichever the religion happened to be. The rituals that honoured the dead, and paid homage to all that man could never explain or control. Innocent ceremonies that were a stitching together of a community, and a propitiation of the unknown.

It is to Edingthorpe church that Georgia heads for the Norfolk wedding which draws *Echoes of War* to a close in a scene of celebration and family unity.

Sheringham

'I grew up in an atmosphere of belief curiously mingled with apprehension,' says poet and critic **Stephen Spender** (1909–95) in his autobiography *World Within World* (1951). Spender's first contact with Norfolk came when the family decided to lease a spacious country house here 'at the extreme edge of the town on the cliffs and adjoining fields' known as The Bluff. Life was far from luxurious, as Spender notes: 'We lived in a style of austere comfort against a background of calamity'. His mother Violet was frequently ill, and the move was partly aimed at improving her deteriorating health. 'I remember her lying on a chaise-longue in Sheringham complaining about debts,' writes the poet.

Nevertheless, for the Spender children (and especially for Stephen, whose ambition was always to be a naturalist), their time here must have been magical; transported as they were from the noise and grime of London to the sea, woodland, caves and crumbling cliffs of north Norfolk:

Stephen Spender

> Near Sheringham there were woods and the common, covered with gorse and heather. In the woods at spring there were the pale damp primroses with their scent of sublimated mould and a buttery thickness which one could almost taste. Then in summer there was the heather, brittle flowers like tiny purple beads on gnarled charcoal stems, flooding over the burnt-looking soil, on which bees descended in thousands to lift away the honey. Beyond the heather, near blackberry hedges, the gorse lay like gold armour, or like fleece of fire all round me, on bushes of spiky green thorns.
>
> Stephen Spender, *World Within World*, 1951

'This poet with his soul upon his shoulder
Trudging up a world's steps to bring those
Who shiver by the embers of their optimism
The hundredweight of his pity'

George Barker, 'To Stephen Spender' *Eros in Dogma*, 1944

But this was the summer of 1913, and with the first rumblings of war came the shadows of zeppelins 'paddling in the evening light' across Norfolk skies. As for so many others at this time, the outbreak of the First World War was to have a significant impact on the life of the young poet.

While Stephen's mother 'had a sense of catastrophe', his dictatorial and bellicose father Harold entered fully into the recruitment and training of the Norfolk Volunteers, later recalling: 'The first bomb of the war fell in a garden just behind my house'. With his father out patrolling against the 'Boche', five-year-old Spender learned that his uncle had already been killed in action, and pondered the impact of these events on his sickly Jewish-German mother.

That Stephen was being kept away from 'bad influences' only enhanced his feelings of alienation, as demonstrated by his poem 'Rough' (later re-titled 'My Parents'): 'My parents kept me from children who were rough / Who threw words like stones and wore torn clothes'. The poem re-lives Spender's fear of the 'salt coarse pointing' of local boys, who teased and bullied him and 'copied my lisp behind me'. His tormentors also 'threw mud while I looked the other way, pretending to smile'.

Things went from bad to worse when Spender abandoned his **East Runton** kindergarten to follow his older brother Michael to the Old School House, then the preparatory wing of Gresham's School at **Holt***. Here, in a school that **W H Auden*** termed a 'Fascist state', Spender could never settle and he soon found himself dubbed 'The Backward

Son' (used later as the title of one his books). Fortunately, Spender was withdrawn from the Old School House at the beginning of 1920, when the family finally gave up the tenancy of The Bluff, severing their Norfolk connections.

Opposite: Sheringham Park – 'My childhood was the nature I remember', writes Stephen Spender – who as a child endlessly explored the landscape here.

As he pursued an immensely successful career as poet, novelist, critic and literary editor, Stephen Spender never lost his sensitivity or his love of nature, shaped so early by the Norfolk landscape. His lasting memories of Norfolk were of blissful days ranging across the windswept scrubland and crackling bracken in pursuit of butterflies – his imagination running riot as he created mountains out of Norfolk's wide skies:

> At evening, floating above the flat Norfolk landscape, there appeared range upon range of mountains with gulfs and valleys between high peaks, which stayed motionless, sculptured on the sky out of clouds. Sometimes, also, at midday, in the sky whose blue was as solid and opaque as the flushed green of a field of young corn, perfect white pictures would appear, as on a screen. 'Look, a milk jug, a white milk jug. It is exactly like a milk jug,' I would cry. 'No, silly,' my sister would say. 'It's a cat, a white cat, can't you see?'

In the late 1950s, playwright and novelist **Patrick Hamilton*** (1904–62) and his second wife Ursula (a novelist herself, nicknamed 'La') arrived here from **Blakeney*** where Hamilton had spent 'a *hideous* period' that had sent his alcohol intake rocketing. Their home here in Sheringham, 'Martincross', had a view of the sea and Hamilton became very attached to it. A keen golfer in his youth, he was pleased to discover that 'the golf course can be cut into (dodging the Club House) by walking for about three minutes'. Sadly, however, the house became the theatre for his decline, as Hamilton slowly drank himself towards immobility and then death, finally forsaking the 'very much *over-rated*' world.

Patrick Hamilton

'One of the best English novelists ... What is he like? ... Where is he now? Is he happy?',

John Betjeman

Hamilton's fame rests upon successful plays, including *Rope* (1929) and *Gaslight* (1939) – both adapted for the screen by Alfred Hitchcock – and on dark novels such as *Craven House* (1926) and *The Slaves of Solitude* (1947). 'His novels give you an idea of what it is like to enter a dark Brighton pub on a gloomy afternoon in March,' says fellow theatre writer **Adrian Wright***. Influenced by Marxism, Hamilton treats his fictional characters with respect, regardless of their dead-end existences, though all his novels draw upon the drink that ruined him in the end. Patrick Hamilton's plays are still performed today, while his novels await rediscovery.

John Betjeman* counted Hamilton as one of his 'literary heroes', and one who continued to shun the limelight: 'I have never heard anything about the personality or appearance or age of one of the best English novelists, Patrick Hamilton ... What is he like? Has he a moustache or is he clean shaven? Where is he now? Is he happy?' Hamilton's closest friend on a literary scene from which he remained alienated was **Michael**

Moving from **Winterton, Mary Mann*** (1848–1929) came to rest in Sheringham and stayed at her 'Greenlands' home until her death in 1929.

Sadleir, literary editor with Hamilton's lifelong publisher Constable and founder of *Rhythm* magazine with **John Middleton-Murry** in 1911.

It was Hamilton's wife Ursula, writing as **Laura Talbot**, who paid off a literary debt to the location of her husband's happiness, by setting her last novel in a Norfolk village. *The Last of the Tenants* (1961) tells the melodramatic story of a woman living alone in the village and believed to have killed a baby. When she is connected with the death of another baby, she drowns herself during a flood.

Towards the end of his life, Hamilton constantly quoted a stanza of 'The Garden of Proserpine' by **Algernon Swinburne***, who had arrived at the Norfolk coast some eighty years earlier:

> From too much hope of living,
> From hope and fear set free,
> We thank with brief thanksgiving
> Whatever Gods may be
> That no life lives for ever;
> That dead men rise up never;
> That even the weariest river
> Winds somewhere safe to sea.

Sidestrand

Miller Jermy waiting to greet his literary visitors at the gate of Mill House *c*.1880

In 1883, unable to find accommodation in Cromer, **Clement Scott*** (1841–1904) strolled out of the town, along the cliff top and 'through the cornfields towards a cluster of farms and a distant village'. Attracted

by a 'ruined church tower', Scott arrived in Sidestrand and, 'secluded and in peace', found himself lodgings at Mill House – the home of the miller Mr Jermy and his daughter Louie.

The ruins that Scott saw when he first approached the village were the remains of Craske's tower, left behind when the church of St Michael's was moved, brick by brick, from its perilous position and rebuilt at a safer distance inland. The 'folly' of Craske's curious and ill-fitting round tower was left to its lonely fate on the cliff tops and finally tumbled down the cliffs in 1916.

It is this tower, surrounded by gravestones from St Michael's churchyard, that Scott uses as the central image for his most famous poem, 'The Garden of Sleep':

> On the grass of the cliff, at the edge of the steep,
> God planted a garden – a garden of sleep!
> 'Neath the blue of sky, in the green of the corn,
> It is there that the regal red poppies are born!
> Brief days of desire, and long dreams of delight,
> They are mine when Poppy-Land cometh in sight.
> In music of distance, with eyes that are wet,
> It is there I remember, and there I forget!
> O! heart of my heart! where the poppies are born,
> I am waiting for thee, in the hush of the corn.
> Sleep!   Sleep!
> From the Cliff to the Deep!
> Sleep, my Poppy-Land,
> Sleep!
>
> In my garden of sleep, where red poppies are spread,
> I wait for the living, alone with the dead!
> For a tower in ruins stands guard o'er the deep,
> At whose feet are green graves of dear women asleep!
> Did they love as I love, when they lived by the sea?
> Did they wait as I wait, for the days that may be?
> Was it hope or fulfilling that entered each breast,
> Ere death gave release, and the poppies gave rest?
> O! life of my life! on the cliffs by the sea,
> By the graves in the grass, I am waiting for thee!
> Sleep!   Sleep!
> In the Dews of the Deep!
> Sleep, my Poppy-Land,
> Sleep!

These were the words, later set to music, which spawned a whole Poppyland industry and saw a rash of souvenirs flood on to the market. Despite a great increase in development in the village, and especially at

neighbouring **Overstrand***, Scott continued to visit and returned to Mill House for fifteen consecutive years; thereby inspiring a host of Bohemian Victorians to do the same.

In September 1883, **A C Swinburne*** (1837–1909) came with his great friend and fellow poet **Theodore Watts-Dunton** (1832–1914) to stay at Jermy's Mill House, his curiosity aroused by Scott's *Telegraph* article some two weeks earlier. Scott had been resident at Mill House up to the very day that Swinburne and Watts arrived and before his departure for London, left a note with some of his poetry for the new arrivals, as Swinburne wrote on 18 September:

A C Swinburne

Following in Clement Scott's footsteps, he first arrived at 'the delicious little refuge' of Mill House in autumn 1883.

> Yesterday we left the metropolitan splendours of Cromer for the delicious little refuge from whence I write … On entering I find an envelope directed to me, left by the outgoing tenant [Scott] … containing a copy of verses of a most fervent and flowery description, adjuring me to confer fame upon this lonely country – which verses I find to be the production of the author of the very article in the *Daily Telegraph* which sent us hither. It appeared on Aug. 30th under the highly 'aesthetic' title of 'Poppy-land', and on my showing it to Watts and saying, 'This must really be a delicious sort of place, in spite of this worthy man's florid style of cockney enthusiasm,' he set his heart on coming here in case the weather were suitable; and it has been very favourable hitherto. But is it not funny we should have got into the very house occupied till last evening by the man who has unconsciously induced us to come into the country? … The whole place is fragrant with old-fashioned flowers, sweet-william and thyme and lavender and mignonette and splendid with great sunflowers. We have bathed once or twice – the sea is much better than at Southwold.

No doubt mindful of Swinburne's volatile nature, sharp tongue and reputation for 'moral excesses', the more conservative Scott may have been wise to have made good his escape. Swinburne was a controversial figure whose great metrical skills were dominated in his early work by a preoccupation with sado-masochism and *femmes fatales*. Part of the Pre-Raphaelite movement, he openly courted controversy, and though his later work was more subdued, Swinburne continued to be a celebrated and influential figure.

By the time he arrived at Cromer, the forty-seven-year-old Swinburne's health had been seriously damaged by heavy drinking, though the downward spiral of his health had been halted by the caring intervention of Theodore Watts-Dunton, with whom Swinburne was to live for many years.

Watts-Dunton had given up a legal career to pursue his own writing and poetry reviewing, and shared a passionate interest in gypsy life

'*Opposite:* The Garden of Sleep' and 'Craske's Tower'; which finally slid into the sea in 1916.

(encompassed in his novel *Aylwin*, 1898) with **George Borrow***, whom he had met and admired. Regular seaside trips for 'sea and air bathing' were his prescription to put Swinburne on the road to recovery, and the dusty track out towards Sidestrand became a particular favourite.

> Seaward goes the sun, and homeward by the down
> We, before the night upon his grave be sealed.
> Low behind us lies the bright steep murmuring town,
> High before us heaves the steep rough silent field.
> Breach by ghastlier breach, the cliffs collapsing yield:
> Half the path is broken, half the banks divide;
> Flawed and crumbled, riven and rent, they cleave and slide
> Toward the ridged and wrinkled waste of girdling sand
> Deep beneath, whose furrows tell how far and wide
> Wind is lord and change is sovereign of the strand.
>
> A C Swinburne, 'The Cliffside Path', 1884

Mill House today remains much as it first appeared to Scott – a 'little red-brick house' with a welcoming look and a well-tended garden, set slightly back from the main coast road.

Trunch

Sid Kipper, aka Chris Sugden

'Probably the county's finest ambassador', on stage and still spinning yarns.

The fictitious parish of 'St Just-near-Trunch' is home to Norfolk's redoubtable folk hero **Sid Kipper**, alias **Chris Sugden** (1952–), whose inimitable style and irreverent humour are epitomised by *Prewd and Prejudice* (1994). This is the hilarious mock diary of London lady Miriam Prewd, who, after the death of her husband in 1903, walks into a publisher's London offices looking for work. They recommend that she write a diary of an Edwardian lady stranded in the country, which she reluctantly agrees to do.

The house she then rents, we learn, was 'built as a toll house on the **Suffield-Mundesley*** turnpike', but 'the project was abandoned when the backers realised that no one actually wanted to travel from Suffield to Mundesley, let alone pay for the privilege'. Putting her feelers out at the rectory of St Just's, she fails to gain an interview with the vicar who is 'busy attending to a fallen woman', and turns instead to the Saxon splendour of the nearby church:

> Norfolk, I have been told, is a county rich in beautiful churches, and just such a gem is wasted here on those without the refinement to appreciate it. I spent an hour looking round the building. I was accompanied by a pathetic, cringing wretch, who I took at first to be a homeless beggar, but later found to be the curate. The church is especially noted, I gather, for its magnificent Saxon doorknob.

In her traumatic year of 'Norfolk exile', Miriam Prewd struggles through All Idiot's Day, Old Soaks' Day, Flinthenge, and the Pedants' Revolt. Her crush on the local worthy, Doyley Silver-Darling, and her attempts at reforming the locals by starting up a Temperance Group to abolish 'The Goat' (the local pub) achieve nothing but a deepening in the alienation between parties.

Written in Kipper's typically deadpan style, *Prewd and Prejudice*, thrice reprinted, takes up most of the current preconceptions about the Norfolk countryside and its populace and, while happily self-deprecating, always succeeds in turning them against the jaundiced vision of the London lady. As the author himself recalls, 'the national papers seemed to think that it took the mickey out of country people, while the Norfolk papers thought it ridiculed Londoners!'

Trunch – but no sign of Sid Kipper here

Chris Sugden was born in **West Runton**, moved to **Wells-next-the-Sea** four years later and then on to **Norwich*** when he was eleven. Despite going into teacher training close to the city, and studying for a PhD at the **University of East Anglia***, he always held on to his 'special connection with the north-east of the county'.

Much of Sugden's work, though using the 'certain thoughtfulness and a love of word play' typified by his native county, aims to promote 'rural life in general'. Nor is Sid Kipper, Sugden's disreputable alter ego, merely a local celebrity; a folk-singing, story-telling character from St Just-near-Trunch, he features on albums with titles such as 'Like A Rhinestone Ploughboy', has broadcasted on Radio 2's 'Lateral History Programme', and has compiled an unpublished rhyming dictionary of Norfolk places for song-writing purposes. Although resident in Halifax now, Sid's creator frequently returns to Norfolk, and, he says, 'most of my writing is still Norfolk based'.

In 1996 *The Ballad of Sid Kipper* was published, detailing the Trunch Tradition alongside the biography of his alter ego. The *Ballad* opens in the year 1936, at which time 'the whole village sighed with relief when Sid's parents ... married each other, because it meant that nobody else would have to marry either of them.' Happily installed at 'Box Cottage' on the edge of St Trunch, they never wanted children, really, 'but at the outbreak of the Second World War they saw the advantage of the extra rations that a child would bring' and registered a 'Sid' who wasn't to see the light of day until after the war was finished. As Sid explains, life in the post-war years was far from easy:

> I sort of got the feeling that I weren't wanted when the rationing got eased. What give me that feeling was when my mother used to leave me in shops or on buses, or anywhere in fact. I once spent three days in a cake shop in North Walsham before they managed to trace her and make her take me back ... Eventually I learned to keep an eye out for her trying to sneak off. I reckon that must be where I picked up the habit of following women home.

Nevertheless, Sid Kipper survived the trauma of his childhood and continues to haunt the fringes of showbiz, while Chris Sugden is following up his song-writing on the legendary rivalry of the Cromer-Sheringham Crab Wars with a play and a book. And for fellow Norfolk author, broadcaster and *Eastern Daily Press* columnist **Keith Skipper**, Sid Kipper remains 'probably the county's finest ambassador', someone who 'captures the true spirit of Norfolk, teaches it tricks, then sends it to run riot across the land.'

CHAPTER SIX

Heartland

LITERARY LINKS

Brian Aldiss, Elspeth Barker, George Barker, Raffaella Barker,
George Borrow, Kate Charles, Geoffrey Chaucer, William Cowper,
Lionel Fanthorpe, Magdalen Goffin, H Rider Haggard, L P Hartley,
Augustus Jessopp, John Cowper Powys, Anna Sewell, George Szirtes,
Christopher Woodforde, Parson James Woodforde

Bawdeswell

Heading north out of **East Dereham*** and across the Wensum, the gently
sloping road to Bawdeswell passes through some of the county's most
beautiful countryside. This area would have been known to **Geoffrey
Chaucer** (*c.*1343–1400) whose character Reeve Oswald, one of the
'Canterbury Pilgrims', lived in a house shaded with trees just outside
'Baldeswell'.

It is claimed that Chaucer's uncle was rector in the village, and that
the old timbered house which stands in Bawdeswell's main street, almost
opposite the church, was once his rectory. In his earlier days, Chaucer
himself served in the household of the patron of this living, the Duke
of Clarence, and it is suggested that he might therefore have stayed from
time to time at his uncle's rectory. Whatever truth lies behind the legend,
Chaucer certainly knew of the village from where his 'choleric' Reeve
heralds, and the timbered house with its overhanging upper storey is
still known as 'Chaucer House' today.

> The Reeve was old and choleric and thin
> His beard was shaven closely to the skin,
> His shorn hair came abruptly to a stop
> Above his ears, and he was docked on top
> Just like a priest in front; his legs were lean,
> Like sticks they were, no calf was to be seen.
> ...
> When young he'd learnt a useful trade and still
> He was a carpenter of first-rate skill.
> The stallion-cob he rode at a slow trot.
> Was dapple-grey and bore the name of Scot.

Geoffrey Chaucer

His Norfolk connections have
become woven into local lore.

He wore an overcoat of bluish shade
And rather long; he had a rusty blade
Slung at his side. He came, as I heard tell.
From Norfolk, near a place called Baldeswell.
His coat was tucked under his belt and splayed.
He rode the hindmost of our cavalcade.

Geoffrey Chaucer, from 'The Reeve's Tale',
*c.*1387, trans. Neville Coghill

The rope is almost paid out
here. Bawdeswell
and the ghost of its foul reeve
left to stew,
I drive down cool green naves,
and soon the lanes
begin to ripple ...

Kevin Crossley-Holland
'An Approach to the Marsh',
1983

We meet the Reeve again in 'An Approach to the Marsh' by **Kevin Crossley-Holland*** (1941–), from *Time's Oriel* (1983). Here the poet takes apart a few of Norfolk's most beloved images, as pilgrims are 'shuffled off to the shrine at **Walsingham**'* and 'screaming poppies' line Crossley-Holland's drive up towards his own 'heartland' on the coast, 'where nothing is as it seems or not for long'.

Bradenham

One of the most prolific writers of his day, **Henry Rider Haggard*** (1856–1925) was born at Wood Farm, Bradenham on 22 June 1856 – the eighth child of William Haggard, a flamboyant and bellicose Norfolk squire. A sickly child, Rider was raised in the bustling household of the Haggard country seat at Bradenham Hall. At the time of his birth, the hall itself was let, thus Rider was the only son born 'on a farm' (as his mother Ella would laughingly remind him), meaning that 'the land would hold him all his life'. Certainly Rider Haggard loved his family home, which helped to cultivate the 'dynastic sense' so evident in later life. Standing on some of Norfolk's highest and then most heavily wooded land, the south-facing Georgian square of Bradenham Hall overlooked some four hundred acres of family land.

In 1875, despairing of his son's seeming lack of both ambition and ability, William Haggard packed nineteen-year-old Rider off to South Africa as an unpaid secretary to Sir Henry Bulwer. It was the beginning of a lifelong fascination with that continent. Rider's time in Africa, in a tough, dry and often dangerous environment, his encounters with Boers and Zulus, and his first-hand experience of war, provided him with much of the material for his early novels. With Rider's respect for Zulu culture came the realisation that he could provide them with a written history, and his writing career commenced with *Cetewayo and His White Neighbours* (1882) which was published on Rider's twenty-sixth birthday.

Forced to abandon his earlier attempts at ostrich farming in Natal, Rider returned to England for a marriage typical of his vigorous and adventurous life. His wedding to 'Louie' Louisa Margitson in 1880 was only possible after Rider had won a legal battle with her guardian. The

Henry Rider Haggard

Novelist, traveller and Norfolk farmer – his mother had told him that 'the land would hold him all his life'.

move to the land of Louisa's inheritance – the south Norfolk soil of **Ditchingham*** – proved to be perfect for Rider, who saw himself transformed almost overnight into a literary sensation, with *King Solomon's Mines* (1886) and *She* (1887) spearheading his relentless drive into new territories of adventure romance.

Rider's returns to Bradenham were always nostalgic and it delighted him to find everything 'completely and satisfyingly the same'. However, after the tragic loss of Rider's only son, Jock, and the death of his father a year later in 1893, things were set to change. Rider declared himself 'utterly weary of a retired life and the writing of books' and, perhaps in memory of his forceful and irascible father, decided to enter the political fray.

Bradenham Hall – Rider Haggard returned to his childhood home in 1918 and writes in his *Diaries*: 'It is odd at the end of life coming back to houses at which one has spent one's beginnings, for then such become one vast and living memory. Every bit of furniture, every picture on the walls, every stone and tree bring forgotten scenes before the eye, or find tongues and talk.'

In typically forthright style, Rider turned down the relatively safe seat of **King's Lynn***, and opted instead to contest the 'difficult' seat of East Norfolk. After a long and acrimonious campaign and faced with unimagined hostility and organised violence, he lost by a mere 200 votes and returned once more to his writing and to the green fields of his estate.

During the First World War, Rider saw that Bradenham Hall had become an impossible burden for his brother Will and that its sale would soon be inevitable. In August 1918, the loss of the family seat was complete: 'The remoter parts of Norfolk are no longer desirable as places of residence,' Rider wrote sadly at the time. This traumatic end to the Haggard dynasty was later recalled by his daughter **Lilias Rider Haggard*** in her biography of her father, *The Cloak That I Left* (1951):

> Bradenham Wood was doomed and nearly all the magnificent oaks for which the estate was famous, and which had been the pride of his father's heart, would suffer the same fate. The Hall and its contents were gone, the land was gone, the trees were going – he could no longer bear to see the place thus stripped of everything that had made it beautiful in his eyes. The curtain had rung down for the last time on the scenes of his childhood, leaving only an empty house, an overgrown garden, and some graves in the little churchyard.

Earlier, in an attempt to retain Bradenham Hall, the Haggards had rented it to a family of prosperous coal merchants, the Moxeys. One of their young boys attended Northdown School with **L P Hartley*** (1895–1972) who came to stay with the family during the summer of 1909. Hartley's visit was later developed into one of his most successful novels, *The Go-Between* (1953).

Recalling his intimate knowledge of Bradenham, Hartley renames Northdown School 'Southdown', while the Moxey family name becomes 'Maudsley'. Thus Bradenham ('Brandham') Hall becomes the setting for a cross-class love affair doomed to tragic failure. Hinting at a distant darkness in his own childhood, Hartley once more blurs fact into fiction in tantalising style:

L P Hartley

> To my mind's eye, my buried memories of Brandham Hall are like the effects of chiaroscuro, patches of light and dark: it is only with an effort that I can see them in terms of colour. There are things I know, though I don't know how I know them, and things that I remember. Certain things are established in my mind as facts, but no picture attaches to them; on the other hand there are pictures unverified by any fact which recur obsessively, like the landscape of a dream.

'I did not understand the world of Brandham [Bradenham] Hall; the people there were much larger than life; their meaning was ... obscure to me ... They were, in fact, the substance of my dreams, the realization of my hopes; they were the incarnated glory of the twentieth century.'

The Go-Between, 1953

The story is narrated by the now ageing 'Leo' who, on finding his diary from the year 1900, is drawn back to the dramatic events from his past. The drama of Leo's rites of passage is matched by the superb depiction of Edwardian Britain, as it enters what Hartley dubbed this 'hideous' century. *The Go-Between* is set during the almost tropical heat of the opening summer of the new century, when Leslie Poles Hartley was just five years old. Like **Hunstanton Hall*** in *The Shrimp and the Anemone*, Hartley uses Brandham to represent the social landscape – a gateway to a wealthy and privileged world – though the rich visuals of *The Shrimp and the Anemone* are not matched in *The Go-Between.*

Hartley's social aspirations were a constant source of frustration to him. He was not ashamed of his middle-class origins, but yearned to surmount the barriers dividing him from the upper class which, despite his best efforts, he could not. This is the overriding message of *The Go-Between*: social barriers may be ignored at our peril.

Acting initially as an unwitting, and later complicit, 'Postman' between Marian Maudsley and the working-class Ted Burgess, Leo is unable to avoid the immense burden of guilt when tragedy occurs. On his thirteenth birthday, Leo is forced to follow Mrs Maudsley out of the house in search of the missing Marian. That they find her 'spooning' with Ted in the outhouse is bad enough, but the trauma of what follows is enough to push Leo towards a nervous breakdown.

In 1971, *The Go-Between* was made into a film by Joseph Losey, with a screenplay by **Harold Pinter** and shot entirely on location in Norfolk. During the filming, Hartley hinted that he himself had been in a similar position to young Leo, though whatever truly happened at Bradenham, he never disclosed.

Buxton/Lamas

Anna Sewell* (1820–78) only wrote one book in her lifetime, but her much-loved children's classic, *Black Beauty, His Grooms and Companions – The autobiography of a horse translated from the original equine by Anna Sewell*, has now sold well over 30 million copies and has been continuously in print since it was first published in 1877.

Anna learned to ride as a child when staying with her grandparents at Dudwick Farm in Buxton, which was on the estate owned by her aunt and uncle. Today there is a public footpath leading towards Dudwick House (rebuilt), through the beautiful parkland (with its many grazing horses) that is thought to be the original of 'Birtwick Park' in *Black Beauty*.

Dudwick Park today – the original of 'Birtwick Park' in *Black Beauty*. 'The first place that I can well remember was a large pleasant meadow with a pond of clear water in it. Some shady trees leaned over it, and rushes and water-lilies grew at the deep end.'

Anna Sewell, *Black Beauty*, 1877

Anna Sewell's driving instructor was her aunt, **Mrs Wright**, who had a passion for natural history and published *The Observing Eye* in 1850, a correspondence with her younger relatives on subjects of natural history. The book enjoyed some success; Queen Victoria read it and endorsed its use in the royal nursery.

It was Black Bess, ridden up each week to Dudwick from **Catton*** by Anna's brother, who provided the model for 'Black Beauty'. Grazing in the meadows around him were the models for the other horses, including Black Beauty's mother, 'Duchess', and his brother, 'Rob Roy', who is tragically killed in a hunting accident. Sewell's compelling moral tale, about a loyal and long-suffering horse which is cruelly exploited before finding a happy home, made a lasting impression on animal welfare in late Victorian society and led directly to the abolition of the bearing-rein.

Anna Sewell's commemorative stone at Lamas.

Anna Sewell never lived to see the enormous success of *Black Beauty*, which took her six years to complete, and died only a year after its publication. Not far from the grazing horses of Dudwick Park, across the Bure Valley Railway and Walk, her grave lies among the Irish yews by the chapel of Lamas, and is commemorated by a stone tablet built into the brick wall near by.

Cawston

The imposing churches of Cawston and Salle are old favourites with church expert and clerical mystery writer **Kate Charles*** (1950–), who sets her *Evil Angels Among Them* (1995) in the fictional village of 'Walston' in the Cawston area. The action of Charles' fifth clerical mystery very much revolves around the church of 'St Michael and All Angels', a composite creation of various churches in that area, with its spectacular angel roof and medieval Doom painting over the chancel arch.

Kate Charles

'I first went to Norfolk in search of churches – and found an abundance of wonderful ones.' The ecclesiastical mystery writer combines work with pleasure during her church visits.

Just a short, woody walk from the church stands 'Walston Manor', while the village pub, the 'Queen's Head', with its sign featuring Anne Boleyn, references the Boleyn family's long connections with the area. The pub windows are double-glazed below the inevitable satellite dish, but other more time-honoured features of Kate Charles' village life are very much in evidence: notably the twitching lace curtains and the 'bush telegraph' at the service of village bigotry.

There is certainly some serious curtain-twitching when the two newcomers to Walston turn out to be a lesbian couple bringing up a six-year-old girl. But, as the church prepares itself for Easter, there is someone in the village who intends considerably more harm than just spiteful gossip. And once again Charles' amateur sleuths – solicitor David Middleton-Brown and his lover, the artist Lucy Kingsley – find themselves in the middle of a mystery.

St Agnes Church, Cawston –
'not the sort of church
one might have expected
to find in a small, rather
undistinguished Norfolk
village like Walston; its size
bespoke past glories of which
scarcely a trace remained.
Built in the Perpendicular
style, its exterior, crowned
by a massive square tower,
was a marvel of flushwork in
Norfolk flint, and the interior,
with its vast expanses of clear
glass in the side aisles and the
deep clerestory, was irradiated
with the sort of light that is
found only in East Anglia, as
if the sky had somehow found
a way to invade the church.'

Kate Charles,
Evil Angels Among Them, 1995

East Dereham

In October 1796, after moving around various locations in Norfolk (which was believed to be beneficial for his health), the poet **William Cowper*** and his constant companion, Mary Unwin, arrived at the home of the then curate of East Dereham, Cowper's cousin Johnny Johnson. By this stage, Mrs Unwin's health was deteriorating rapidly, and she died soon afterwards, in December that year. It was a devastating blow to Cowper, who himself had suffered many severe bouts of illness and depression, and one from which he never truly recovered.

William Cowper

Cowper's creative output had been much-damaged by ill health, but he continued to work here on his intensely moving poem 'The Castaway', inspired by his time at **Mundesley***. In December 1799, Cowper was moved from Johnson's home overlooking the Market Place to another house nearby and it was here that he died some four months later. He is buried in the Chapel of St Thomas of Canterbury (formerly St Edmund's Chapel) in the church of St Nicholas and commemorated by the magnificent stained glass Cowper Window, depicting the poet with his pet hares. A stone memorial here bears an epitaph from Cowper's first biographer, **William Hayley**: '... Here, to devotion's bard devoutly just, Pay your fond tribute due to Cowper's dust!'

'No voice divine the storm
            allay'd,
No light propitious shone;
When snatch'd from all
            effectual aid,
We perish'd, each alone:
But I beneath a rougher sea,
And whelm'd in deeper gulphs
            than he.'

from 'The Castaway', 1799

The Cowper Memorial Congregational Church, squeezed in between shops on the Market Place, occupies the site of the red-brick house 'three doors down ... with a charming garden, well-planted with wall-fruit' that was Cowper's final Norfolk home. A plaque pays tribute to the 'patient friends' who cared for him during his periods of depression – which were partly caused by his firm conviction that he was predestined for the fires of Hell and that a huge gulf was separating him from God ('Hell within creates a Hell without').

Cowper remains much-admired and the power of his poetry lies as much in its humility, humanity and humour as in its technical merit. Cowper's writing also gives rise to many expressions used to this day – 'Variety's the very spice of life', 'God made the country, and man made the town' and 'God moves in a mysterious way' (written as a hymn) all originating from the poet's pen.

The Cowper Memorial Church on the Market Place – this was the site of the house in which William Cowper spent his last months, dying here in 1800.

In the mid-nineteenth century, the American writer **Elizabeth Barrett Browning** dedicated her poem 'Cowper's Grave' to the memory of the writer, poet and champion of the oppressed:

It is a place where poets crowned may feel the heart's decaying;
It is a place where happy saints may weep amid their praying.
Yet let the grief and humbleness, as low as silence, languish;
Earth surely now may give her calm to whom she gave her
                                                anguish.

Overgrown, but still visible outside the west door of St Nicholas, is St Withburga's Well, from which Cowper is said to have drunk every day in the hope of allaying his melancholy. The seventh-century Saint Withburga's remains were snatched by monks from Ely in the tenth century and a well with curative properties sprung up from her tomb.

George Borrow

'I love to think of thee, pretty, quiet D——, thou pattern of an English country town, with thy clean but narrow streets branching out from thy modest market-place, with thine old-fashioned houses, with here and there a roof of venerable thatch.

Lavengro, 1851.

During his travels in Wales, the polyglot Borrow was once mistaken for a Welshman. 'I am not a man of Llydaw,' he said, 'but of Norfolk where the people eat the best dumplings in the world, and speak the purest English.'

George Borrow, *Wild Wales*, 1857

Though he travelled widely throughout his life, eccentric Victorian novelist **George Borrow*** (1803–81) always remembered his native Dereham with fondness – tempered only by the knowledge that within the 'venerable church ... moulder the mortal remains of England's sweetest and most pious bard'. Borrow could never quite forgive the town for the latent unhappiness of Cowper's last years; for his 'crushed and gentle spirit'.

The military career of Borrow's father regularly moved the family around Britain, setting the pattern of the writer's itinerant lifestyle from an early age. Borrow's parents married here in 1793 and were tenants in Norwich Street at the time of his birth, but tradition holds that his mother returned to her parents' home in nearby **Dumpling Green** for the event. At the end of a pot-holed, unmade-up road, off the B1135 opposite a thatched house, stands an impressive red-brick Georgian farmhouse, which, apart from a couple of fir trees and a satellite dish, looks much as it would have in Borrow's day. Regardless of any dispute over his birthplace, Borrow himself simply claims East Dereham as the place where 'I first saw the light'.

George Borrow was a contradictory and restless soul. Unusually tall, strong and robust, an excellent swimmer and keen rider, he was also prone to fits, or 'the horrors' as he called them. Though evidently an egotist, Borrow also admitted to being 'shy and cold' and though never handsome, with his head of white hair he possessed, as **Theodore Watts-Dunton*** was to describe, both a 'strangeness' and a 'remarkable beauty'. Borrow's legendary rudeness was reserved largely for the 'gentility nonsense' he despised – always an awkward socialiser, Borrow was happier conversing with servants, workers or travelling folk.

Learning to ride – today's equivalent of passing a driving test – opened up the world to Borrow and increased still further his yearning for travel. His genuine affinity with foreign tongues – he had a working knowledge of at least sixteen different languages – aided by a remarkable memory, was to earn Borrow the title 'Lavengro' or 'Word-master' from his gypsy friends. Proud and fiercely independent, Borrow abandoned any thoughts of a legal career and in 1824 he left Norfolk, aiming to earn his living as a writer. But his translations of often obscure foreign works earned him little money or praise.

A decade later, his work for the British and Foreign Bible Society (fuelled more by adventurous curiosity than evangelical zeal) finally fulfilled his ambition to travel widely abroad. Borrow was a good field

The poet William Cowper, pictured with his pet hares in the Cowper Window in St Nicholas Church, East Dereham, not far from where his 'crushed and gentle spirit escaped from a world in which it had known naught but sorrow'

Overleaf: An aerial view of Scolt Head, looking towards Burnham Overy Staithe – the 'Waterslain' land of poet Kevin Crossley-Holland and a 'frayed margin of opportunity and possibilities' to naturalist Richard Mabey

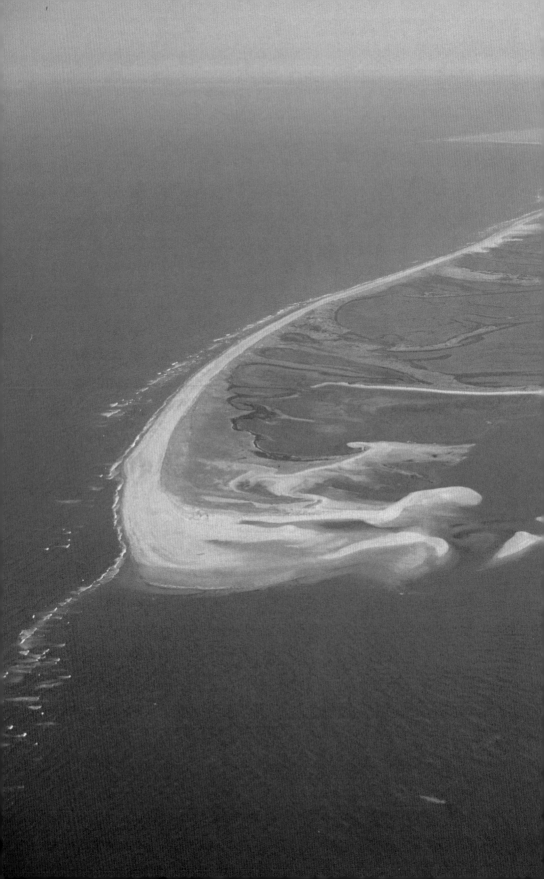

The Church of St Peter and St Paul, Salle – 'the finest church in Norfolk' is a firm favourite with ecclesiastical mystery writer Kate Charles and crime novelist Brian Cooper

worker – bold, daring, and a strong communicator – and it was this employment which provided him with the material for the book with which he made his name as a writer, *The Bible in Spain* (1843). Written in the lively, direct and readable style of his literary hero **Daniel Defoe***, Borrow's *Bible* earned him great acclaim.

Borrow returned to his roots for his next book: *Lavengro* (1851). Rapidly covering the writer's formative years in Norfolk and with blatant disregard for chronological ordering, *Lavengro* soon reveals itself to be a fascinating account of life on the road. Through his vigorous and unaffected prose, Borrow presents a series of events by which he presents himself as a 'fictional' character within his own autobiographical novel. Within the imaginative space of *Lavengro* – 'In the following pages I

The farmhouse in Dumpling Green reputed to be George Borrow's birthplace

'Sometimes he would say to his wife after breakfast', writes **Peter Sager** in *East Anglia*, '"Beloved, today is a day to go walking." And often he would not come home until months later ... with the remark: "Beloved, a fine walk."'

have endeavoured to describe a dream' – Borrow transforms himself from a lad fishing in Norfolk streams to a seasoned traveller leaving much of his real life behind in his brilliantly conceived encounters. Borrow was the first to describe the everyday life of gypsies without romanticising excessively.

Romany Rye (1857) continues along the same road of irony and ambivalence. Though *Lavengro* and *Romany Rye* are the books on which his literary fame rests today, they received very mixed reviews at the time. Victorian England demanded 'authentic' autobiography and distrusted the major 'omissions' from his life presented by his blend of fact and fiction. Borrow never truly recovered from the mauling he received at the hands of the critics. He continued to translate, and travelled widely around Britain but always remained an outsider from Victorian Society. His remaining years, which included a spell in **Great Yarmouth***, were clouded by loneliness and uncertainty, aggravated by the death of his wife Mary in 1869. He died alone at his home in Oulton Broad in 1881.

Brian Aldiss

'I cannot remember when I was not making books.'

The stained glass scene, still visible in the rear bay window of the old Aldiss family flat – representing Norfolk with its 'gentle hills, woods, humble houses and ... sea'.

Not far from the Cowper Congregational Church, standing opposite Norfolk Street in Dereham's busy High Street is the old shop of H H Aldiss – once a drapery and today forming the entrance to Aldiss Court. It was here, in the large flat above the shop floor, that science-fiction writer and novelist **Brian Aldiss** (1925–) was born. 'Whether I like it or not, my roots are buried behind the façade [of] ... my grandfather's shop' says Aldiss, who remembers the flat as a 'paradise of a place for a boy'.

The joys of living above a thriving shop, including a crush on the young lady from the hat department, were wrenched away from Aldiss when his father was forced to sell up his share of the business after the death of H H Aldiss. In *Bury my Heart at W H Smith's – A Writing Life* (1990), Aldiss recalls that 'the shadow of necessity, the spectre of poverty' was always present. The move from Dereham into a small terraced house at **Gorleston*** was not a happy one.

However, it was when he was sent away to boarding school, at the 'tender age of seven', that Brian Aldiss found himself becoming a 'champion storyteller'. He never looked back, and went on to become a most versatile writer with international best-sellers such as *The Hand-Reared Boy* (1970), *A Soldier Erect* (1971) and the acclaimed science-fiction of *The Helliconia Trilogy* (1982–5).

'I cannot remember when I was not making books,' says Aldiss, relating his writing to an 'acute visual sense' and remembering clearly one particular childhood sight: 'H H Aldiss's shop, and our flat ... had been redesigned after the First World War by my architect uncle ... In our square bay window with its comfortable window seat, he had set a little scene in stained glass. It represented Norfolk, with its gentle hills, woods, humble houses and – not least – the sea. For the first twelve years of my life, I looked at that motif every day when I was at home.

Amazingly, despite all the changes, the window still exists.' This simple and colourful stained glass scene can indeed still be seen today, above the flat roof of the shops at the back of the old H H Aldiss store. The store itself has altered almost beyond recognition from the austere but friendly outfitters shop that stood here in the early part of the century. Only the framing of the windows and the neat 'Aldiss' mosaic in the old doorway remain.

The 'Norfolk' years of Brian Aldiss 'have been influential' in his writing; witness the novellas *The Saliva Tree* (1966) and *Brothers of the Head* (1977) and the recently re-released 'Squire' quartet. These later novels set the 'difficulties and pleasures of family life against a changing political background and world-wide scene ... whilst always returning to East Anglia'. They also draw upon the disorientation caused by Aldiss' childhood upheaval, focusing on male protagonists 'who have no place in the world and had to find a place through various alien environments'.

Life in the West (1980) uses the fictional 'Hartisham' near the **Walsinghams***, *Forgotten Life* (1988) disguises East Dereham as 'Nettlesham', and *Remembrance Day* (1993) opens in **Yarmouth***. In the final 'Squire' volume, *Somewhere East of Life* (1994), Roy Burnell's dangerous and action-packed travels take him through Germany, Hungary and the old Soviet empire in search of his missing memory. Eventually, the 'dry and crumbling' façade of 'Diddisham Abbey' (based upon a house for sale outside Dereham a few years ago, 'a couple of miles from Quebec Road'), provides a return to normality with his family and friends in Norfolk. Situated in 'flat bland agricultural country' close to the village of **North Elmham** (north of East Dereham), the Burnell family home houses the remains of a 400-year-old abbey.

Under an 'unyielding' Norfolk sky, Burnell walks through the 'flinty skeleton' of the ancient abbey's remains, contemplating a reunion with his estranged wife. The return to his native Norfolk seems to offer Burnell a chance of a reacquaintance with his former life, loves and memories – a chance for redemption. Meanwhile, Brian Aldiss continues to write, and a large portion of his autobiography, *The Twinkling of an Eye* (1998), consists of 'a whole-hearted reconstruction in words of my grandfather's business and ... East Dereham as it was in the thirties'.

The old H H Aldiss shopfront still standing in the High Street. The first-floor flat above the shop was the birthplace of Brian Aldiss, who as a youngster could 'escape through the window' on to the flat roof below, 'and climb to any part of the shop as I pleased without my feet ever touching the ground'. He recalls attending the Cowper Memorial Church, where the family had their own pews, and being forbidden to look at the posters advertising films at the cinema opposite.

A colleague of Brian Aldiss and fellow native of East Dereham, the **Rev. Lionel Fanthorpe** is reputedly the most prolific science-fiction writer in the world and a triple record holder for the most words written in twenty-four hours in Prose, Drama and Poetry. To prove his point, on 10 August 1995, the former head teacher and author of over 200 books undertook another twenty-four-hour writing marathon at **Norwich*** Central Lending Library, churning out well over 24,000 words on his Norfolk childhood.

Through a part share in Quay House at **Blakeney***, Brian Aldiss still maintains his Norfolk links. This 'stately stone building', standing back from the quay, takes up where the stained-glass scene of his childhood left off: 'From its windows we look out over the cut and the marshes to the North Sea'.

Erpingham

The 'good white head' of the soldier **Sir Thomas Erpingham**
(1357–1428), this 'most kind gentleman' figures in **Shakespeare's***
Henry V, when the king borrows Erpingham's cloak to sound his
troops' morale. A supporter of John of Gaunt, he commanded the
archers at Agincourt in 1415 and lived at **Blickling** and **Norwich***,
where he had the Erpingham Gate facing the Cathedral built
(1416–25). Although he has a tomb monument in Norwich
Cathedral, he is now said to be buried at Erpingham.

Four centuries later, Erpingham was to house an unhappy Italian exile
whose true story, pieced together from letters and diaries, was written
by her granddaughter **Magdalen Goffin**. A touching memoir of an
uprooted existence, *Maria Pasqua* (1979) tells the incredible tale of
Maria Pasqua, born in 1856 and taken by her father, when she was six
years old, on a hitch-hiking journey from Rome to Paris, never to see
Italy again. Once in Paris, Maria became a small sensation in the
painters' circle, with Hébert and many other artists painting the
likeness of this exceptionally beautiful child.

The English Countess who subsequently bought Maria Pasqua off
her father at the age of seven ('She would have the original'), seems
to have walked straight out of an overheated imagination: 'Madame',
this curious blend of benefactress and tyrant, never travels when the
wind is blowing from the east and swears by red glass windows and
the beneficial effects of cows' breath.

In 1881, Maria married Philip Shepheard, a Norfolk doctor nearly
twenty years her senior. Their first home was Bridge House, in the
remote, low-lying village of **Gayton** near **King's Lynn***, where Maria
was made unwelcome by both her husband's sister and servants: 'They
heartily disliked foreigners, had no desire to go abroad, did not speak
French, nor approve of artists'. Maria found the few visitors here
'as dull as they thought her strange', and the trees outside the drawing-
room, planted too near the house, appeared to close in around
her life.

With Maria withering and longing for her home in Italy, the move
in 1884, to Abbot's Hall, a small, square, red brick house off the main
road between Erpingham and **Aylsham** (now the A140) appeared to
be a wise one. In addition, the fairy tales which Maria had started
writing in her long hours of boredom had finally been accepted by a
publisher. But, with the death of her son and the continuation of her
so evidently mismatched marriage (in the equally mismatched
environment of Norfolk), there was to be no happy ending to the story
of Maria Pasqua's life.

Itteringham

Bintry House, a seventeenth-century flint and brick National Trust farmhouse on the Blickling Estate, is the home novelist and reviewer **Elspeth Barker** (1940–) shared for many years with the poet **George Barker*** (1913–1991), whom she married in 1989. Born Elspeth Langlands, in Scotland, and later educated at Oxford, Barker admits that moving here from London wasn't easy: 'It took me a while to get used to Norfolk.' Her own writing career started late – the five children she bore George Barker leaving little time for such dubious pleasures – but was encouraged by both George and their eldest daughter, the writer **Raffaella Barker** (1964–).

An article on 'Hens I have known' in the *Observer* led to an immediate approach from a publisher; her first novel, *O Caledonia*, was released to great acclaim in 1991. Of her work, Barker says: 'landscape is very important to me when I'm reading, and … most important in my writing … landscape inflicts a shape on people's lives'.

As for life in Itteringham, the 'state of mutual suspicion' with her fellow villagers has long been lifted: 'we're among the village's oldest inhabitants now', Barker observes wryly. Her new novel is set in Norfolk and includes the drumlin of **Beeston Hill** and windows 'the colour of sea water' in **Cromer*** church. Elspeth Barker also edited an anthology on the theme of *Loss* (1997), six years after the death of her husband.

Once described as 'the oldest *enfant terrible* in the world', George Barker matched a reputation for his poetry (he has been compared to **Dylan Thomas** in particular) with a reputation for a wild Bohemian lifestyle virtually second to none. After his much-publicised relationship with **Elizabeth Smart** (who fell in love with Barker through reading a volume of his poetry), Barker's arrival in this remote village in the Norfolk heartlands – together with a procession of children and animals, and a steady flow of visitors – must have turned a few heads.

This was the late 1960s, and Barker's standing as a poet was already well established. Having decided at the age of sixteen that he wanted to be a poet, Barker received early encouragement from **John Middleton Murry***, which led to the publication of his first collection *Thirty Preliminary Poems*, published by David Archer in 1933. Barker's second collection, *Poems*, was published by **T S Eliot** in 1935, and was an immediate success.

Norfolk was now Barker's home, and away from the riotous gatherings, drunken binges and fearsome hangovers, the poet responded to his surroundings with renewed creative vigour. Each Thursday, the expanding Barker family would head off to explore Norfolk churches; as Elspeth Barker remembers, 'they're perfect for toddlers'. Combining his roles as father, poet and storyteller, Barker produced his marvellous first collection for children, *To Aylsham Fair* in 1970, while his visits included the hauntingly beautiful church of All Saints at **Thurgarton**.

Elspeth Barker

The award-winning novelist, who took time adjusting to life in Norfolk, pictured with Lily, the youngest daughter she bore the poet George Barker.

George Barker

The dawn has brightened the
shallows and shadows and
the Bure sidles and idles
through weed isles and fallen
willows, and under
Itteringham Mill, and
there is a kind of rain-
drenched flittering in the
air, the night swan still
sleeps in her wings and over
          it all
the dawn heaps up the
          hanging
fire of the day.

George Barker, from 'Morning in
Norfolk' *Poems of Places and
People*, 1971

Lost in the outback of Norfolk, this thatched, towerless church becomes the scene for Barker's deeply moving requiem *At Thurgarton Church* (1969), dedicated 'To the memory of my father'.

Barker's poetry has often been labelled 'romantic'; revealing an intimacy and personal extravagance at odds with the 'social conscience' of the largely anti-romantic movement of the 1950s. Nevertheless, aside from brief spells as a visiting professor at Japanese and American universities (he received no formal education himself), Barker earned his often precarious living from his poetry alone. Brimful of all-too human frailty and passion, the eloquence of Barker's work is often overwhelming in its simplicity – and bound together by an unfailing sense of place.

'George loved Norfolk', says Elspeth, and in his later years he liked nothing better than to be driven around the countryside to his favourite

Bintry House, Itteringham

Home to Elspeth and George Barker, this is the scene of a chaotic upbringing for 'Gabriella' in Raffaella Barker's *Come and Tell Me Some Lies* (1994).

Thurgarton Church

At Thurgarton Church the sun
burns the winter clouds over
the gaunt Danish stone
and thatched reeds that cover
the barest chapel I know.

I could compare it with
the Norse longboats that bore
burning the body forth
in honour from the shore
of great fjords long ago.

The sky is red and cold
overhead, and three small
sturdy trees keep a hold
on the world and the stone wall
that encloses the dead below.

I enter and find I stand
in a great barn, bleak and bare.
Like ice the winter ghosts and
the white walls gleam and flare
and flame as the sun drops low

And I see, then, that slowly
the December day has gone.
I stand in silence, not wholly
believing I am alone
Somehow I cannot go.

George Barker, from
At Thurgarton Church, 1969

haunts. His last book of verse, *Street Ballads*, was partly written in Aylsham Cottage Hospital. After his death in 1991, George Barker was buried on the hill in Itteringham churchyard, from where, as Elspeth says, 'he can still hear people in the house talking'.

> **Lindsay Clarke***, in his novel *The Chymical Wedding* (1989), bases the character of the fearsome poet Edward Nesbit on the real-life George Barker. Clarke lived for a while in nearby **Aylsham** and helped tutor Raffaella Barker for her A levels.

The chaotic life of the Barker tribe is the stuff of myth and legend, and fuels Raffaella Barker's strongly autobiographical debut novel *Come and Tell Me Some Lies* (1994). This charts the eccentric and often bizarre upbringing of 'Gabriella' (Raffaella), living in the Norfolk village of 'Mildney' as she struggles to come to terms with her Bohemian family and her own identity. Truth is often stranger than fiction and as Barker points out, 'the myths of my family, favourite fables told again and again, are brought out like battered photographs, nostalgia-scented and made alive by scrambled memory.'

There are stories of her father, 'Patrick', a frequently drunken poet and his dreaded 'drinking nights', of her mother who dons a blonde wig every time she drives the van she is not legally permitted to drive, and of trips across the border into Suffolk to visit 'Liza' (Elizabeth Smart). 'Jim', the scar-faced Belfast man with bank robber potential returns as the protagonist of Raffaella Barker's second novel *The Hook* (1996), and she continues to combine writing novels with journalism from her home at **Thurgarton**.

Raffaella Barker

She writes of family life becoming 'fairy-tales, fantasies grown from a seed of truth into something wild and overblown.'

Scarning

A passionate local historian, the **Rev. Augustus Jessopp** (1824–1914) worked hard to place Norfolk history within a national and international context. Jessopp researched and wrote *One Generation of a Norfolk House* over a period of fifteen years – linking Norfolk life with sixteenth-century religious intolerance and persecution, as he unfolds the tale of the Jesuit priest Henry Walpole, put to death at York in 1595.

Educated at Cambridge, Jessopp began his career teaching and working as a curate before moving to Norwich School in 1859 as headmaster. Relinquishing his headship twenty years later to join the ranks of the literary Norfolk clergy, Jessopp struggled at times to adjust to the parish he called 'Arcady' – Scarning was very different from the 'high' society he had moved in during his time at Norwich.

Jessopp's *Arcady for Better for Worse* (1887) includes fine descriptions of the district and, drawing from his contributions to *The Nineteenth Century* periodical, focuses on the local community as he experienced it. Rather rashly, Jessopp once wrote of his frustration with the provincialism of Norfolk village life, declaring that 'The East Anglian is, of all the inhabitants of these islands, most wanting in native courtesy, in delicacy of feeling, and in anything remotely resembling romantic sentiment'!

Needless to say, this prompted some angry responses, including a poetic rebuke from a certain 'Daughter of Arcady': 'Nowadays in Arcady / Dwells a shepherd – wise is he! / On all subjects recondite / Scholarly the man can write. / Just a bit beyond his ken / Is the theme of brother men'. Nevertheless, Jessopp worked hard to be accepted by the taciturn Scarning folk and soon became a popular figure who, according to **Arthur Mee**, was 'still remembered in the village' in the early 1970s.

If *One Generation of a Norfolk House* is seen to be Jessopp's most important work, the collection of essays forming *The Coming of the*

Augustus Jessopp

The writer, historian and clergyman was a keen scholar who had won a prize when only nine years old for reciting 700 lines of **Ovid** from memory!

Mary Mann* relates in a letter how Jessopp's speech at a village wedding left his audience nonplussed: 'A brilliant speech; his elocution is perfect, his air (altho' he is by birth as great a commoner as we) high-bred and refined. I pitied him: this speech was immensely witty – not a creature smiled. He made point after point – not the slightest applause.'

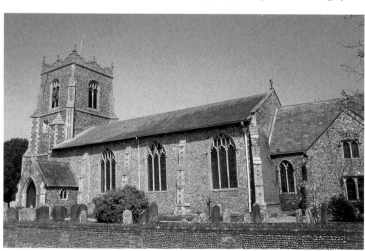

St Peter and St Paul's Church – where Augustus Jessopp was rector for thirty two years

Friars (1889) remains his most popular. The title essay traces the history of the Franciscan order's success in Norfolk from 1226, under the leadership of Norfolk man Richard Ingworth, as the order became 'the most learned body in Europe' – until the suppression of the monasteries. In 'Six hundred years ago', Jessopp displays his concern for country people to understand their past, in a lecture to a group of villagers:

> Consider for a moment – who are we, and what do we mean by *Ourselves*? When I meet a ragged, shuffling tramp on the road (and I meet a good many of them in my lonely walks) I often find myself asking the question, 'How did that shambling vagabond come to his present condition? Did his father turn him out of doors? Did his mother drink?'

Jessopp makes history tangible for the locals by asking them questions about the daily life of their forebears: What did they eat? What did they drink? What would the local beer have tasted like six hundred years earlier? What type of clothes would they have been wearing and would the crime rate have been similar to today's? Like **Mary Mann***, Jessopp was prepared to represent the often difficult and squalid lives of his parishioners. A granite cross marks his grave in the churchyard.

In *Arcady for Better for Worse*, Jessopp describes how he befriends 'Loafing Ben', a labourer who apparently 'never changed his clothes, and never washed himself, never tasted any liquid but beer, nor any food but dry bread for years'. Through persistence, Jessopp gains Ben's confidence and learns of his harsh and strange existence.

Weston Longville

That the name of **Parson James Woodforde*** (1740–1803) should become so well known in literature today would certainly have astonished this ordinary and unexceptional man. The son of a West Country rector, Woodforde was educated at Winchester and Oxford before receiving the living at Weston Longville in 1774, although he did not actually take up residence here until 1776. By this stage, Woodforde's diary, which he had begun as an undergraduate in 1758, was already in full flow and excepting a few early omissions, would be continued for forty-three years, up until a few weeks before his death.

Like the **Paston Letters***, Woodforde's *Diary* provides a wonderful insight into the domestic and social life of his times. It is packed with details of Woodforde's daily routines, the food and drink consumed, the illnesses suffered, and the friendships, trade and social circles of eighteenth-century Norfolk. When much-edited extracts were published as *The Diary of a Country Parson* in 1924, a still war-weary public received this glimpse of an age of innocence forever lost with delight and surprise. The success of this best-seller lies in its period charm and in the very ordinariness of Woodforde himself.

Woodforde lived an unspectacular bachelor life in a quiet Norfolk village. He achieved neither fame nor notoriety, wrote no books and, like most of us, seemed destined only for obscurity. But his unpretentious and often amusing writing style, combined with his diary's unusually complete account of everyday Norfolk life still has a strong

Parson James Woodforde

Clergyman and diarist – he was an ordinary man whose writing has proved to be extraordinarily popular.

Literature was not among Parson Woodforde's main interests, although he did read **Fanny Burney**'s* *Evelina*, which he considered 'very cleaver and sensible'.

appeal. Woodforde records the carrying out of his church duties, visiting the sick and poor, and dining frequently with the local squire. We hear about his conversations at the Hart Inn near the church, the open buying of smuggled tea and rum, and how he managed to get his 'two large Piggs' drunk on his home-brewed beer.

Though very close to **Norwich***, Weston Longville today retains the isolated rural beauty it had in the eighteenth century. However, at the time the swamps and stagnant waters of the undrained Norfolk land carried the risk of malaria for the inhabitants, despite Woodforde's attempts to dose his household against the 'Whirligigousticon'.

The heartlands of Norfolk, in the reigns of George II and George III through which Woodforde lived, supported a largely agricultural society with great discrepancies between the lives of the wealthy and the poor. Reformists such as **Thomas Paine*** were campaigning for more equality, but as America gained independence and the monarchy fell in France, life in the parish of Weston Longville seemed relatively untouched. Parson Woodforde cherished his daily routine, and apart from the occasional visit to **Yarmouth***, Norwich or nearby parishes, many entries in his *Diary* are of the 'I breakfasted, dined, supped and slept again at home' variety. He fishes in his pond, goes hare-coursing, gambles and enjoys good food. What his diary also shows is that his culinary interests follow him even into the world of his dreams:

> I dreamt last Night that I went to Weston Church with a Corpse after me, and just as I came to the Church Yard Gate, saw another Corpse bringing from Morton Road way, and which had died of the small Pox. The corpse that I attended on seeing the other, I ordered to be carried into the Chancel, till the other was buried. When I returned to the Chancel, I thought I saw a most elegant dinner served up – particularly fish...

The Parson Woodforde pub sign, standing almost opposite the village church

Woodforde's rectory no longer stands and though the old, thatched Hart Inn endures as a private dwelling, precious few buildings have survived from his time. The thirteenth-century tower of All Saints' Church remains the oldest part of the village, and has become something of a shrine to Woodforde's memory as visitors come to visit his grave at the north-west end of the chancel (indicated by a diamond-shaped tile) and the memorial above it. A painting of Woodforde by his nephew Samuel hangs on the north side of the Tower Arch. Opposite the church, **The Parson Woodforde** pub features an impressive cast-iron mantrap on the wall as a reminder of the less savoury side of the past, while offering its Parson's Bitter to the thirsty literary pilgrim.

The owner of **Parson Woodforde**'s original *Diary* manuscript and a descendant of his elder brother, the **Very Revd Dean Christopher Woodforde** (1907–1962), was not only an authority on stained glass

(*The Norwich School of Glass Painting*, 1950), but also the author of supernatural tales for boys with a very definite sense of place. His enjoyably old-fashioned stories originally told to public school boys and collected in *A Pad in the Straw* (1952) earned him a reputation as a writer of 'different but delightful' (**John Betjeman***) tales, usually revolving around old churches, old inns and schools, where the supernatural can strike at any moment.

Combining an antiquarian's interest in the past with a teacher's didactic skill, Woodforde conjures up goblins, spectres and other manifestations. In 'Roderick', a dragon appears on an air-strip and gobbles up all air crew within reach, but releases them safely after a good talking to by a young lad whose dragon skills baffle everybody. 'Michael' is set in 'Bressingthorpe' and told by a churchwarden as a mysterious stone from a monument in Bressingthorpe church becomes instrumental in the apprehension of an arsonist.

'Malcolm', another Norfolk story, involves an Oxford student and amateur painter, whose annual visit at 'Cawsby Hall, near the north coast of Norfolk' to see his uncle goes terribly wrong. When Malcolm's sketches of the Hall change to ghastly scenes executed in blood-red paint, it takes a trip into **Norwich*** and 'Haddescoe's Bookshop' to solve the mystery of the Judas tree of Cawsby Hall.

Woodforde was also curate at St Margaret's (with St Nicholas) in **King's Lynn*** and at **Drayton**, near Norwich. His last book, *Record of John*, about a few months in the life of a sixteen-year-old grammar school boy, was published in 1962, the year he died.

Christopher Woodforde

'It seemed to me that no one had made a sustained effort to offer to boys of the ages of 13–14 stories which combined their natural love of the uncanny, the unknown, and the somewhat gruesome with their natural and rightful heritage of English history and the English countryside.'

Wymondham

Budapest-born poet **George Szirtes** (1948–) moved to Norfolk in the summer of 1994 to take up a position teaching and co-ordinating Creative Writing at the Norwich School of Art & Design. Arriving in England in 1956, Szirtes has since established himself as a chronicler of the human and the intimate, usually within a domestic environment, and one whose sympathies and vision lie with Europe as a whole and with Hungary and England in particular.

His most recent work, including *Portrait of My Father in an English Landscape* (1998), reveals a gradual integration of Szirtes into the Wymondham community, though his 'Norfolk' poems tend to focus more on the people and buildings here than on the landscape. 'Tinseltown' describes the scene in the local newsagent at Christmas and 'Gunsmith' references the shop directly opposite Szirtes' house, while 'Mouth Music' is written in memory of botanist Harold Woolhouse whose 'wonderful' garden is still maintained further down Damgate Street: 'But we want him here with us, just as he has been / just as we hope that we ourselves will be, where the wind / sings in the

George Szirtes

'I suppose the truth is I am an urban creature, born in one capital city (Budapest) and brought up in another (London), so natural landscape has had to filter slowly into my imagination.'

attic and the water seeps through the stones in the cellar / here where we sit and make noises of talking'.

Only 'Rabbits' touches on the physical landscape – 'The rabbits are about their business / of softening. They congregate in gangs / by hedgerows as if waiting for an event / of greater softness to overtake them'; but the animals Szirtes watches in the fields at dusk are observed with a certain detachment from the window of his carriage on a passing London train. As Szirtes himself notes: 'I have probably drawn more on memory and imagination than on direct observation of landscape'. In this respect, Szirtes seems happier exploring, with depth, sensitivity and humour, the rich and varied landscape of the human mind and the 'unresolved balance between beauty and terror'. It is left to 'Backwaters: Norfolk Fields' (1998), a series of sonnets and sonnet sequences, to explore the 'Broad fields out of town. The slow unravelling / of a long reel where everyone is travelling':

> On a high-cloud day, you could drown in sky
> round here. You see the gentle swaying
> of leaves along a wall. Something under
> the water, under the sky-light, in the dry
> cabin under the ocean is quietly playing
> a music of muted bells in soft thunder.

David Middleton-Brown, the amateur investigator in **Kate Charles**'* ecclesiastical mysteries lives in this busy market town, and Wymondham's Abbey Church 'with its striking double towers' visited as a young boy sparked 'a life-long love affair with this church' and with ecclesiastical architecture in general.

Yaxham

This village, strung out along the B1135 just south-east of Dereham, can boast of a connection with both **William Cowper*** and a distant but no less distinguished relative, **John Cowper Powys*** (1872–1963). Born and raised in the dales of Derbyshire and the eldest of eleven children, Powys came from a long line of country parsons on both sides of the family and his mother was related to the poets William Cowper and **John Donne**. In his *Autobiography* (1934), Powys recalls his childhood visits to his maternal grandfather's rectory here at Yaxham and the impact of 'another and very different landscape' that 'imprinted itself' on to his 'simple and sensuous, if not passionate nature' as a young child:

Opposite: Yaxham House – hidden away behind St Peter's churchyard, the old rectory of John Cowper Powys' grandfather stands at the end of the same avenue (lined by yews and still pitted with puddles when it rains) that John Cowper Powys describes in his *Autobiography*.

> In this country, lying almost at sea-level, and where nothing but poplars and alders and willows obstruct the rising and sinking of the sun, I remember at an age when my stature made it hard for

me to see over the tops of the ears of full-grown wheat-fields, being transported with delight ... by the feeling of absolute and unbounded power I got... pretending to be one of those Great Eastern Railway engines.

It was not until Powys was in his fifties that his writing career really began to take off, with the publication of his poetry and historical romances to great critical acclaim. He returns to Norfolk in his passionate novel, *A Glastonbury Romance* (1932), which uses the fens surrounding **Northwold*** as a setting for the early action.

Powys' writing always has a philosophical edge to it, and even as a five-year-old boy playing at trains, fishing for newts and tadpoles in Yaxham village pond with his brothers, he became aware of the early shaping of his 'vaguely grandiose' character, of being observed by others, wondering at his 'wayward and mysterious purpose'. Later Powys describes hearing of the death of an uncle and remembering 'the exact look of the rain, making little pyramids of water as it fell in the puddles by the side of the avenue that led to my grandfather's house'. Today, the old rectory (privately owned) still retains its understated grandeur, along with its great lawns, ancient trees, tame deer, and loudly meowing peacocks.

John Cowper Powys

The Norfolk landscape 'imprinted itself' into his young mind.

CHAPTER SEVEN

The Edge

LITERARY LINKS

W H Auden, E F Benson, Brian Cooper, Kevin Crossley-Holland,
Lilias Rider Haggard, Patrick Hamilton, Jack Higgins, Angela Huth,
John Lanchester, Richard Mabey, Captain Frederick Marryat,
Katherine Pierpoint, William Rivière, Stevie Smith, Henry Sutton,
Sylvia Townsend Warner, Henry Williamson

Blakeney

First 'smitten by a landscape' as a teenager in the Chilterns, it was to a 'landscape every bit as devious and demanding as I remembered it' that one of Britain's foremost nature writers **Richard Mabey** (1941–) returned in the early 1980s. 'Running wild in north Norfolk', Mabey gleaned an understanding of the abstraction that he refers to as 'The Edge' between humanity and nature – 'just a frayed margin, of opportunity and possibilities'.

In Mabey's autobiography *Home Country* (1990), he describes arriving in Blakeney to stay with friends on the Dilemma X, an 'ancient lifeboat, converted into a liveable craft by an overgrowth of cabins' moored at Blakeney quay. Mabey is spellbound by the view from his porthole:

Richard Mabey

What I saw was an astonishing panorama – a mile of saltmarsh shimmering under a high tide. The whole landscape seemed to be on the move. Terns hovered feet above the water, and arrowed down for small fish. Spikes of cord-grass and sea-lavender bounced about in the current. Swirling geometric figures opened up on the surface of the water, stretched and then closed again. Even the mud seemed alive, and slid out of the ebbing water with the moist shine of a newborn animal. Out in the distance, framed against the breakers, we could just make out Blakeney Point, the shingle spit that was all that separated the harbour from the German Ocean. It was a sight that has kept me in thrall to this coast ever since, a liberating vision of being at the edge of things.

'I'd found the marsh landscape incomprehensible at first, too huge and incoherent to be anything other than a backdrop. But it had that twice-daily refashioning by the tide, and as I got used to its rhythms, it began to seem less foreign.'

Home Country, 1990

Blakeney Creek – the world here 'seemed to be all possibility' to Richard Mabey. In the distance is the old coastguard's hut on Blakeney Point, used to eerie effect in E F Benson's short story 'A Tale of an Empty House'.

Blakeney went on to become Mabey's 'second home' throughout the sixties, and the days spent scouring the shoreline for samphire, wild sea-spinach, fennel and mushrooms provided the inspiration for his first book, *Food for Free* (1972), written in a spacious cottage in High Street.

Just a short bike ride away at **Cley**, Mabey used to go bird-watching with the inspirational ornithologist and illustrator Richard A Richardson – 'a cross between Mr Punch and a weatherbeaten rocker'. The combination of Richardson's 'exhaustive knowledge of local natural history', the beauty and tranquillity of the north Norfolk coast, and Mabey's own successful writing career provided the lifestyle he had always dreamed of.

Today, Mabey continues to champion the cause of nature, while his affection for the shape-shifting shores of the north Norfolk coast remain faithfully recorded through the pages of *Home Country*:

> A little higher up the shore, where the ground was firmer, I would sit and watch the tide coming in over this moist green pelt in something close to a trance. I'd screw up my eyes and peer obsessively for the turn, fixing on an identifiable pattern in the sand or a clump of cord-grass, and trying to spot the first signs of its disappearance ... Tide-watching became as compulsive as peering into a fire – except that here, when the ebb came, everything re-emerged, soft-edged, as good as new, but with a subtly altered geography that had never existed before.

The unique beauty and solitude of this coastline were well known to popular author **E(dward) F(rederic) 'Fred' Benson*** (1867–1940) who was a regular visitor and bird-watcher here. On one occasion, Benson writes of his thrill at catching a rare glimpse of a solitary avocet, which, sadly, was shot a few days later.

However, bird-watching was not the prolific Benson's only preoccupation here – the sometimes bleak and mysterious nature of the area inspiring several of his ghost stories, which first appeared in *The Room in the Tower and other Stories* (1912) and were followed by the better-known *Spook Stories* (1928) and other collections. Although the author of numerous novels and other works, Benson's ghost stories are probably his most enduring, and the Norfolk landscape lends itself perfectly to using changes in scenery or sound to evoke feelings of unease in his readers.

'Outside the Door' finds a disbelieving narrator 'at a little village north of Sheringham', listening to the ghost story of his friend's wife, Mrs Aldwych. Outside, in the 'transparent half light' of the evening, Mrs Aldwych relates the tale of the poor murdered wretch who haunts their house. To the accompaniment of 'whispering ripples' from the nearby sea, she tells of the night, one month ago, when she awoke, terrified, to a shuffling sound: 'feet feeling their way in the dark were coming downstairs to my passage: I could hear also the groping hand slip and slide along the bannisters'.

Mrs Aldwych explains her theory that the victim's brainwaves, 'as she groped along her lost way' pursued by her murderers, somehow still remain in the house. 'Every wave of whatever kind leaves its mark, does it not?' she puts to the still sceptical narrator, before making him an offer: 'Shall I give you a room on the route of the poor murdered harmless walker?' Our narrator answers swiftly, 'I am very comfortable, thanks, where I am.'

More spine-tingling still is 'A Tale of an Empty House' which exploits the distinctive and superbly rendered locales of Blakeney to the full.

In early 1998, Mabey rediscovered the Dilemma X – sitting in a field near Glandford, waiting, as he puts it for the 'Last Great High Tide.'

E F Benson

The prolific popular novelist enjoyed exploring the 'amphibious meadows' of this area; birdwatching and plotting further 'spook' stories.

'Towards evening the raucous cries of the gulls are still, the terns cease their chiding, and the only bird-sounds are the voices of the curlews whistling or giving out the liquid bubbling note which always connotes to me the fall of dusk on the lonely marshes, their huge emptiness and their ineffable magic.'

E F Benson, *Final Edition*, 1940

Travelling towards 'Crowthorpe' in filthy weather, our narrator decides
to overnight at a hotel in the village of 'Riddington' (Blakeney). He
awakens to an unexpected view: 'a limitless expanse of shining grasses
with tufts of shrubby growth, and great patches of purple sea-lavender.
Beyond were tawny sand-banks, and further yet a line of shingle and
scrub and sand-dunes. But the sea which I had expected to fill the whole
circle of the visible world till it met the sky on the horizon had totally
disappeared.'

Opting for a walk, swim and some bird-watching, the narrator sets
off for the 'exhilarating solitude' of the peninsula 'Riddington Point'
(**Blakeney Point**). Here he spots signs of human habitation for the first
time; a deserted coastguard's house standing on a 'stony spit of ground
that ran like some great rib into the amphibious meadows'. Pausing at
the house for his lunch, our narrator falls asleep only to be awakened
by the footfall of a strange, lame man. When staff at the hotel later
inform him that the house has long been uninhabited, his curiosity and
unease are aroused. Little realising that a terrible murder had once been
committed there, he returns the next day with his friend Jack. The two
men shelter at the house from a sudden storm, only to find themselves
overwhelmed by an 'awful spiritual presence' which plunges them into
a 'horror of great darkness'.

Jack Higgins (1929–), aka Harry Patterson, opens his best-selling novel
The Eagle Has Landed (1975) with a visit by the author to the same
'amphibious meadows' explored by E F Benson. Based at the Blakeney

Hotel for his research, Higgins stumbles across the secrets of 'Studley Constable' which lies close to Blakeney and **Cley** – a quiet and intriguing village and 'one of those places that seem to turn up in North Norfolk and nowhere else'. Though 'Studley' is actually based upon a village on the Thames, the sense of place evoked in Higgins' thrilling wartime tale is distinctly Norfolk.

Based upon a plot Higgins heard of during his own military service, the audacious plan by German special forces to assassinate Winston Churchill when he visited the area in 1943, is lent credibility by the isolation and natural camouflage offered by the **Glaven Valley**. It is a landscape well-suited to the dramatic plot of secrecy and concealment, as the German's local spy, Joanna Grey, notes with satisfaction:

Jack Higgins

The Eagle Has Landed effortlessly blends fact and fiction in the 'strange alien world' of north Norfolk.

> It was a strange alien world of sea creeks and mudflats and great pale barriers of reeds higher than a man's head, inhabited only by the birds, curlew and redshank and brent geese coming south from Siberia to winter on the mud flats ... In the distance she could see the Point on the other side of the estuary, curving in like a great bent forefinger, enclosing an area of channels and sandbanks and shoals that, on a rising tide, was probably as lethal as anywhere on the Norfolk coast.

In his own inimitable style, Higgins interweaves fact with fiction; the enemy forces drop into a territory very similar to the pine-fringed coastline at **Holkham** (the American military base of 'Meltham' appears to be based here), while the 'medieval cathedral in miniature' of Studley Constable closely resembles the church of St Nicholas here in Blakeney.

Using the mist-shrouded seclusion of the windswept marshes, Higgins ladles out excitement, romance and violence in a typically gripping narrative which begins and ends in the remote Norfolk churchyard of 'St Mary and All the Saints', Studley Constable: 'the kind of village that you find by accident one day and can never find again, so that you begin to question whether it ever existed in the first place'.

Pillboxes at Holkham – situated close to where Steiner's men parachute into England in *The Eagle Has Landed*, these are some of the many wartime reminders scattered around this exposed area.

Katherine Pierpoint

Having spent 'year after year' holidaying here, her poetry brings a new intensity of vision to the salt marsh.

As a young child, the poet **Katherine Pierpoint** (1961–) used to holiday around the Blakeney area with her parents where she loved 'paddling in the salt marshes'. With memories of watching 'a duckling, so small it's about the size of a bee sculling around a salty puddle', Pierpoint describes one holiday visit in 'Up the Brook', from her prize-winning collection *Truffle Beds* (1995). Leaving the sanctuary of their boat, the Sea Cow, to explore the coastline, Pierpoint describes feeling 'a pliant sack of huge thrills / At being the only set of footprints on this island; / At running with another old dog, this one black, / Taking possession by the nose of the beach and dunes.'

Katherine Pierpoint studied languages and worked in publishing and television before winning a Creative Writing Fellowship in 1993. With her move from London's bustling urbanity to East Anglia's 'toughness of the land and the weather ... and sense of history in the landscape' came a heightened perception in her writing, exemplified by the deftness of touch and sensory awareness of her recent poetry.

Her intensity of vision is revealed in 'Saltmarsh and Skylark', where, in a landscape 'with light pouring everywhere', even the slightest of hollows in the marshy terrain lends an equal sense of isolation and exposure:

A man sits in a bowl of sunlight on the saltmarsh, clearly alone.
A slight hollow brings shelter on this husky threshing floor,
Stamped out flat by heavy, working weather.

The marshes are etched by veins of water so salt
It rustles faintly as it flows; sequin platelets buffed bright by acid –
So salt it iceburns, with the stick and pull of skin on frosted metal.

The water is carding its knotty white strings slowly
Through the blue brown fish-flesh of the mud.
Slowly laces and unlaces the filaments in the corridor of gills.

The marsh is a scribble of tough whip-grass and matted vetch;
Cross-hatched collage of God's leftovers;
Odd peelings from the plughole, pilled tweed
And steel wool, glued on in tufts by a nervous understudy.

Dry brown curves of grass, bowing down in pools of white light;
A crumbling-rusk-in-skimmed-milk landscape.
The man squints upwards into larksong and closes his eyes.

As he tilts, he inhales the song all the warm way up the light.
The eyelids thinly filter, impressing into hot blood-orange,
Then melting crabshell, embossed in pink and greening bronze;

Strange bunching and wellings, expansive dissolution;
The matt black stamen of the skylark's turning tongue,
The brain-stem's softly-bound bouquet of pulses.

Brancaster

'Norfolk is my talisman', says novelist and short-story writer **Angela Huth***, who has been coming to the 'ribbed distances' of Brancaster since she was twelve years old, when her parents first had a cottage here. Huth's intriguing novel *Invitation To The Married Life* (1991) explores the tranquillity and stability of life on the north Norfolk coast, presenting a stark contrast to the frustrating and often frantic existences led by her characters elsewhere around the country. Focusing on September Ball invitations issued to various couples, the plot revolves around the machinations of a motley collection of failing marriages and infidelities.

Here in Brancaster, however, postman Yacksley cycles along the country lanes towards 'Church House', looking over to the marshes where the wind bends the reeds, past the abandoned and crumbling old grey stone church, until he reaches the neatness of Bill Lutchins' log pile. Bill and his wife Mary retired to Norfolk ten years ago, returning to the home of Mary's childhood and to the scene of their marriage half a century earlier. The lure of the 'wind-torn skies' and sweeping coastline is irresistible. Walking along Brancaster beach, braced against the 'edgy breeze', Mary ponders the salt-smudged familiarity of her surroundings and the 'gradual disintegration' of the 'once sturdy shell' of a Second World War shipwreck, a metaphor perhaps for her own old age and increasing physical frailty:

> It had succumbed slowly to barnacles, seaweed, lashing storms and strong currents. Now, when the tide was out, just a few posts of blackened steel remained – too few even to indicate the former shape of the ship's bones. At high tide the two or three small posts protruding from the water could be missed by all those unfamiliar with the disappearing skeleton. There was a high tide this afternoon: sea dull as an elephant's shank in moments when the cloud obscured the sun. Then, when the sun passed, herbaceous blues and greys and greens of a sophisticated garden border.

Huth herself admits to treasuring the precious solitude offered by the Brancaster beach out of season, particularly those 'glorious' winter days 'with bright blue skies, sunshine like diamonds and the sand dazzling on the beach'. In an interview she once described 'standing quite alone' here one Christmas, 'looking at the great emptiness and thinking there is nowhere on earth more beautiful'.

In *Invitation To The Married Life*, the 'luminous grey sky' he sees in a beautiful watercolour painting in a Nottingham gallery lures amateur artist, collector and hopelessly unfaithful husband Thomas Arkwright to the Brancaster coastline. Stunned by the pure 'simplicity' of the watercolour *Norfolk: Early Morning*, he finds himself both admiring and envious of the artist's talent. But it's not just the scenery that

Angela Huth at Brancaster

'It's the sense of continuity in Norfolk that I love so much. It's not a fashionable one-year-in-out-the-next kind of place ... I've found everything I needed here in Norfolk.'

Thomas is after. Always on the lookout for perilous new love affairs, here in the 'brick and flintstone' surroundings of 'Marsh Cottage', he soon finds another object for his insatiable desire, in the form of the Norfolk landscape artist Rosie Cotterman (whose name bears an uncanny resemblance to that of the Norfolk painter John Sell Cotman) – a tiny, older and 'strange' woman for whom he immediately falls.

Thomas' affections are not reciprocated however, and the Norfolk character of Rosie Cotterman remains calmly aloof, capable and fiercely independent. Thomas' sudden arrival, an 'overweight ... uncomfortable-looking man shuffling and slipping down the dunes' disturbs Mary, who is pondering her own mortality, and the rending of her own marriage that death will inevitably bring:

Mary loved the beach, its ankle-high gusts of sand stinging her boots, its ribbed distances scrunchy with shells, its wind-wrinkled pools blinking fast as troubled eyes. But she did not like the sea. It made her think of death, endings, the remorseless indifference of Nature.

She climbed the dunes, making her way along paths scratchy with marram grass and sea gorse. At the top she stopped to survey the high tide, the empty sweep of the beach. Through the thickness of her jersey she felt the sun. She made her way down to the sands. There, in the sharp morning light, each small stone and shell made its particular shadow. A single seagull kited above her, rising and falling, pulled by an invisible string. How many more times can I have all this, she wondered?

As the summer passes, and the couples don their ball gowns and dinner jackets in readiness for the ball, each relationship seems to reach its crisis point. But from this assortment of perceptively drawn and often humorous pairings, and despite a tragic death, something like hope seems to emerge through the 'quixotic skies' of north Norfolk.

The village of Angela Huth's childhood holidays might be 'very dead' now, peopled as it is mainly by weekend and holiday cottages, but it still provides a perfect writing refuge. Working from a converted barn in the centre of the village, overlooking the shimmering marshland, Huth often enjoys long afternoon strolls around the coastline; across the Brancaster sands and through **Burnham Deepdale**.

Moving between settings in Brancaster and New York City, Huth's earlier novel, *Wanting* (1984), offers readers a first sight of the symbolic wreck on Brancaster beach, used here in a powerful scene of reverie and loss as Huth's protagonist Viola Windrush finds herself walking out towards its 'jagged black outlines', soon after the death of her parents:

As she walked on the firm wet beach the entire compass of her eyes was filled with the soft translucent light. Feeling the ribs of sand beneath her feet she remembered that as a child she had imagined they were the imprints of the bodies of underwater monsters who liked to lie on the sea-bed when the tide was high, unseen ... She had often wondered if she might one day see the monsters, woken from their sleep by the pull of an outgoing tide, scurrying after it in fright. But her father, who was so often up early duck-shooting, had never mentioned any such sight, and she had not liked to ask.

While Viola Windrush ponders the wisdom of her decision to keep on the old rectory that was her parents' house, her dilemma is paralleled with that of Mr Baxter, who, after the death of his wife, now faces lonely retirement. But *Wanting* still favourably compares the quiet, quintessentially English surroundings of Brancaster with the fast,

'It had succumbed slowly to barnacles, seaweed, lashing storms and strong currents' – the Brancaster wreck, lying far out on the sands at low tide.

artificial world of New York City whose characters cannot understand Viola Windrush and her exiled brother Gideon's fascination with their 'old seaside dump'. 'Norfolk stinks,' exclaims the sad figure of theatre producer Harry Antlers, as he weaves through narrow country lanes in pursuit of the elusive object of his unrequited passion. There are missed opportunities along the way, but in the end, most characters succeed in satisfying their 'wanting' in some way.

Burnham Overy Staithe

The austere beauty of the marshes here proved to be the 'ideal landscape' for novelist and playwright **Patrick Hamilton** (1901–62) late in the 1930s, when his first wife Lois found them a cottage in the village. The godchild of **Arthur Conan Doyle***, Hamilton found the 'sombre flatness' of Burnham the perfect place to work on his novel *The Siege of Pleasure* (1932), the story of a young servant girl slipping into prostitution and the second part of Hamilton's London trilogy *Twenty Thousand Streets Under the Sky* (1935).

Patrick Hamilton

'[His] great achievement was to portray, and to create, a vivid, fantastic world of comic horror, of rented accommodations and temporary refuges, lodging houses, pubs, cinemas and tea houses, where the lost, failed and forgotten meet and bore each other and seek some respite.'

Sean French, *Patrick Hamilton, A Life*, 1993

There were no great comforts in the Overy Staithe cottage, indeed it would get extremely cold in the winter, with no indoor lavatory 'nor much in the way of utensils to eat with', as Hamilton warned his brother, detective novelist **Bruce Hamilton**. But his work went well in what was, according to his second biographer **Sean French**, 'his refuge, a small community, mainly of labourers, ideal for the isolation in which he could best write'.

While the Norfolk landscape never entered the work of this vagrant existence, the bleakness of the landscape certainly matched the bleakness of his vision, exacerbated by a disfiguring accident a few years before he arrived here. Although today his novels are little read, this most talented offspring of a literary family was a rising star in his time.

In 1937, Hamilton became increasingly dispirited by the isolation of Overy Staithe, and when he moved away a year later, it was with a determination 'not to sink back into the Norfolk rut'. Nevertheless in1955, despite worries expressed to his brother that 'the part of the world you and I knew is now overrun with GIs (raping girls right and left) and aeroplanes', Hamilton decided to return to Norfolk.

Hamilton and his second wife Ursula ('La') rented Highfield House in **Blakeney***, a large property facing south, 'with an absolutely unspoiled view of miles of the most rural part of Norfolk – a garden big enough to turn into a miniature Golf Course (which I've done) – some goldfish, believe it or not, in a sort of stone pond – what more could you possibly want?', he says in a letter, 'feeling better that I've ever felt in my entire life.'

Hamilton's last years were spent in **Sheringham***, but after his death from alcohol-related illnesses in September 1964, his ashes were scattered on the lonely plains of **Blakeney Flats**.

When poet, Anglo-Saxon scholar and children's writer **Kevin Crossley-Holland** (1941–) returned to live in the 'Waterslain' land of his childhood in 1994, it was with a sense of 'anchorage', of coming home. Now based in the nearby literary and arts centre of **Burnham Market**, much of Crossley-Holland's writing focuses on his spiritual 'heartland' here on the north Norfolk coast.

Kevin Crossley-Holland

The poet and Anglo-Saxon scholar whose spiritual 'heartland' is here at 'Waterslain'.

There is a great feel of 'looking back to move forward' about Crossley-Holland's work, visible in the accomplished translations of *Beowulf* and *The Exeter Riddle Book* and reflected too in his adept re-working of traditional English folklore for children in *The Old Stories: Folk Tales from East Anglia and the Fen Country* (1997).

Legends, as Crossley-Holland reminds us, begin like 'a piece of grit in an oyster' – producing the gleaming pearl of a story after many years of accumulation. In his literary pearl-diving, Crossley-Holland displays a genuine affection and respect for the past, and especially for the 'out-and-out heroism, a dogged refusal to surrender' of his favoured Old English literature. And no landscape better epitomises this sense of stubborn resistance than the ancient state of 'flux' of the 'Waterslain' (an old Norfolk word meaning 'flooded') marshlands around Burnham Overy Staithe.

In his study, Crossley-Holland cherishes an aerial shot of **Scolt Head**, the island he 'graduated to' from the 'first island' he conquered as a child, 'only a minute's gallop from my grandparents' house':

> The first island to make its mark on me lies in the middle of a creek in that part of England I love best, North Norfolk. It is perhaps a hundred yards long, twenty yards wide, a long grassy hummock fringed by reeds and samphire and mud. Day after day through my early childhood my sister and I used to paddle or row across to it, depending on the state of the tide; it was ours, and

with great ceremony we christened it 'Kenwood' in honour of the chocolate bars we had taken to eat there.

'The First Island', from *Pieces of Land: A Journey to Eight Islands*, 1972

Burnham Overy Staithe – 'Waterslain'

'This indeterminate and empty / quarter, this mesh of sanding and marsh and creek'

Kevin Crossley Holland, 'Eastern Light', 1986.

Some of Crossley-Holland's most spare and evocative poetry can be found in *Waterslain* (1986). This is a collection peopled by the past; his childhood self standing alongside such characters as 'salt shepherd' Billy Haines, Mrs Riches 'leaning right across her counter' at the post office to recount all the local gossip, and 'Diz', the old woman with webbed hands and feet who 'reeks of kelp' and catches her meals in the saline coastal pools. Taken from *The Painting-Room* (1988), and perhaps Crossley-Holland's most significant and representative work – the fruit of many walks across the 'sky-wide fields', along the dyke at Burnham Overy Staithe and out towards the sea – is 'Here, at the Tide's Turning':

You close your eyes and see
                              the stillness of
the mullet-nibbled arteries, samphire
on the mudflats almost underwater,
and on the saltmarsh whiskers of couch-grass
twitching, waders roosting, sea-lavender
faded to ashes.

                    In the dark or almost dark
shapes sit on the staithe muttering of plickplack,
and greenshanks, and zos beds;
                              a duck arrives
in a flap, late for a small pond party.

The small yard's creak and groan and lazy rap,
muffled water music.

                    One sky-streamer,
pale and half-frayed, still dreaming of colour.

Water and earth and air quite integral:
all Waterslain one sombre aquarelle.

From the beginning, and last year, this year,
you can think of no year when you have
not sat on this stub of a salt-eaten stanchion.

Dumbfounded by such tracts of marsh and sky —
the void swirled round you and pressed against you —
you've found a mercy in small stones.

This year, next year, you cannot think
of not returning: not to perch in the blue
hour of this blunt jetty, not to wait, as of right,
for the iron hour and the turning of the tide.

You cross the shillying and the shallows
and, stepping on to the marsh, enter
a wilderness.

                    Quick wind works around you.

You are engulfed in a wave of blue flames.

No line that is not clear cut and severe,
nothing baroque or bogus. The voices
of young children rehearsing on the staithe
are lifted from another time.
                              This is
battleground. Dark tide fills the winking pulks,
floods the mud-canyons.

                    This flux, this anchorage.

Here you watch, you write, you tell the tides.

                    You walk clean into the possible.

Success came gradually to this poet, master storyteller and 'guardian of the Anglo-Saxon matter' (**Seamus Heaney**), rather like 'a drive in Norfolk', says Crossley-Holland: 'just when you think you're getting somewhere – you get caught in traffic!' One of many successes coming from braving the bumps and bends of a writer's road is his children's story *Storm*. The winner of the 1985 Carnegie Medal, this is a haunting tale of childhood initiation. Annie Carter is used to playing on her own; her parents are rather old and Annie's mother blames the marshes for her arthritis, feeling 'as stiff as a whingeing hinge'. The family cottage is on the edge of the great marsh, two miles from 'Waterslain' (Burnham Overy Staithe) and Annie loves to go off exploring, unconcerned by rumours of the ghost said to haunt the ford, playing tricks on people. One Christmas when her sister Willa returns home, Annie finds herself offered a ride by a tall, silent horseman. Will she accept?

> Just on the edge of the village, with grounds stretching down to the creek, stands a large, long brick and flint building – now divided into separate properties – which once accommodated guests as the Old Moorings Hotel. It is to this rambling old retreat that estranged wife Clare Lyall and her lover Joshua Heron come together in **Angela Huth**'s* first novel *Nowhere Girl* (1970). From here the couple go for long walks through the adjacent cabbage fields and out on to the 'scrawny dunes'. But even here, in the middle of 'nowhere', as dawn breaks like 'edges of burning paper' in the vast Norfolk sky, there are still many questions about their relationship which must be answered.

Standing on the edge of the fields, just off the coast road, the skeletal arms and shadowy bulk of Burnham Overy Mill overlook the 'Waterslain' land and the marshes beyond. It is here that contemporary novelist **Henry Sutton*** (1963–) places the very disparate characters of his unsettling second novel *Bank Holiday Monday* (1996).

Angst-ridden Henderson, the organiser of the Bank Holiday weekend break, returns to an all-too familiar landscape with his wife, Laura, and their young son, Tristram. Still haunted by visions of his childhood holidays and a terrible event that occurred here, Henderson steels himself for a confrontation with the traumas of his past.

Arriving with them is Laura's relative Alice, who serves as the emotional litmus paper for the group and is herself running from a disastrous relationship back in Australia. Seeing the 'vastness of the marshes spreading out in front of her', Alice already has suspicions about the real motive behind their visit.

Drawn from childhood summers spent at his grandparents' house here, Henry Sutton's intimacy with the landscape is used to depict an area 'that's both primeval yet oddly sophisticated, or at least intense'.

Henry Sutton

His *Bank Holiday Weekend* explores the 'repressed, difficult' landscape here.

'[Alice] could smell the sea, hear its murmur. Though she couldn't see it now. And it occurred to her then that perhaps the sea wasn't what Henderson had brought them all this way to see, but this repressed, difficult land that sunk slowly into it.'

Henry Sutton, *Bank Holiday Monday*, 1996

And the 'stale sweetness' of the windmill – once a working structure linked to the land by its trade, now standing still and aloof from the surrounding farmlands – is a powerful reminder of historical transition.

Windmills, as Tristram reminds us, are 'like sailing ships that don't go anywhere', but while the sentinel mill remains rooted to terra firma, the action of the book moves all around the north Norfolk coast. When Francis and Carey join the others at the mill, the group is soon heading off to **Burnham Thorpe** (for a drink at the decidedly eccentric local pub), **Titchwell** (Britain's busiest bird sanctuary), **Wells** (inevitably to fetch some fish and chips from the harbour front), and out towards the shallow sea at **Holkham Bay** – all cross-referenced with the natural history of the area, its seabirds, shellfish and samphire.

After a lengthy tramp out of Burnham Overy Staithe and along the embankment, Henderson's pilgrims are greeted by the 'purple shimmer' of the marsh and the sun-drenched sands of Holkham Bay. Picnicking in the shell-scrunchy dunes of **Gun Hill**, it all seems quite idyllic – until Tristram goes missing and the group take an unfortunate detour back through marshes becoming fast-filled by the incoming tide. Across the water which appears 'like mercury rising onto the shingle banks', are the 'marram-tufted bluffs' of **Scolt Head**, but the party are soon trapped by a large creek 'filled with fast-moving water, patches of swirling brown scum'.

The story is infused with the past, and as Alice, armed with her crumpled old coastal map, attempts to steer the party home, visions of the ancient geology of the coastal region are very much in her mind:

> She could hear no human sound. Just the marshes breathing or waves breaking. Whatever it was. Then she wondered what sound glaciers made advancing over land. A terrible, shuddering, earthquake sound, she thought. But it would be so slow no one would hear it. Waves of frozen sound.

Throughout *Bank Holiday Monday*, Sutton remains faithful to the unsettled landscape of this part of Norfolk and its myths and legends – all very much in tune with the state of emotional flux he creates. In an atmosphere of sexual static and almost constant tension, everyone is looking for something, everyone is escaping from something.

Tiptoeing around the fragile structures of their separate relationships, so much of the characters' communication is implicit; despite the apparent kinship and bonds between them, there remains a terrible Englishness about their self-denial and inability to discuss their problems with each other. And if Henderson and Alice at least find a form of anchorage here, the others spend most of their time bogged down. As Sutton's characters prepare to head their own separate ways, Alice's observation of the now redundant windmill represents a degree of optimism for them all: despite severe weathering 'it was enough that it had survived' – and perhaps it should be enough that they have too.

Henry Sutton's symbolic and 'stoically still' structure is today owned by the National Trust and available for holiday lets – perfect for bank holiday weekends.

Holt

The sea and salt marshes some five miles distant provided a welcome escape for the young **W[ystan] H[ugh] Auden** (1907–73) who enrolled here as a pupil at **Gresham's School** (founded 1555 and one of the oldest schools in England) in September 1920. In his essay *The Old School* (1934), he called himself a 'typical little highbrow and difficult child'.

Initially judged to be a bright rather than brilliant scholar, Auden soon progressed with ease through the academic system, winning a scholarship and regularly receiving praise for his English essays. Still, his five years here were marred by the anxiety of life under the repressive 'Honour System' – a system of 'civilised' moral conduct and informing against transgressions – which he later claimed was so deeply flawed that it had real potential for turning boys into 'neurotic innocents'.

Auden's own thoughts of the future were still less than certain at this stage; he was fascinated by motorbikes and photography and entertained thoughts of a career as a mining engineer. But in early 1922, a boy he admired asked the teenage Auden a question which was to redirect his life:

W H Auden

His essay 'The Old School' (1934) describes his time at Gresham's.

> Kicking a little stone, he turned to me
> And said, 'Tell me, do you write poetry?'
> I never had, and said so, but I knew
> That very moment what I wished to do.

Stephen Spender* attended the preparatory wing of Gresham's but, teased and dubbed 'the backward son', became very homesick and retreated into an introverted solitude. He refers to this time of terror in his strongly autobiographical novel *The Backward Son* (1940). Spender and Auden later met at Oxford University and went on to become firm friends.

Tarquin Winot, a manipulative, snobbish cookery fanatic suffering from delusions of grandeur, is the central character and narrator of *The Debt to Pleasure* (1996) – an extraordinary debut novel from ex-Gresham's pupil **John Lanchester** (1962–). Winot apparently spent parts of his childhood in an unspecified village in Norfolk, and in all likelihood owes his more appalling traits to Lanchester's fellow Gresham's pupil Jeremy Bamber (who was imprisoned for murdering his family).

Lanchester, the Deputy Editor of the *London Review of Books* and one-time restaurant critic of the *Observer*, portrays Winot as a larger-than-life character, as full of appreciation for W H Auden's martinis as of contempt for iceberg salad and taste-free tomatoes. In this elegantly hilarious first novel (translated into twenty-one languages), loosely organised around the theme of seasonal menus, Norfolk is used as a

John Lanchester

As a teenager he commuted between Hong Kong and Holt for eight years, and returns to the 'isolation' of Norfolk in his best-selling novel *The Debt to Pleasure*.

Gresham's School in Holt – the famous school which has seen W H Auden, Stephen Spender and John Lanchester pass through its gates.

'Autumn in Norfolk can have a quality of absolute melancholy, of isolation. The year's sap is shrinking, the leaves are sere, one's heart is tugged downwards like a barometer in lowering weather.'

John Lanchester,
The Debt to Pleasure, 1996

pretty drab foil against which Tarquin's spiritual home of Provence can shine all the stronger.

'Fresh down from Norfolk', Winot meets up with Laura, who is helping to write his fastidious memoirs, but their collaboration has disastrous consequences as, assisted by the *The Mossad Manual of Surveillance Techniques*, Winot sets out to shadow Laura and her fiancé (loathed by Tarquin) on their honeymoon.

Whatever the merits of Tarquin's culinary expertise, everybody coming in contact with him remains tainted or worse: cooks mysteriously fall on to railway lines, Tarquin's neighbour in Provence gets herself shot, while his parents back home in Norfolk perish in a gas explosion, to mention but a few. Gastronomic digressions aside, one thing is certain – Tarquin Winot is up to no good.

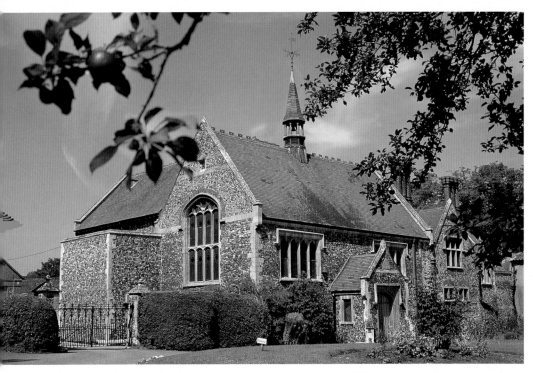

Thetford Grammar School – the political reformer Thomas Paine and novelist Colin Middleton Murray count amongst the pupils educated behind the flintwork of one of England's oldest schools

The distinctive banded cliffs of Hunstanton, – towering over L P Hartley's Eustace at play amongst the seaweed-clad rockpools in *The Shrimp and the Anemone* (1944)

A blaze of Breckland colour near Watton – the 'unique and curiously intimate' landscape portrayed in Michael Home's *Autumn Fields* (1944)

Middle Fen at South Lopham, close to the rising of the Waveney – 'If you know our countryside you'll understand how still it can be in the evenings, how soft and hushed, almost as if it were listening for something' (Barbara Vine, *The Brimstone Wedding*, 1996)

Sunset over the Morston Salt Marshes – the final 'swathes of golden light' washing across the 'land so nearly sea' of William Rivière's *Watercolour Sky* (1990)

Langham

In his early fifties, the novelist and seafarer **Captain Frederick Marryat** (1792–1848) moved into Manor Cottage on Cocksthorpe Road, here in this inland village. Shortly before the transfer from London in 1843, the author of *Mr Midshipman Easy* (1836) and *Masterman Ready* (1841–42) and temperamental father of eleven children, had successfully turned to children's writing.

Marryat's pre-Langham novels tend to be picaresque tales, incident-packed, strong on characterisation and owing their immediacy and veracity to the author's twenty years at sea. At Langham, living what he called a 'Robinson Crusoe sort of life', Marryat wrote *Settlers in Canada* (1844) and his more famous *The Children of the New Forest* (1847), about the fate of four aristocratic children hiding from Cromwell's troops.

On his farm, Marryat was surrounded by animals: Ben Brace the bull, Dumpling, the cream pony, various dogs and fowl and acres of not very good farmland. A reformed poacher in a fur cap ran the Decoy Lake whose yield of wild-fowl made it about the only really profitable venture on Marryat's land, before it too was abandoned.

Captain Frederick Marryat

The seafaring novelist lived a 'Robinson Crusoe sort of life' at Langham.

At Langham, Marryat tackled some less welcome animals, remarking on the size of 'our Norfolk rats ... quite as large as well-grown guinea pigs'. There were games of picquet, which Marryat adored, and there was dancing and fun for the children, with whom he was as good as he was with animals.

Every day, after careful arrangement of the sixteen clocks and chronometers he cherished and which would sometimes chime together, Marryat would sit down at the dining table to write. In the evenings, he often read novels – sometimes re-reading his own work, not ill-pleased by what he found ('What's this? Bless my soul if it isn't mine!'). While his temperament mellowed with his settlement in Langham, Marryat stayed creative and curious all his life, even planning a (later abandoned) scheme to drain the nearby salt marshes.

Marryat's death in August 1848 was marked by **Virginia Woolf**[*] who paid a moving tribute to the quiet end to Marryat's rough and active life in her essay 'The Captain's Death Bed'. Marryat spent the spring and summer of that year facing the long windows of the boudoir room; 'a room whose ceiling had been painted to imitate the sky, and whose walls were painted with trellis work covered with roses upon which birds were perching.' Together with the mirrors let into the doors, the effect must have been stunning, and 'the village people called the room the "Room of a Thousand Pillars" because of its reflections'.

Marryat's tomb in St Andrew and St Mary's churchyard – after a life at sea and at the writer's desk, his last words were 'It is now half-past nine o'clock. World, adieu.'

Marryat, described as a 'survivor from the eighteenth century', but whose works were savoured by a large readership spanning all echelons of nineteenth-century society, was buried in Langham churchyard. He is commemorated by a marble tablet on the north wall of the church nave. Marryat's gabled Tudor Gothic manor with its heavy chimney-stacks, latticed windows and overhanging thatch was pulled down in 1883, and the rebuilt Manor Cottage today houses a Carmelite convent.

Morston

William Rivière

He displays his intimate knowledge of the landscape here in his *Watercolour Sky*.

Norfolk-born novelist **William Rivière*** (1954–) opens his debut novel *Watercolour Sky* (1990) with the annual 'Battle of Morston Creek' boat race. The significance of the day is not lost on Kit Marsh and Alice Dobell, as they are transported, in a taut narrative, through adolescent angst to adult anguish.

Almost every element of life in this salt marsh and sea land is incorporated into this bitter-sweet romance, as the protagonists swim, sail and ride across deserted sands. Rivière also uses the Norfolk landscape to instil moods of quiet and disquiet, as Kit ponders what 'the flatness of the marsh, ... this wide emptiness' could portend?

William Rivière spent his childhood a few miles from the sea at **Dilham Grange** near **North Walsham** where his family still lives. Although currently teaching in Italy, Rivière still spends time in Norfolk and takes obvious delight in his 'very happy links' with the area: 'In summer we galloped our ponies across the stubble fields, in winter we shot pigeon in the woods, ... sailing offshore at Morston and on **Barton Broad**.'

Through his writing, Rivière exploits his intimate knowledge of the coast, well aware that even to locals, the landscape can sometimes look less than appealing:

> Here the farm land came to an end, joined almost flush against scalloped summer sea. No more wheatfields, woods, villages. No more rivers snaking through water-meadows past headless windmills, down cascades of watermills where decayed wheels hadn't turned for years, past rushy banks over which sails apparently without hulls dragged themselves across lowlands apparently without water. No more churches standing over fens where grebe and bittern breed, where marsh harriers tilt over reedbeds, where old vessels along dykes sink at their moorings. ... Here churches were gaunt fortresses against gales; they reared exposed from the last salt-bitten acres. Where the few copses that survived were stunted, every tree's back bowed, shoulders craven, arms hunched to protect cowed head ...
>
> Godawful flat charmless countryside, Emma Dobell thought. What was it doing, this lump sticking out into the least appealing of seas?

Opposite: 'Sails far away across salt marsh, far away in Blakeney creek in evening light'

William Rivière, *Watercolour Sky*, 1990

Despite the ebbing and flowing tides of human emotion that swirl around *Watercolour Sky*, Kit and Alice's love affair endures, as does the appeal of the shape-shifting north Norfolk landscape.

Salthouse

Sylvia Townsend Warner

Wintering here with Valentine Ackland, she writes of the east wind that 'sobs and whimpers like a Brontë in the kitchen'.

Salthouse at dusk – with 'the true voice of the sea' in the air, the town becomes 'Loseby' in Sylvia Townsend Warner's symbolic novel *The Flint Anchor*.

In a typically impulsive move **Sylvia Townsend Warner** (1893–1978) decided to rent the Great Eye Folly – a former coastguard station – on the edge of the pebble beach near Salthouse from October 1950 to March 1951. Together with Valentine Ackland, Warner found herself housed in an ugly, castellated fortress of a building, totally exposed to the elements.

Warner was working here on her last and certainly one of her finest novels: *The Flint Anchor* (1954), which follows the family fortunes of Victorian merchant John Barnard in the Norfolk coastal town of 'Loseby'. Set between 1790 and 1863, *The Flint Anchor* (named after the flint crest 'centred between the first-floor windows' of Anchor House, the Barnard family seat) focuses on the hypocrisy and self-deceit inherent in the rigid morals and values which typified the Victorian and late Georgian era in England. Not long arrived in Loseby, John Barnard feels the pressure of other people's expectations upon him:

> Turning again in his walking to and fro, he saw that the western sky was drained of its sunset, only a rusty tint remaining on the clouds that had burned so long and so brilliantly. Lighted windows peered out, and the smell of the town came greasily puffing towards him. Six months ago he had not even heard of Loseby. Now it was the place where he must be his father's son.

Much of the power of this historical and symbolic tale lies in the way Warner intertwines the central themes of obsessive love and flawed family values with the difficulties of strait-jacketed life in a small Norfolk fishing community. Prosperous families such as the Barnards and the Kettles live side-by-side with the fisherfolk and the poor of Loseby – 'weavers from **Norwich*** thrown out of work by the new manufactories in the North of England, or cottagers dispossessed by an Act of Enclosure'.

Swirling through the story, rising and falling with the narrative shifts, is the omnipresent ocean. History itself changes with the tides, a process of constant writing and rewriting, of smoothing waves or raging storms, depending upon whose voice is believed. For the luckless and much-maligned Thomas Kettle, the sea offers a sense of abstraction and escape from the claustrophobia of Loseby:

> He turned about, and saw the solemn dusk of the eastern sky, the unshining sea, the riding-lamp that had been lit on the fishing-boat. A man standing in the boat called to him, 'Will you come for a sail, bor?'
>
> A night at sea, among strangers, the cool air blowing between himself and his thoughts ... He did not hesitate, and jumped into the boat ... As they drew away from shore he relaxed ... and breathed more deeply, staring overhead and speculating which were the constellations that showed piecemeal between the clouds. The sea was calm, and the wind so light that it barely filled the sail. Of all the things held in that globe of night sky only the stars traversing the gaps between the clouds seemed to move and have purpose.

For Warner, perched precariously in her fortified station, with no electricity and no water (except for pumped sea-water), this was a location both daunting and exhilarating in equal measure. During the winter, surrounded by ice and with the waves freezing on the shore, she writes of the east wind that 'sobs and whimpers like a Brontë in the kitchen'.

Her Norfolk 'wilderness' home proved to be inspirational for Warner, who some months earlier had defeated a bout of writer's block with 'The Sea is Always the Same', a short story based on a visit to **Cromer***, and *The Flint Anchor* is crafted around the Norfolk coast with subtlety and vision. As John Barnard contemplates his own death, his mind turns once more to the sea:

> The noise of the sea came rolling solemnly through the dark, and he thought how all his life it had been in his ears and yet he had seldom been much aware of it. When he listened, it was almost always for some practical reason, a storm or the forecasting of a storm, a shift in the wind, the state of the tide ... And so he had never given ear to the true voice of the sea, the waves travelling to the shore, languidly, or with light gaiety, or confusedly and in violence, but always to break, uttering the word, *Now!*

'A frittering day – and one of the coldest I have ever known. A south wind, again: a steady stealthy boring wind; and no sign of it, on this clean-shaved landscape, except on the sea.'

Sylvia Townsend Warner, *Diary*, 2 February 1951

On 8 March 1951, Warner and Ackland return from **East Dereham***, where Sylvia has visited the Norfolk artist John Craske. There is a strong wind blowing as Warner writes: 'the sea was almost up to the gap, with nearly three hours to run … I rang up the coast guards, who said Prevention was better than Cure. Not seeing how one can cure the state of being cut off from the mainland, we made a swift dusky get-away – and left for **Winterton*** with the spindrift whirling after us.'

In the same Norfolk neighbourhood, a few years earlier, was **Lilias Rider Haggard** (1893–1968), who writes in her *Norfolk Notebook* (1947) of a grey, sunless day in the troubled times of the Second World War, when she can still marvel at the natural beauty around her:

> The pale masses of the bents [grasses], thick and soft as cream-coloured fur. The brilliant emerald patches of young grass round the pools of flood water. The browns and umbers and golds of the reeds, standing with rain-straight stems and dark plumed heads all leaning one way like the sheaves which bowed down [towards us]. The light shining silver along the spear points of their leaves. Grey November and the thraldom of winter's hand upon the land. The cry of the redshank and the distant snarl of the tide on the shingle. The long line of woods and rounded hills behind – the pewter-grey sea before – this corner of England which once it holds your heart is more lovely than any place on earth. Beautiful with a hint of secrecy which haunts it, as the memory of a dark and tender sadness clouds the brilliance of a summer day.

The Salthouse Folly that Sylvia Townsend Warner and Valentine Ackland rented was built by Onesiphorous Randall in the mid-nineteenth century, but fell victim to the terrible floods of January 1953, which swept away its rear walls leaving only a hollow shell. In **Brian Cooper**'s* *Messiter's Dream* (1990), Salthouse becomes 'Thorpe-next-the-Sea' and the Salthouse Folly 'Hampton's Folly'. The stormy night of 31 January 1953 provides the climax:

The Salthouse Folly, home to Sylvia Townsend Warner and locale for Brian Cooper, before its destruction in 1953

> That was the night when the driver of a train from Hunstanton to Lynn was amazed to see a huge wave careering towards him, bearing a bungalow high on its crest; when a motorist, driving by the park wall at Holkham, met a rampart of water that swept across his car; when a farmer at Burnham Overy, a mile inland, opened his door to see waves already lapping the step; when a villager at Cley, peering out into the storm, found a boat from Blakeney quay, a mile and a half away, floating outside his dining-room … That was the night when Purdy's prophesies, regarded till then as nothing but the ravings of a crazy old man, assumed a terrifying truth; and Hampton's Folly, pounded by the waves, crumbled into the marshes and sank beneath the sea.

Stiffkey

In the New Year of 1936, as winter strengthened its icy grip on the north Norfolk coast, novelist **Henry Williamson** (1895–1977) arrived feeling weary and dissatisfied with life. Staying with his publisher at nearby **East Runton**, Williamson was prompted to look at The Old Hall Farm with its 235 acres of land for sale further round the coast at Stiffkey.

It was probably more nostalgic curiosity – recalling his childhood holiday spent cycling Norfolk lanes some twenty-four years earlier – than genuine intent that brought the best-selling author of *Tarka the Otter* here. Indeed, Williamson was unimpressed by the dilapidated property and its overgrown and untended farmland, yet, incredibly, he soon found himself bidding for the plot. Against the best professional advice, and certainly against his own judgement, Williamson suddenly found himself a Norfolk landowner in the midst of a severe agricultural depression.

Henry Williamson

'The farmer takes on the character of his fields, even as his fields are part of an expression of his spirit'

As Britain braced itself for another cataclysmic world war, Williamson was to spend the next decade battling his barren Norfolk fields, fighting to establish his credentials as a farmer and seeking to fulfill his vision of true harmony with the land.

Williamson's *The Story of a Norfolk Farm* (1941) was written between the spring of 1937 and the summer of 1939 and draws heavily upon his experiences and the characters he met here. It also became the focus for his increasingly fluctuating and volatile emotions. Williamson scarcely bothers to fictionalise his locales, with The Old 'Castle' – 'faded brick and flint ... pinnacles and round towers' – being located so close to 'Whelk-next-the-Sea' (**Wells**). The impact of the landscape here is immensely significant too, and Williamson is often spellbound by the natural beauty around him.

In his determination to succeed against all odds, Williamson displays similar fortitude and single-mindedness to that other famous literary farmer **Henry Rider Haggard***. Unfortunately, Williamson lacked Haggard's resources and *The Story of a Norfolk Farm* is littered with the anxieties of expense accounts. Nevertheless, Williamson seemed to thrive on the pressure and, though alternating between ecstasy and despair ('Sometimes I found reality temporarily unbearable; the gulf between aspiration and reality was too great'), was occasionally able to find peace:

> The sea was half a mile from the village, and the field ended in a plantation or land-fringe of stunted trees, and then steeply down to a pebbly shore and a creek where a fisherman's boat was moored. We sat down on the grass, gazing out over the marshes, one vast gut-channelled prairie of pale blue sea-lavender. Afar was the sea merging in summer mist and the palest azure sky. There was no sound: the air was still: not a bird was stirring. This was the sun I remembered from boyhood days, the ancient harvest sunshine of that perished time when the earth was fresh and

summer seemed an illimitable shining that would never end, the reapers moving round the fields and setting up the stooks of golden corn. And sitting there, it was as though the past and present were one again, and I had entered upon my heritage of happiness.

'Now there was a width and depth in the sky and on the earth and sea, and I knew why so many artists had come to paint along this coast, with its clear lights and distances. It was a land of far-extending marsh and watery dykes, windmills, grey North Sea, and teams of horses drawing plows.'

Henry Williamson, *The Story of a Norfolk Farm*, 1941

Any thoughts of pastoral bliss were soon obliterated as the organised chaos of the Second World War descended upon north Norfolk. Unfortunately, Williamson had already given his outspoken approval to Oswald Mosley's British Union of Fascists and refused to accept that Hitler would wage war against Britain. Daubing Mosley's lightning flash symbol on his cottage wall cannot have helped Williamson's cause and served to further isolate him from a community in which he was so often to find himself a 'furriner'. Williamson, who had himself experienced the appalling conditions of the Somme as an infantry transport officer in the First World War, even suffered the indignity of being arrested and questioned as a possible German spy.

For Williamson, his farming project represented much more than just an alternative lifestyle for him and his family. It represented a direction that he hoped the whole country would take; a pride in the land, in its heritage and traditions, while moving forward with the 'fundamental spirit of a new, clean, healthy, mentally fearless Britain'. In his opinion, a country that 'neglected its soil, neglected its soul' and Williamson saw this interaction with the land, between humanity and nature, as vital for the future – and represented it through much of his writing: 'The farmer takes on the character of his fields, even as his fields are part of an expression of his spirit'.

Williamson was justifiably proud of his success in converting the sadly neglected and dilapidated farmland and buildings into a home and fully operational farm. But the strain of his work, the disintegration of his marriage and his increasing disillusionment with farming life were to prove too much. In October 1945 his farm was auctioned and Williamson moved his family to Botesdale near **Diss*** and himself away back to Devon. It was a tragic end to a long but not altogether happy relationship with Norfolk.

Nevertheless, the county still survives through the characters and stories of Williamson's later fiction. He had already written much of 'A Norfolk Farm in War-time', as a sequel to *Story of a Norfolk Farm*, before being forced to abandon it. Williamson later builds the body of this work into *The Phasian Bird* (1948) and *Lucifer Before Sunrise* (1967) – drawing deeply on his wartime diaries and memoirs. In *Lucifer*, featuring his alter ego 'Phillip Maddison', writer turned farmer, Williamson recreates perfectly the sense of continual unease and alienation experienced in the wartime farming community of Norfolk.

Despite its disquiet, *Lucifer* reveals a grudging admiration for the processes of Norfolk agricultural life and demonstrates a gradual

'One heard, near and from afar, the sad piping of wading birds, as though within their feathered bodies were spirits, grievous that water found nowhere any rest upon the land it helped to make.'

Henry Williamson,
Lucifer Before Sunrise, 1967

integration into the landscape and community here, accompanied as ever by Williamson's great awareness of both natural and local history. A sombre but detailed historical narrative, *Lucifer* is also a first-hand account of life in Britain during the war years, with occasional moments of calm scattered like infertile seeds among the months of relentless toil on the barren land: 'to farm land is to plan and to sustain a war', writes Williamson.

Some twenty years earlier, in *The Phasian Bird*, Williamson presents 'Wilbo', an artist accompanied by his exotic pheasant Chee-Kai, who struggles with a near-derelict Norfolk farm, is imprisoned for his political beliefs, and suffers a tragic and symbolic death along with his pheasant. Fortunately, Williamson himself survived his Norfolk experiences and went on to complete over fifty books before his death in 1977.

'From here could be seen distant marshes and the North Sea. It was a beautiful view, for anyone with an unencumbered mind; but with the chronic feelings of things never being right – the everlasting difference in ideas between himself and his fellow men – Phillip could seldom enjoy the view.'

Henry Williamson,
Lucifer before Sunrise, 1967

Wiveton

Stevie Smith

'English holidays –
"She loves, adores 'em", can't
be torn away from coastal
marshes (... Norfolk) ... sea
everywhere, empty country
... walking, walking (like all
melancholics) walking ...'

Letter to Kay Dick, 1953, from
*Me Again – The Uncollected
Writings*, 1984

Like many people, the poet and novelist **Stevie Smith** (1902–71) first encountered Norfolk on her childhood holidays and it made a lasting impression. Confined by illness to a children's convalescent home for some three years, young Stevie's trips to Norfolk provided her with occasional respite and allowed her to spend time with her mother. This established a pattern to be repeated throughout her life, with Norfolk providing a regular 'bolt-hole', especially when visiting friends and staying at a cottage in Marsh Lane at Wiveton.

Though permanently based with her aunt in north London, Smith always enjoyed escaping to Wiveton, which was a world apart from the rather stifled suburban seclusion of Palmer's Green. Smith loved the smell of the sea air, the eerie, empty landscape and the solitude it afforded, once writing in a letter: 'There are parts round the Norfolk coast that look like nobody had ever been there before just dunes and sand and sea and nobody at all.'

Stevie Smith first made her name as a novelist, with the stylised and poetic *Novel on Yellow Paper* (1936), followed by *Across the Frontier* (1938) and *The Holiday* (1949) – strongly autobiographical works using lucid but unconventional prose. As a poet, she is probably best remembered for her 'Not Waving but Drowning' – the title piece of her 1957 collection which epitomises the barbed wickedness of her humour: the waving signals of a drowning man are first misinterpreted and then ignored, leaving his body to be washed up on the beach. In many ways this seems to have been true of Smith's life too: 'I am becalmed in a deep sea / And give signals, but they are not answered.'

Like **Edward Lear*** before her, Smith also enjoyed sketching simplistic line drawings and cartoons to accompany her poetry; and like Lear, she laced her shrewdly farcical comedy with magic and loss.

In 'Archie & Tina' from *Collected Poems* (1975), Smith recalls the joy afforded by her seaside holidays in the 'such sharp bright air' of Norfolk, where she used:

> To paddle the samphire beds; fish
> Crabs from the sea-pool, poke
> The anemones, run,
> Trailing the ribbon seaweed across the sand to the sea's edge

Such joyous innocence is far from the mood evoked by 'The Old Sweet Dove of Wiveton' from *Not Waving but Drowning* where, through 'the sombre day and the beginning soft rain', the sound of the solitary 'old dove' sitting 'high in the chestnut tree' is heard as a melancholy murmuring of pain, 'Crying; Love, love'.

Stevie Smith was noted for her remarkable reading performances which transformed her work and belied her small-framed, slightly mousey appearance. Whether at the Edinburgh Festival, or the tiny

Nonconformist chapel at **Cley**, the audience was held rapt by her curious tone, her exaggerated cheerfulness and the occasional bursts of slightly off-key warbling. Yet Smith only really gained acceptance in the 1960s, when poetry was back in fashion and producers such as **George MacBeth*** promoted her work.

Fame arriving so late in life puzzled Smith and although her social life was far from empty, she lived much of her life as an isolated eccentric, on the fringes of literary society. Perhaps this is why life on the Norfolk coast held such a fascination for her, wandering the coastline, feeling at once both outside of life – 'happier far where the night winds fall, / And there are no doors and no windows at all' – and yet being able to return to the comfort and very genuine hospitality of her hosts.

After the death of her aunt, Stevie Smith returned again to Wiveton, this time spending almost a month here. She had always linked visions of death with the restless sea and powerful, irresistible tides and some time later, while picnicking with friends on **Blakeney Point**, Smith had a presentiment of her own death. Wandering across the marshes alone, she encountered a boatman who asked if she wanted to be ferried across the water. She declined, but in the fading light which highlighted the lonely chill of the marshes, Stevie Smith saw the scene as powerfully reminiscent of Book VI of the *Aeneid* – a crossing over to death. A year later, aged sixty-eight, Stevie Smith died of a brain tumour.

Her life is perhaps best summarised by 'The Hostage' (1957), 'just a talk, not really a confession' with an imaginary priest before her execution, where Smith presents the paradoxes of human existence and the feeling of constantly being held hostage by her fits of melancholy. Despite the 'beauty' of life in both town and country ('Have you ever seen the sun getting up in the greenery/ Of a summer day, in Norfolk say'), contentment remains agonisingly beyond her reach:

> Life bustles in the country, you know; it should be easy.
> But I was outside of it, looking, finding no place,
> No excuse at all for my distant wandering face.

'It's heavenly here, really too marvellous. I do nothing at all but sleep, eat and go for short trots over the saltings ... I am becoming fat and agreeable and quite incapable of reading.'

Stevie Smith, letter from Wiveton, March 1965, from *Me Again – The Uncollected Writings*, 1984

CHAPTER EIGHT

Pilgrim's Progress

LITERARY LINKS

Alan Brownjohn, Sandy Brownjohn, Kate Charles,
Erasmus of Rotterdam, Margaret Fountaine, L P Hartley,
S T Haymon, Pocahontas/John Smith, John Timpson,
Horace Walpole, P G Wodehouse

Kate Charles

For her the 'extremes of emotion, and the extremes of conviction' of the area make it a 'perfect setting for a murder mystery'.

Opposite: The National Pilgrimage procession at Walsingham – pilgrims have been heading to this part of Norfolk for centuries.

East Barsham

A few miles north of Fakenham en route to the shrine at **Walsingham***
there is a cluster of three 'Barshams' – the small villages of **North**, **East**
and **West Barsham**. There is no 'South Barsham', but for **Kate Charles***
(1950–), this fictitious village provides the setting for her novel *The
Snares of Death – A Clerical Mystery* (1992). South Barsham, a 'middling-
sized' village, is the Anglo-Catholic parish inherited by Evangelical priest
Bob Dexter. Reverend Bob Dexter is a conceited and quarrelsome
nuisance who speaks about himself exclusively in the third person and
whose lips curl at the slightest mention of the Virgin Mary.

Arriving at his new parish, Dexter is determined to stamp out all
signs of the 'popery' and 'idolatry' he finds at St Mary's Church. So when
he finds a picture of Our Lady of Walsingham bearing the inscription
'A lamp burns for this church at the Shrine of Our Lady of Walsingham',
he feels he has to act: "'Not for long, it doesn't," Dexter said aloud, seizing
the poster by the corner and ripping it down. He immediately felt better.'
As Dexter's intolerance and reformatory zeal continue unabated –
"'Worshipping a piece of bread!" he thundered. "I've never seen anything
so ... so shocking in my entire life!"' – there are strong rumblings of
discontent among the residents of Dexter's 'primitive backwater'. So
there are plenty of motives and no shortage of suspects when the
Reverend meets his maker. But when Dexter's death is followed by a
drowning in suspicious circumstances during the annual pilgrimage at
Walsingham, it becomes clear that the case is more complicated than it
at first appeared.

Onto the scene comes the investigative team of amateur artist Lucy
Kingsley and her partner David Middleton-Brown (based in

Wymondham* with a solicitor's job in **Norwich***). These complex and believable characters were first introduced in *A Drink of Deadly Wine* (1991) – Charles' inaugural tale of clerical blackmail, distress and death.

What first brought Kate Charles to Norfolk was the opportunity to indulge in her favourite hobby of visiting churches, one which she shares with her protagonist David Middleton-Brown. Those at Wymondham, **Salle, Cawston***, **South Creake** and **Norwich*** Cathedral count among her favourites. As Charles continues her successful series of stories brimful with ecclesiastical detail and carefully interspersed biblical quotes, Norfolk – 'a great influence on me personally and in my writing' – maintains a high profile.

Heacham

The expanding village of Heacham, close to Hunstanton is linked to one of the great modern myths – that of the Indian Princess Pocahontas. The legend has been written and rewritten through innumerable texts: from Captain John Smith's dramatic first-hand accounts of the early seventeenth century, through **Shakespeare*** and **Dryden** to nineteenth-century romance and the insipid melodrama of the recent Disney film.

The true story begins in 1607 with the founding of Jamestown on the north-east coast of North America by an English expedition representing the Royal Virginia Company. Jamestown was a vital colonial outpost for an expanding empire and was to develop into a major supplier of tobacco to the thriving home market. On that first expedition was Captain John Smith, a shrewd but abrasive adventurer who had managed to make sufficient enemies to get himself arrested for conspiracy to mutiny before his ship even saw shore. Smith was soon freed from his shackles and while the colony floundered under illness, sloth and sheer incompetence, proved himself to be a capable negotiator with the indigenous Indian population.

The area was under the control of the Supreme Indian Chieftain Powhatan who kept a respectful distance from the settlers. The young Pocahontas was the favourite of Powhatan's ten daughters – her name derived from an adjective meaning playful or mischievous – Smith's *Generall Historie (The Third Book)* of 1624 (published 1662) reveals that, when he was captured by Powhatan's Indians on a foray up river, only the dramatic intervention of the ten-year-old Pocahontas saved his life.

It was to be the first of Pocahontas' many contacts with the English and she was to save Smith's life on more than one occasion. Much has been written of the romantic connections between the two, but of more significance was the bridge that Pocahontas represented between two totally alien and generally hostile cultures. Her constant mediation and supply of provisions enabled the imperilled colony to survive for many years. In return for her kindness, Pocahontas was kidnapped by the

'Two great stones were brought before Powhatan: then as many as could layd hands on him [Smith], dragged him to them, and thereon laid his head, and being ready with their clubs, to beate out his braines, Pocahontas, the Kings dearest daughter, when no intreaty could prevaile, got his head in her armes, and laid her owne upon his to save him from death.'

John Smith, *Generall Historie (The Third Book)*, 1624

English colonists as insurance against attack from her father, while Captain Smith fled back to England without so much as a nod in her direction. Still Pocahontas kept faith with her captors and when John Rolfe arrived in 1613 it was the start of a friendship which bloomed into intimacy.

The Country wee now call **Virginia** beginneth at Cape Henry distant from Roanoack 60 miles, where was Sr Walter Raleigh's plantation: and because the people differ very little from them of Powhatan in any thing, I have inserted those figures in this place because of the conveniency.

King Powhatan comands Cr Smith to be slayne, his daughter Pokahontas beggs his life his thankfullness and how he subiected 39 of their kings. reade y̆ history.

Pocahontas adorns the
Heacham village sign

Although Pocahontas herself
enjoyed the patronage of
Queen Anne, the Royal Court
was no place for John Rolfe –
King James I abhorred tobacco
and saw smoking as an evil
vice second only to witchcraft!

Rolfe was an educated man from a Puritan Norfolk family of landed gentry with its roots at Heacham Hall. He had travelled to North America in the summer of 1609, only to lose his wife and child after being shipwrecked off Bermuda. Rolfe's ambition and industry were focused on the tobacco industry and he soon established successful plantations to rival the Spanish suppliers from the West Indies. John Rolfe and Lady Rebecca, as Pocahontas was known after her christening, married in 1614 and the following year their son, Thomas, was born.

With the Virginia Company struggling to attract investors and interest in the colony fading, the owners 'invited' Pocahontas back to England – a publicity stunt they could not afford to miss. Her reward was a lifetime stipend from the company and a six-week sea voyage in cramped and primitive conditions. If the journey back to England was bad, then the crowded, smog-bound, stench-filled streets of a London bursting the seams of its medieval walls must have been a nightmare for Pocahontas and her long-suffering Indian companions. Huge crowds gathered wherever they went, but it was the then common diseases – tuberculosis, smallpox, measles and typhoid – that posed the greatest threat to the defenceless visitors.

With several of the Indian group quickly succumbing to illness, and Pocahontas herself falling sick with a respiratory disease, John Rolfe made a return to his native Norfolk. By all accounts 1616 was a year remarkable for its good weather and Pocahontas would have seen this isolated corner of England at its verdant best. Although a long way from Jamestown and the lush green vegetation and cool clear waters of the Virginia forests, the golden sands and bracing sea air of Heacham must have reminded Pocahontas of home.

Quite what the Rolfe family made of this 'Noble Savage' will never be known. Certainly her appearance in the conservative backwaters of rural Norfolk would have caused as great a stir as it did in London. It is likely that the first 'Red Indian' ever to grace the walks of Heacham met with disapproval and even hostility from a provincial Puritan community fully conversant with an Old Testament that warns about the taking of 'strange wives', and not a single mention of Pocahontas exists in the Rolfe family records. Heacham Hall, a modest but spacious residence with substantial gardens was destroyed by fire in the 1940s, though family tradition insists that the giant mulberry tree shown in an early sketch is 'Pocahontas' Mulberry Tree', presumably planted by her.

Pocahontas was never to return to Norfolk. Although John Rolfe arranged for his family to travel with him to the New World, Pocahontas' health deteriorated to the extent that she had to be set ashore in Gravesend, which was to be the final resting place of the twenty-two-year-old. John Rolfe remarried but only outlived Pocahontas by some five years, while their son Thomas remained in North America as a member of the colonial militia which was to contribute greatly to the extinction of his mother's people. Today the legend lives on, with

Heacham contributing its own small part – in St Mary the Virgin Church, tucked out of sight behind a pillar in the north aisle is an alabaster portrait of a frowning Pocahontas, while in 1960 a village sign depicting the princess was erected just opposite the lavender fields for which Heacham is famous.

Houghton

Horace Walpole

The prolific letter-writer and originator of the Gothic novel only late in life found a good word for Norfolk.

The largest country house in Norfolk, Houghton Hall was built by Sir Robert Walpole (1676–1745), Britain's first Prime Minister. In the park is the parish church of St Martin where Sir Robert and **Horace Walpole** (1717–97) are buried without memorials. During his undergraduate years and again in 1743–5 Horace Walpole passed summers here in the Palladian mansion of Yorkshire stone built by his father. He did not find country society congenial and wrote:

> Only imagine that I here every day see men, who are mountains of roast beef, and only seem just roughly hewn out into the outlines of human form, like the giant-rock at Pratolino! I shudder when I see them brandish their knives in act to carve, and look at them as savages that devour one another. I should not stare at all more than I do, if yonder Alderman at the lower end of the table was to stick his fork into his neighbour's jolly cheek, and cut a brave slice of brown and fat.

Horace Walpole, 4th Earl of Oxford was, like **Bulwer-Lytton***, of Norfolk blood and London birth and it was the cosmopolitan lure that the

Houghton Hall – Horace Walpole described his father's country house as a 'monument of grandeur'.

flamboyant, homosexual politician and socialite found most irresistible. His visits to Houghton were few and, apart from the magnificent gardens which he loved, Walpole found life in Norfolk stagnant, and full of unpleasant reminders of family misfortunes.

As an MP, Horace Walpole represented both **Castle Rising** and **Lynn***, but he lived mainly in London, making a name for himself in politics and transforming his villa at Strawberry Hill (Twickenham) into a legendary Gothic mansion. The publication of his 1774 *Description of the Villa of Horace Walpole* strongly influenced the movements for Gothic architecture and landscaping, but his novel *The Castle of Otranto*, published ten years earlier, was at the forefront of the new literary genre, the Gothic novel. Although he followed this success with *The Mysterious Mother* (1768), he published no further fiction and focused instead on his sometimes unreliable memoirs and engaging, manipulative letters (his self-confessed 'propensity for faction' was used skilfully for political manoeuvring).

Walpole was a prolific letter-writer covering wide-ranging topics: politics, history, literature, antiquarian matters and social gossip. He wrote very much with publication in mind and today some four thousand letters remain – with numerous others lost or destroyed – as testimony to his vast output. In time, Walpole became more reconciled with Houghton, and in a letter to George Montagu, his tone is one of nostalgia and sad reflection:

> Here I am at Houghton and alone in this spot where (except two hours last month) I have not been in sixteen years! ... Here I am probably for the last time of my life, though not for the last time – every clock that strikes tells me I am an hour nearer to yonder church – that church into which I have not yet had courage to enter ...
>
> When I had drunk tea I strolled into the garden – they told me it was now called the pleasure-ground – what a dissonant idea of pleasure – those allees where I had passed so many charming moments are now stripped up or overgrown; many fond paths I could not unravel. I met two game-keepers and a thousand hares! In the days when all my soul was turned to pleasure and vivacity ... I hated Houghton and its solitude – yet I loved this garden, as now with many regrets I love Houghton – Houghton, I know not what to call it, a monument of grandeur in ruin.

Hunstanton

As a child, the layered sandstone cliffs, sweeping sands and shallow waters of Hunstanton made this a magical place for novelist **L[eslie] P[oles] Hartley*** (1895–1972). Hartley was later educated at Harrow under George Warner, the father of writer **Sylvia Townsend Warner***, but it was as a child playing here, with his sister Enid among the shimmering seaweed-clad rock pools, that Hartley found the inspiration for *The Shrimp and the Anemone* (1944), which forms the first part of his powerful *Eustace and Hilda* trilogy:

> Eustace bent over the pool. His feet sank in its soggy edge, so he drew back, for he must not get them wet. But he could still see the anemone. Its base was fastened to a boulder, just above the water-line. From the middle of the other end, which was below, something stuck out, quivering. It was a shrimp, Eustace decided, and the anemone was eating it, sucking it in.

L P Hartley

Hunstanton becomes 'Anchorstone' in his *Eustace and Hilda* trilogy, which his publisher encouraged him to develop as a 'study of childhood'.

Hunstanton cliffs – the young L P Hartley played under this crumbling façade, little knowing that fifty years later he would be faithfully re-creating the landscape in the pages of his books.

'Eustace gazed about him ...
On his left was the sea,
purposefully coming in;
already its advance ripples
were within a few yards of
where they stood. Ahead lay
long lines of breakers,
sometimes four or five deep,
riding in each other's tracks
towards the shore. On his right
was the cliff, rust-red below,
with the white band of chalk
above and, just visible, the
crazy line of hedgerow
clinging to its edge ...'

L P Hartley, *The Shrimp and
the Anemone*, 1944

As the Hamlet-like Eustace deliberates his next move, his sister Hilda moves decisively to save the shrimp – which, 'a disappointing sight', is dead anyway – and in the process kills the anemone. It is a striking and allegorical opening to a novel which goes on to expose the full potency of the psychological warfare that childhood involves, and how we carry our injuries into later life. 'Why not think of our *Shrimp and the Anemone* as a study of childhood?' suggests Hartley's publisher in a letter to the author and this is precisely what Hartley achieves – with disturbing effect. Depicting the destructive nature of love, Hartley continues his central themes of 'unbearable intimacy' and 'man's immortal longings and mortal weakness' as he moves his protagonists into adulthood. In *Eustace and Hilda*, Hartley focuses on the power of the landscape around 'Anchorstone' (Hunstanton) to great effect. Even as Eustace sits in Venice, fingering his paperweight – a carved fragment removed from the ruined chapel back in Norfolk – his thoughts return home:

> Of all the places in Anchorstone Hall this was his favourite, perhaps because, being a roofless ruin and belonging to the past, it did not repel his imagination with the pride of alien ownership. They had laughed at him, at home, for bringing away the carved fragment ... but Eustace had a strong feeling for relics, and it should earn its passage by acting as a paper-weight. The stability of paper-weights appealed to him. They tethered things down, they anchored the past. The Anchor Stone!

In *The Shrimp and the Anemone*, nearby **Snettisham** ('Frontisham') has a similarly stunning impact on the sensitive young Eustace. Sitting with his family for tea in the Swan Hotel, Eustace marvels at the wondrous west window of Frontisham church:

> Within the massive framework of the grey wall seven slender tapers of stone soared upwards. After that, it was as though the tapers had been lit and two people, standing one on either side, had blown the flames together. Curving, straining, interlocked, they flung themselves against the retaining arch in an ecstasy – or should we say an agony? – of petrification ... Pictures of saints and angels, red, blue, and yellow, pressed against and into him, bruising him, cutting him, spilling their colours over him.

Though the landscape of north-east Norfolk is skilfully interwoven into the *Eustace and Hilda* trilogy, what Hartley really creates is a powerful psychological landscape. Touched by an intangible darkness, Hartley's novels are frequently a medium for autobiographical exorcism as his own fears and anxieties bleed to the surface. Hunstanton Hall comes to represent both the social aspirations and social exclusion felt by the deeply class-conscious Hartley, while his struggle to come to terms with his own homosexuality is exposed through the sexual static and deep-

rooted anxieties of his writing. The only biographer to have got close to the enigma of L P Hartley is Norwich-born **Adrian Wright*** (1947–) whose excellent *Foreign Country* (1996) strengthens the Norfolk connection. Wright was the only biographer permitted to access the 'great archive' of Hartley's private papers which were recently burned as instructed by Hartley's sister Norah. And as to Hunstanton's appeal, Wright is certain: 'It was the stillness of the pools that so attracted Leslie, who never much cared for the sea; it was the *placidity* of water that thrilled him.'

The Old Lighthouse Teashop as L P Hartley would have seen it.

Like many seaside resorts in England, Hunstanton ('Hunston' to locals) remains 'anchored' to the past, as Adrian Wright describes: 'Today the little watering-place retains much of its grandeur, inevitably faded, its lordly architecture rising up above the promenade.' Nothing remains of the 'storm-bent hedge which clung giddily to the uttermost verge of the cliff' in *The Shrimp and the Anemone*, but the 'decapitated ... hideous maroon' lighthouse seen in *Eustace and Hilda* as 'The Old Lighthouse Teashop' still stands, now tastefully redecorated as a private residence. Meanwhile, the 'treacherous' cliffs with their distinctive bands of colour continue to crumble above the 'dun-coloured' shore 'not meant for lounging on ... scoured by stiff breezes challenging the blood'. On top, the blue-painted Victorian shelters used by Eustace and Hilda remain as colourful reminders of time past, while the nearby red-brick water tower which Hartley was unable to walk past without imagining 'it would burst' has now been converted to flats.

P G Wodehouse

The many works he focuses here make Norfolk the 'official' Wodehouse county.

Hunstanton was familiar territory for light humorist and popular novelist **P[elham] G[renville] Wodehouse** (1881–1975), affectionately known as 'Plum'. Having started his working life with the Hong Kong

Hunstanton Hall – 'It's one of those enormous houses, about two-thirds of which are derelict. There is a whole wing which has not been lived in for half a century.' P G Wodehouse, writing from Hunstanton Hall in 1926.

and Shanghai Bank, Wodehouse soon moved into journalism and short-story writing, but his real success was to come as a comic writer of immensely popular novels and musicals. By the time he died, on Valentine's Day 1975, Wodehouse had produced some ninety-six books, over 300 short stories and much humorous verse. He also saw involvement in some sixteen plays, twenty-eight musicals and half a dozen films. In his lifetime, he had become one of the most widely read authors this century.

Wodehouse's deceptively casual style belied a real sense of industry which gave rise to some of the best-loved characters in English literature, not least the ingenious and stoical butler Jeeves and his foppish master Bertie Wooster. These two characters first appeared in a short story in September 1915 – the same month that saw the creation of the popular Blandings Castle in *Something Fresh*. Many years and many 'Blandings' novels later, Wodehouse was to discover a 'real-life' Blandings here in north-west Norfolk: Hunstanton Hall, complete with park, lake, moat and thousand-acre estate. With fact and fiction blurring exquisitely in the novelist's mind, Wodehouse writes on 27 April 1929:

> It's wonderful being back at Hunstanton Hall again, though things aren't so frightfully bright at the moment, as host has had a row with butler, who has given notice. The butler is a cheery soul who used to be the life and soul of the party, joining in the conversation at meals and laughing appreciatively if one made a joke, but now he hovers like a spectre, very strong and silent. I'm hoping peace will be declared soon. I think I like Hunstanton Hall as well in winter as summer, though of course I don't get the moat in the winter months. I laid the scene for *Money for Nothing* at Hunstanton Hall.

With a decent map to hand, it is possible to trace virtually every spot described in *Money for Nothing* (1928) including the moated hall, the stream and its little bridge, and the path across the fields to the village. This was not the only novel Wodehouse set at Hunstanton and as the Chairman of the P G Wodehouse Society, N T P Murphy, declares in his exploration of Wodehouse country, *In Search of Blandings* (1986): 'Norfolk is the 'official' Wodehouse county'. Murphy explains that there have been Wodehouses in Norfolk for centuries (the ancestral home is at **Wymondham***) and that 'it was from Norfolk that Wodehouse's grandfather set out to fight in the Napoleonic wars'. With Plum evidently enjoying his visits here over an eight-year spell (1926–33), it is easy to see why so many of his characters have 'Norfolk' names: Lady Wroxham, Lord Heacham and Jack Snettisham, to name but a few.

Wodehouse based much of his work upon incidents and places from his own life, and with further exploration it is possible to unearth an even wider range of Norfolk – and especially Hunstanton – references in his writing. Whether it is the 'Octagon' standing in the middle of the island at 'Woollam Chersey' in *Very Good Jeeves* (1930) or the daughter of a Blandings parlour-maid in *A Pelican at Blandings* (1969) – the final Hunstanton reference in Plum's work – it is safe to assume that there is some Norfolk influence at work. But the enduring image of Wodehouse's time here comes in a letter dated 26 June 1926 where Plum delights in discovering not only the ancient moat, but also a punt in which to work:

> I spend most of my time on the moat, which is really a sizeable lake. I'm writing this in the punt with my typewriter on a bed-table wobbling on one of the seats. There is a duck close by which utters occasional quacks that sound like a man with an unpleasant voice saying nasty things in an undertone. Beside me is a brick wall with the date 1623 on it. The only catch is the water is so full of weeds, so I can't swim in it as I would like to.

South Acre

Margaret Fountaine

The intrepid adventurer closes her diaries with the dedication: 'To the Reader, maybe yet unborn, I leave this record of the wild and fearless life of one of the South Acre children…'

Bordering the River Nar, this village is the birthplace of travel diarist and lepidopterist **Margaret Fountaine** (1862–1940). A fairly dull and conventional Victorian childhood spent here as the daughter of a country clergyman was followed, after the death of her father in 1878, by a long spell at Eaton Grange House, **Norwich***. It was there, aged sixteen, that she started the diary which she was to maintain until just a few months before her death.

After suffering a bout of unrequited love for a semi-alcoholic Irish singer, and financially secure through a legacy, Margaret went off to travel the world and to hunt down better love and as many butterflies as she could lay hands on. When the butterfly net fell out of her hands – literally – in Trinidad, at the age of seventy-eight Margaret Fountaine had written over a million words and collected some 22,000 butterflies. Her ten mahogany display cases full of butterflies, together with the twelve volumes of her diaries were bequeathed to the Castle Museum, Norwich. Under Fountaine's instructions, her diaries were only opened in 1978, releasing *Love among the Butterflies* and *Butterflies and Late Loves* into the publishing world in 1980.

Acquaintances of the tall, angular Fountaine told the *Sunday Times* how she 'would suddenly get up and go off on an expedition, leaving the breakfast things on the table'. Shopping at Harrods in London, Fountaine would 'buy half-a-dozen pairs of plimsolls at a time to take abroad with her. "I don't think you'll get very far in the jungle with those … What about the leeches?" "Oh, they don't bother me," she said. "They don't like creosote." She bathed in creosote.'

Stanhoe

Contemporary poet **Alan Brownjohn** (1931-) and his wife Sandy, both keen walkers, are particularly fond of the 'long beaches and green lanes' around this corner of Norfolk, where they have had a cottage since 1976. Already familiar with the Norfolk landscape from his earlier stays at the old **Sedgeford Station** just east of **Heacham***, Alan Brownjohn explores the 'contradictions' of the Norfolk seasons to the full in his keenly-observed and often hard-edged poetry.

'In January', from his *Collected Poems* (1988), finds Brownjohn seeing in the New Year, lost amongst the salt marsh and 'Raw silence of reeds and waters' – until he is drawn by the lights of a distant television mast and an underlying 'deep drone / Of generators'. For a moment he is tugged back into the past, to 'revisit a lost hour', before breaking from his reverie to 'suddenly return / To the path over the marshes'.

Writing 'In the Visitors' Book', Brownjohn arrives at an 'exhausted, exalted coast', observing that 'The spring tide in April is / No resurrection of crested energies, but / A cagey, persistent ripple towards us', while

'Song' utilises simple visions from a walk down a Norfolk lane to conjugate the 'detail' of love: 'Turned soil rests and waits in the damp, clean and unharried; / The concealing flat cloud glows, in foreground to the sun; / One gust flicks beads of wet from the grass at crazed angles; / *I love you through detail*'.

In *The Observation Car* (1990), Brownjohn shifts seasons again – this time to witness the cooling down of 'September Days':

> There is only me in this landscape. There was only me
> This morning, in the brightness of the beach,
> And I thought I still had strength to run against
> Those droves of white sand raised by the same wind . . .
> Should I bow, in winter's direction, like the grass?

The holder of a Modern History degree, with his background in education and Labour politics, Alan Brownjohn has been called 'the best of our social poets' and meshes together his central themes of 'love, politics, culture, time'. Besides his poetry, Brownjohn is also the author of a prize-winning first novel, *The Way You Tell Them* (1990), of translations and adaptations of **Corneille** and **Goethe**, and of teaching anthologies with his wife Sandy. Incorporating the more positive post-colonial values offered by the English language ('rationalism, democracy, and humanity'), Brownjohn is not ashamed to note that 'it's the English-ness of what I write that strikes me most as I look back at it'.

The wide-ranging work of Brownjohn's ninth collection, *In the Cruel Arcade* (1994) continues his reflection on Britain's shifting social fabric, which is occasionally viewed through a Norfolk window. In 'January to April', Brownjohn returns to the 'cold plain stretch' where earlier in the year he had disturbed a Norfolk shooting party – a 'project whose business / Was impersonal slaughter'. Even with the arrival of spring, Brownjohn can only view the April rain as 'a distillation / Of the palest hope earth could ever seek and find' – but he still succeeds in lending the muddy Norfolk soil sufficient compassion and humanity to have pleased his fellow poet and anti-hunt sympathiser **William Cowper***some two centuries earlier.

Alan Brownjohn

'… each field and hedge / Looks green and living still, as I stride away' – the poet pausing for breath on the North Norfolk Coastal Path.

Christmas at Holkham
One crossbill hides from
  twitchers
Who all look alike.

Sandy Brownjohn, from
'A Norfolk Haiku Bestiary', 1996.

Sandy Brownjohn's children's poetry also 'draws on our love affair with the area'. *Both Sides of the Catflap* (1996) watches geese flying in formation like 'waves in dream water', tells the story of Rufus Lupin Chester the ginger cat with ' nowhere to go' roaming the lanes of **Catton** before finding a home in **Norwich***, and features an A-Z 'Norfolk Haiku Bestiary'.

Walsingham

Following the visions of Lady Richeldis de Fervaquere, all the English monarchs from Henry III to Henry VIII came on a pilgrimage to this world-famous shrine. Having experienced a strange dream in which she was transported to Palestine and shown the room where the Archangel Gabriel made the Annunciation to Mary, Richeldis went on to duplicate the building at Walsingham. The exact location arrived with her second dream, detailing the two pieces of land, which remained dry after a heavy dew, here in a Walsingham meadow close to a pair of ancient wells (the source of miraculous cures). Building work initially proved difficult, but after much prayer, all the materials were reassembled exactly how she had seen them in Palestine.

The ruins of Walsingham Priory – Henry VIII completed the pilgrimage to the Shrine of Our Lady shortly before his Dissolution resulted in the destruction of the shrine in September 1534 and the decay of this once powerful priory.

Writing in 1511, the Dutch humanist **Erasmus** (*c*.1467–1536) describes Walsingham as a 'dissolute place, living almost entirely on its visitors ... and many held that its low standard of conduct arose from the demoralising traffic with the crowd of pilgrims, many of whom must have been offenders against good manners; otherwise they would not have needed to go thither as penitents.' Erasmus, who antagonised Church dignitaries with his satire *The Praise of Folly* (1511) also wrote the colloquy *Peregrinatio religionis ergo* at the expense of the monks he saw as being lazy and 'thick-headed'.

Just two decades later, the Dissolution reduced the powerful priory to the ruins still visible today. The desecration of Walsingham's magnificent ecclesiastical buildings and shrine is decried in an anonymous poem often ascribed to **Philip Howard, Earl of Arundel** (1557–90):

> Bitter was it oh to see the seely sheepe
> Murdered by the ravenginge wholves, while the
> > sheephards did sleep
>
> ...
> Levell, levell with the ground the toures doe lye,
> Which with their golden glittering tops pearsed once to
> > the skye.
>
> ...
> Where weare gates, no gates are nowe; the waies unknown,
> Where the press of peares did passe while her fame far
> > was blowen.
> Oules do scrike where the sweetest himnes lately
> > weer songe,
> Toades and serpents hold their dennes where the palmers
> > did throng.
> Weepe, weepe O Walsingham, whose dayes are nightes,
> Blessinge turned to blasphemies, holy deed to dispites.
> Sinne is where out Ladie sate, heaven turned is to hell,
> Sathan sittes wher our Lord did swaye, Walsingham oh
> > farewell.

Heremytes on a heep with
hoked staves
Wenten to Walsyngham, and
their wenches after,
Grete lobies and longe that
lothe were to swynke;
Clothed hem in copes, to ben
knowen from others;
And shopen hem heremytes,
their ese to have.

William Langland (c.1330–c.1386), from *Piers Plowman*

The unearthing of about fifty urns in a Walsingham field, 'Some containing two pounds of bones, distinguishable in skulls, ribs, jawes, thigh-bones, and teeth, with fresh impressions of their combustion', inspired **Thomas Browne's*** famous meditation *Urn Buriall* (1658).

Sylvia Haymon* (1915–95), writing as **S T Haymon**, uses the 'low standard of conduct' witnessed some five hundred years earlier by Erasmus as the foundation for her detective mystery *Death and the Pregnant Virgin* (1980). Instead of confrontations between rival religious factions, the inhabitants of the 'jam-packed' village of 'Mauthen

Sylvia Haymon

She introduces Inspector
'Valentino' Jurnet to her
readers for the first time in her
'Walsingham' mystery, *Death
and the Pregnant Virgin*.

Barbary' have to contend with murder and personal greed which threaten to destabilise their community. When local squire Charles Griffin unearths the ancient statue of 'Our Lady of Promise' and reinstates the shrine which stood here before the Dissolution, there are mixed feelings among the villagers. Some believe the statue of the pregnant virgin to be a heathen abomination, others believe it to be a miraculous blessing, while one villager sums up the feelings of the majority: 'I reckon we ended up, most of us, proud we had her instead of some other place.'

For the thousands of pilgrims, mainly 'barren', childless couples, descending upon Mauthen Barbary, 'Our Lady' offers something more – hope. For Haymon, *Death and the Pregnant Virgin* offers the ideal opportunity to introduce Detective Inspector 'Valentino' Jurnet to her readers. And with the village packed full of pilgrims and protesters, when the murderer strikes, there is an abundance of suspects for the diligent Jurnet to sift through.

Although Haymon takes care to have her American professor Diefenhaus and his wife arrive 'from Walsingham', there is little doubt that 'Mauthen Barbary' is modelled on the world-famous shrine here. The descriptions of the market cross, the church, a nearby 'manor', the abbey ruins as 'jagged encrustations of masonry like the molars of some primeval monster', the 'barn-like' shrine building and the wattle-and-daub houses all fit Walsingham – even the detail of a visit by Henry VIII shortly before he dissolved the monasteries and ordered the destruction of the shrine here is historically correct.

When Jurnet looks around the deserted streets after the murder, he considers them to be 'like a film set where shooting was over for the day', which is precisely what the picturesque Walsingham has been on at least two occasions – once for the BBC's filming of *David Copperfield*

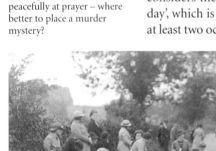

Walsingham pilgrims
peacefully at prayer – where
better to place a murder
mystery?

in 1982 and later for the filming of **Graham Swift**'s* *Waterland*. In *Death and the Pregnant Virgin*, as the pilgrims' procession is brought to a full halt by another grisly murder, Jurnet must penetrate the 'immemorial East Anglian art of self-concealment' before he can unravel the mystery and safely apprehend his villain. Naturally, the statue of the pregnant virgin carries more significance than anyone can guess.

Before writing her ecclesiastical murder mystery *The Snares of Death* (1992), **Kate Charles*** (1950–) visited Walsingham several times, and confirms that 'a trip to the National Pilgrimage in May was an eye-opening experience – especially the confrontation between Anglo-Catholic pilgrims and rabid Evangelical protesters during the procession. The extremes of emotion, and the extremes of conviction, made it a perfect setting for a murder mystery.' And what Charles' amateur sleuth and artist Lucy Kingsley finds when she enters the Walsingham Shrine Church to investigate would be enough to make the character of the reforming Reverend Bob Dexter turn in his early grave:

> ... a collection of minute chapels, each decorated in an entirely different style, stuck out at crazy angles everywhere she looked ... An austerely furnished altar with a sumptuous Flemish-style reredos jostled next to one that was almost flagrant in its campiness; yet another had the blue and white porcelain decor of an old-fashioned bathroom ... At the back of the Shrine church she marvelled at the Chapel of the Ascension, where a pair of brightly painted plaster feet, gory with stigmata but trailing clouds of glory and gilt stars, hovered jauntily overhead. Turning another corner, she gasped at the sight of a plaster representation of Our Lady, transfixed to a pillar with a sword through her heart, arms outstretched in agony, but a look of rapture on her painted face.

Weasenham St Peter

This village, just off the Fakenham-Swaffham road, is now home to one of the most indefatigable pilgrims in all things East Anglian, author and broadcaster **John Timpson** (1928–). Timpson's first impressions of the county gleaned from two early visits hadn't been too favourable, as he wrote in the first of his many articles for the *Norfolk Journal*:

> One was a summer holiday in Cromer, when it rained continuously and the only entertainment was watching the fire brigade pump out the hotel basement. The other was as a National Serviceman during the bitter winter of 1947, when predictably the Army ran out of fuel and we could only warm our hut by burning the chairs, the tables, and even the spare beds; we were working our way through the roof joists when we were finally posted to the comparatively tropical climes of the Austrian Alps.

John Timpson

The writer, journalist and Norfolk pilgrim has completed fifteen books in under twelve years here: 'so whatever [Norfolk] has to offer to writers, it has certainly been a help to me!'

Consequently, when Timpson first came to Norfolk to report for the *Eastern Daily Press* in **East Dereham*** in the 1950s, his friends thought he had taken leave of his senses. Certainly, what they thought of as 'a sort of Dutch Siberia' was as cold as when Timpson had left it three years earlier ('in our pantry the pickled onions froze in the vinegar'), and Norfolk society appeared 'not exactly feudal, but older folk were still tempted to touch their forelocks as the squire rode by'. His eight years in Dereham helped him devise the fictional plots for two novels, *Paper Trail* (1989) and *Sound Track* (1991), set in a provincial newspaper office in 'Toftham'. In *Sound Track*, which sees Charles Benson getting weary of local functions after seven years with the *Toftham and Wettleford Journal*, Timpson describes one of the local worthies holding forth about his trip to Canada:

> Albert Pollitt, secretary of Toftham Rotary Club, local chemist, and ardent traveller to foreign parts, turned another page of his notes. At the far end of the room somebody sighed. Or it might have been a gentle snore. 'Now thass a big place, Toronto. Bigger than Norwich, I'd say. But then, that hent got a castle the same as Norwich. There weren't much call for castles in Canada, I reckon. Not a lot of Norfolk farmers around to cause 'em trouble.'

In the 1980s, Timpson came back to live in 'High Norfolk' – 'which anyone else would call Deep Norfolk, but Norfolkmen like to do diff'rent'. People have a different concept of time here too, as Timpson was reminded while supervising building work on the cottage he planned to move into. Judging by the look of it, things weren't really moving with this local builder in charge:

> A little impatiently, I fear, I asked him how things were going. There was a considerable pause while he surveyed the apparent muddle around us – the heaps of rubble, the trampled mud, the half-built walls and tile-less roof. Then he nodded gently. 'Why', he said, 'thass comin t'gether.' And sure enough, in his own good time, it did.'

Since coming back to the 'working landscape, genuine and honest' that Norfolk represents for him, Timpson has written fifteen books, starting with *Timpson's England* – 'so whatever Norfolk has to offer to writers, it has certainly been a help to me!' he says. Despite the trials and tribulations of living between the threat of suburban sprawl and the conservationist 'drawbridge brigade' (who regret the Fens were ever drained), Timpson is adamant: 'Once you get to know a Norfolkman there is no better friend; once you get to know Norfolk, there is no better place to live.'

CHAPTER NINE

King's Lynn & Fenland

LITERARY LINKS

Edward Bulwer-Lytton, Fanny Burney, John Capgrave, Barbara Cartland, Daniel Defoe, Robert Forby, Robert I Hamilton,Thomas Hood, Margery Kempe, Osbert Lancaster, George MacBeth, John Cowper Powys, Lisa St Aubin de Terán, Dorothy L Sayers, Edward Storey, Graham Swift, Rose Tremain, Anthony Trollope, Fay Weldon, Anthony C Wilson

King's Lynn

Born in the reign of Edward II, when the town was called Bishop's Lynn, **Margery Kempe** (*c.*1373-*c.*1439) was the daughter of a prominent King's Lynn merchant and a close contemporary of **Julian of Norwich***. The story of her unique and eventful life is found in *The Book of Margery Kempe* (*c.*1436) – a historical jewel providing a fascinating insight into mysticism and medieval life. It is significant not least because it appears to be the first autobiography to be written in English – by an almost certainly illiterate woman.

'The more slander and criticism I suffered, the more I grew in grace and the more I would devote myself to holy meditation.'

The Book of Margery Kempe, *c.* 1436

Although Margaret was to bear fourteen children, her first pregnancy was particularly traumatic and led to a complete mental breakdown. The medieval mind had a clear perception of wrong and right and usually viewed physical illness as some sort of divine retribution for sins committed. During her dark period, Margery was pursued and tormented by demons until, in a religious vision, Christ came to her side. She emerged from her 'possession' calm, collected and with a new-found devotion.

For a time Margery Kempe continued with the affluent lifestyle that she had been used to. In her time, Bishop's Lynn was one of Britain's busiest seaports – with regular trade to and from the continent and laden ferries constantly winding their way back and forth along the River Ouse. With her brewing and milling businesses, Margery joined the thriving grain, wool, salt and cloth industries and a multitude of other trades and crafts competing side by side in Lynn town centre.

When her business ventures failed, Margery took this as a sign from God that she should abandon her ways and devote herself to Christ.

St Margaret's Church – Margery Kempe's new-found spirituality became focused here, where her wailing and weeping frequently disturbed services.

Transforming her life through fasting, vigils and prayers, and making visits to the poor and sick in the community, Margery also managed to persuade her husband to share a vow of chastity, which was accepted as being of fundamental importance to her spiritual well-being.

Margery Kempe's new life involved rising at 2 or 3 a.m. and spending many hours in the church, praying and sometimes lying prostrate on the floor. She was readily moved to tears by religious thoughts and visions, and her wailing and sobbing often disturbed sermons and upset the congregation, causing much embarrassment and irritation to those around her. *The Book* tells of one frightening episode when Margery's daily devotions turned to cries of pain:

> On the Friday before Whitsun Eve, when I was in St Margaret's church in Lynn hearing mass, I happened to hear a loud, frightening noise. I was very scared, for I'd been unnerved by people saying that God would take his revenge upon me. I knelt on my knees, bowing my head and holding my prayer book in my hand, and begging our Lord Jesus Christ for his grace and mercy. Suddenly a stone weighing three pounds and a stump of beam weighing six pounds fell from the highest point of an archway, where they had been supporting the central beam, and landed on my head and my back. I thought my back was broken, and I was afraid I hadn't long to live. Promptly I cried out, 'Jesus, have mercy', and my pain disappeared.

Unlike the majority of medieval mystics and spiritual authors, Margery Kempe was a married woman with a large family. But what she lacked in education and 'purity', Margery Kempe made up for in effort, kindness and resilience. In all probability, she was illiterate, but could commit biblical readings to memory, and was able to produce them at appropriate moments to confound her detractors. Accused more than once of Lollardry (Lollards – the followers of **John Wycliffe** – rocked the stability of the English church with their criticism of its greed, corruption and misuse of power), Margery successfully convinced the authorities of her innocence.

Pilgrimages were an important part of pre-Reformation English life, with nearby **Walsingham*** second in importance only to Canterbury. Few had the means to travel, however, and it was a truly courageous act to undertake lengthy and risky voyages overseas. Undeterred, Margery journeyed from Lynn to all the major shrines in Britain and on to Jerusalem and the Holy Land, Rome, Assisi and Santiago de Compostela.

Margery lived into her sixties and, unlike **Julian of Norwich**, whom she met and greatly admired, experienced all the difficulties and delights of the real world outside a cell. Seemingly immune from embarrassment, Margery was an extraordinary person who mingled with archbishops and friars, lepers and thieves, and never lost her great love of humanity. Wherever she went, she recorded the existence of the divine in the human, and behind the frequent melodrama lay a good person whose life became devoted to self-sacrifice.

John Capgrave (1393–1464) was born in Lynn and lived most of his life here. A great scholar, Capgrave devoted most of his time to the old Augustinian friary where he led the order as Friar Provincial from 1453–7 and compiled his numerous religious works and invaluable historical records of fifteenth-century Britain. Capgrave's most important English work is his *Chronicle* of English history up to 1417,

The gateway of the old Augustinian friary outside the Council Offices in Austin Street

'If ye will wete what that I am / My countre is northfolk of the town of Lynne', writes John Capgrave, who received Henry VI here in 1446.

which has been praised for its simplicity of style. The author of *De Nobilibus Henricis* received Henry VI in 1446 at the friary, of which all that remains now is the gateway in Austin Street.

Described as 'a real wonder' by **Dr Johnson**, novelist and diarist **Fanny Burney (Madame d'Arblay)** (1752–1840) was born into a Bohemian family in the 'fascinating society of the Augustan Age' and lived a 'magnificently crammed' life. Probably born at 84 High Street, she was certainly baptised in the fifteenth-century Chapel of St Nicholas – the largest chapel of ease in England.

Although the family moved to London in 1760, Fanny returned throughout her childhood to stay at Dower House, near the churchyard of St Margaret's, with Mrs Stephen Allen (who later became her stepmother). Fanny enjoyed the small garden here, writing that its 'greatest part is quite a grove, and three people might be wholly concealed from each other with ease in it ... it has the most private lonely, shady, melancholy look in the world'.

Fanny's father was organist at the church where, from the shelter of Mrs Allen's house opposite, a young Fanny sympathises with the bride at a very 'publick' wedding, and enjoys a 'very good view of the procession'.

Fanny learned to read and write quite late, but from the age of ten she was conjuring up short stories and kept early diaries, which she wrote in 'The Cabin' at the bottom of the 'long garden that runs along the house' down to the river. The summer of 1768 finds Fanny in her hiding place here, where a friend recalls her being disturbed by 'the annoying oaths of the watermen'.

Fanny's early diaries offer contradictory views of her home town – her resolute defence of Lynn earning her the praise of her stepmother

Prospect of Lynn from the west, *c.*1680

'Here are more gentry, and consequently is more gayety in this town than in Yarmouth, or even in Norwich it self; the place abounding in very good company'

Daniel Defoe, 1724

and grandmother, while later she bemoans the 'chit chat' of a 'Country Town', where 'all the conversation is scandal, all the attention, dress, and almost all the heart, folly, envy, and censoriousness'. Her two 'most favourite pursuits' remain 'reading and writing' and she enjoys walking the surrounding countryside.

No doubt alarmed by her stepmother's warning that to be known as a 'scribbler' would seriously harm her marriage prospects, fifteen-year-old Fanny burnt her romantic manuscripts and resolved to write only her journal. Fortunately, she was unable to keep to her pledge and in 1778 she published *Evelina* anonymously and to much critical acclaim. Fearful of discovery, Fanny had worked secretly on the book for years, scribbling in the darkness which cannot have helped her short-sightedness. But the book was well-received at home and her sister recalls hearing their father read extracts from *Evelina* to his wife as they lay in bed, their laughter echoing around the house.

An inspiration for Daniel Defoe's *Robinson Crusoe*? A memorial slab to a later Robinson Cruso in St Nicholas Chapel.

In his *Tour through the Whole Island of Great Britain* (1724), **Daniel Defoe** (1660–1731) arrives in Lynn to declare it the port with 'the greatest extent of inland navigation' outside London. He certainly seems familiar with Lynn, where, at the west end of its impressive St Nicholas Chapel, lie the black marble tomb slabs of the Cruso family, including at least two Robinson Crusos. Although the *Tour* was published some five years later than *Robinson Crusoe* (1719), it seems likely that Defoe's knowledge of the town may have brought the name to mind when plotting his literary classic. From Lynn, Defoe headed for the 'fenn-country', the 'unwholsom air' of which left him singularly unimpressed.

Fanny Burney

The author, editor and critic **Walter Allen** once wrote: 'To read Miss Burney is rather like having a mouse's view of the world of cats: the cats are very terrifying, but the mouse's sense of the ridiculous could not be keener.'

'For some time past, I have taken a walk in the fields near Lynn of about an hour every morning before breakfast – I have never yet got out before six, and never after seven. The fields are, in my eyes, particularly charming at that time in the morning – the sun is warm and not sultry – and there is scarce a soul to be seen.'

Fanny Burney, *Early Diary*, 1768

Agricultural writer **Arthur Young** (1741–1817) was connected with the Burneys and his country home is mentioned in Fanny Burney's *Camilla* (1796). Young was apprenticed to a merchant's house in Lynn, but soon switched to charting farming methods on his famous journeys through England and Europe.

Fanny Burney's comedies of domestic life, developed around innocent heroines as they enter a sophisticated world, prefigure **Jane Austen***. But the immense success of *Evelina*, a tale of love and fluctuating family fortunes in society, was never fully to be repeated and had at least one unfortunate consequence: the invitation from Queen Charlotte to become Second Keeper of the Robes, where Fanny spent five lonely and frustrating years witnessing the King's 'madness' first-hand.

Although writing actually did little to hinder her prospects, Fanny Burney did not marry until 1793 when she was forty years old. Then it was an 'outrageously romantic' marriage to the French émigré, General Alexandre d'Arblay and, despite separations caused by the Napoleonic Wars, they had one child and remained together for a quarter of a century up to the General's death.

In 1831, poet and humorist **Thomas Hood** (1799–1845) wrote an influential poem on the subject of Eugene Aram, who was arrested in 1758 for murder while employed as an undermaster at the Grammar School. Until 1779, the school was situated above an old Charnel Chapel adjoining St Margaret's Church, in a building that became known as 'The Shambles'. Aram, the misguided and remarkable scholar described so well by **Jessopp*** and Bulwer-Lytton, was executed in August 1759 and his body hanged in a roadside gibbet.

Hood's 'fine and striking' poem is acknowledged by **Edward Bulwer-Lytton** (1803–73) in *Eugene Aram* (1832) – his own dramatisation of the tragedy in which he sets out 'the stoical and dark character of the man'. Though lacking any strong sense of place, Lytton's wordy and largely melodramatic novel, with its shadowy strangers and inevitable romantic entanglements, is nevertheless cleverly plotted and gripping in the run-up to the final 'confession'.

Eugene Aram is depicted as a 'wonderfully learned man' who lives his life in seclusion in 'Grassdale', devoted to study. When he falls in love with the local squire's daughter, a chain of events is unleashed which brings the past back to haunt and, finally, to destroy him. Even with the accusation of murder hanging over him, Aram retains an air of scholarly

> Two stern-faced men set out from Lynn
> Through the cold and heavy mist;
> And Eugene Aram walked between,
> With gyves upon his wrist.
>
> Thomas Hood from 'The Dream of Eugene Aram', 1829

The Shambles on the Saturday Market Place – demolished in 1914, the school above the old Charnel Chapel was where the infamous Eugene Aram reputedly taught Fanny Burney's brother.

detachment and his guilt or innocence is uncertain till the end. It is a classic tale of the inevitability of fate and of the moral improvements available through education and learning, though quite how true it is to the actual events in Aram's life remains uncertain.

> The influential editor, critic and poet **Robert I Hamilton** (1938–) was born in King's Lynn and lived here till the age of thirteen. His works include *Fifty Poems* (1988), a **Robert Lowell** biography and *In Search of J D Salinger*. He was the editor of *The Review* (later *The New Review*) from 1962 to 1979.

In her prize-winning novel *Restoration* (1989), **Rose Tremain*** (1943–) creates the fictional estate of 'Bidnold Manor' as the much-loved home of her flawed hero Robert Merivel. Set in seventeenth-century England, under the newly 'restored' monarchy of King Charles II, Tremain's compelling tale involves much loss and restoration – of friendship, sanity and self-respect. Bidnold, a 'small but agreeable estate' placed here in north-west Norfolk, 'probably not far from King's Lynn', in the author's own words, remains the measure of Merivel's success throughout.

A self-confessed 'glutton for foolishness', Merivel finds favour with the King after curing one of the royal dogs and abandons his medical studies to join the 'Age of Possibility' at the Court. When he is presented with money, a title and land at Bidnold as a reward for 'marrying' Charles II's youngest mistress, Merivel's success seems assured, although he initially appears confused: 'I could not remember how far from and in what relation to … London lay the county of Norfolk.'

Merivel's mixed emotions on arrival at Bidnold ('Though struck by its drabness, I rejoiced in it') are matched by his relief at finding that his 'wife' is 'a woman not at all to my taste'. But as Merivel's passion for the 'perfect space' of his Norfolk home grows, so too does his longing for the 'quiet beauty' of his wife. 'We no longer live in an honourable age', points out Merivel, dallying with impossible ambitions of becoming an 'artist' instead of employing his skills as a physician. But his carnal desires soon prove his undoing and swiftly propel him into the perilous depths of depravity and despair.

While not exploring the Norfolk landscape in detail, Tremain's brushstroke technique captures perfectly the essence of the place. In the murky waterland of the fens, Merivel notes how 'the landscape became, as it were, *less* and the sky *more* and how the creatures most numerous were the birds, who had their existence in both elements'. At Bidnold he treasures 'certain combinations of colour and light … that I do not think exist anywhere in the world but here'. And while Merivel's fortunes ebb and flow like the nearby tides of **The Wash**, Norfolk itself remains calm and solid, awaiting his return.

Rose Tremain

She explores Norfolk's 'Age of Possibility' in *Restoration*.

'In a Norfolk wind, I sometimes feel my sanity flying away.'

Rose Tremain, *Restoration*, 1989

At the 'New Bedlam' lunatic asylum in the fens, Merivel joins his friend John Pearce with hopes of restoring at least a modicum of self-respect. But here in the Quaker community, Merivel's weaknesses are once more cruelly exposed. With the Plague still a very real threat, Merivel heads back to the capital seeking a new start in life. But even as he picks up his physician's instruments and sallies forth into the community, one obsession continues to haunt him – the restoration of his position in the King's favour.

The pocket-sized *Powers of Arrest and Charges* – widely accepted as 'the policeman's bible' – was written by King Lynn's theatre-loving 'Laughing Policeman', Chief Constable **Fred Calvert** (1910–1986).

Merivel's opportunity for redemption arrives in the midst of Rose Tremain's riveting depiction of the calamitous Great Fire of London and offers, perhaps, the return to Bidnold he dreams of:

> There is a fresh breeze and the shadows of fast-moving clouds sail across the grass. The chestnuts are in full candleburst. A cluster of deer grazes under them and, as we come on, the animals raise their heads and look at us.
>
> We round the curve in the drive and there it is: Bidnold Manor in the County of Norfolk, the house snatched from the Anti-Royalist, John Loseley, and given to me in return for my role as cuckold, the house where all my foolishness was contained, Merivel's house.

Fenland

Although divided between three different counties, the fens form a vast, flat, 12,000-square-mile region which recognises no district or county boundaries. Incorporating large tracts of marshland, the area is, in its own way, as distinct and unique as any part of Britain. This is reclaimed land, still gradually sinking, whose pumps, dykes and embankments do constant battle with the forces of The Wash and the North Sea beyond, bidding to recapture land that was once water. This fertile land, criss-crossed with ditches and drains, was originally formed by vast silt deposits; until, as its vegetation decomposed over the centuries, a soggy, swampy land composed of rich, dark peat remained.

When **Anthony Trollope** (1815–82) travelled the Eastern District in his capacity as Post Office Surveyor it was with a jaundiced eye for the flat scenery around him. A lover of mountains and rugged landscapes, Trollope's antipathy for the fenlands and fields of Norfolk is clearly revealed in *The Belton Estate* (1866), his tale of a wilful and impoverished heroine, Clara Amedroz, who must decide whether to marry for money and social position or for love.

Anthony Trollope

He found his novel *The Belton Estate* as uninspiring as the Norfolk fens: 'I seem to remember almost less of it than of any book that I have written'.

A farm in the unappealing remoteness of the fens heralds the romantic interest of her distant cousin Will Belton, in direct competition with her other suitor, the wealthy Captain Frederic Aylmer. Clara's father is unimpressed by 'farmer' Will Belton, even if he does live in the impressively named 'Plaistow Hall' – a fine and picturesque Tudor brick

'You've no conception what an ugly place Plaistow is. The land isn't actual fen now, but it was once. And it's quite flat. And there is a great dike, twenty feet wide, oozing through it, just oozing you know; and lots of little dikes, at right angles with the big one. And the fields are all square. And there are no hedges, and hardly a tree to be seen in the place.'

Anthony Trollope,
The Belton Estate, 1866

Denver Sluice, built by Vermuyden in 1650 – This crucial piece of fenland engineering is visited unflatteringly in Trollope's *The Belton Estate*, tragically in Graham Swift's *Waterland*, and catastrophically in D L Sayers' *The Nine Tailors*.

mansion with 'many gables and countless high chimneys' not far from **Downham Market**. 'They call all the farms halls down there,' he snorts derisively.

Cousin Will isn't too enamoured with his homeland either, and with escape to his West Country inheritance (the Belton Estate) a priority, even a return to Norfolk for shooting is unthinkable as he sets out to convince Clara of the honorability of his intentions. Will Belton holds many characteristics in common with the author himself; energetic, self-reliant, outwardly abrasive and certainly impatient.

One Sunday, as he contemplates the prospect of losing Clara's hand, Will Belton suddenly decides to walk out his frustration along the eight miles to 'Denvir Sluice' and back – in just over three hours! Striding out across the bank of a great dike and down a five-mile straight road, the countryside must have been a blur to Belton, whose outing is summarised as: 'A country walk less picturesque could hardly be found in England.' Fortunately for him, Clara makes her choice with considerably less impatience and, after much vacillation, for romantic rather than financial reasons.

Trollope's social novel, encompassing as it does an entire stratum of society – women without dowry who were destined to marry for money or stay poor – failed to win over the critics, who were more interested

in his immensely successful 'Barsetshire' novels. In spite of Trollope's own dismissal of his novel, and his all-too-obvious loathing for the flatlands of Norfolk, *The Belton Estate* is still an entertaining and much undervalued work.

It is into these wet and wind-scoured flatlands that **Graham Swift** (1949–) places his prize-winning *Waterland* (1983) – a deeply imaginative novel with a haunting sense of locality and touched by the mystery and madness which perhaps best epitomise the writings of this region.

Tom Crick, the protagonist and narrator of *Waterland*, was raised in a lock-keeper's cottage in the fens, and this region represents both an 'empty wilderness' and a 'fairytale land' of windmills and will-o'-the-wisps. Crick's lock is on the 'River Leem', flowing 'out of Norfolk into the Great Ouse', coloured by the 'milky brown of the Norfolk chalk hills' and giving off that smell 'which is characteristic of places where fresh water and human ingenuity meet, and which is smelt over and over again in the Fens'. This smell, a 'cool, slimy but strangely poignant and nostalgic smell ... half man and half fish' lives with Crick into his later years, as he stands before his class as a beleaguered history teacher, using his own fenland life as a lesson:

Graham Swift

He captures the amphibious feel of the fenlands to perfection in *Waterland*.

> And no one needs telling that the land in that part of the world is flat. Flat, with an unrelieved and monotonous flatness, enough of itself, some might say, to drive a man to unquiet and sleep-defeating thoughts. From the raised banks of the Leem, it stretched away to the horizon, its uniform colour, peat-black, varied only by the crops that grew upon it – grey-green potatoes, blue-green beet leaves, yellow-green wheat; its uniform levelness broken only by the furrowed and dead-straight lines of ditches and drains, which, depending upon the state of the sky and the angle of the sun, ran like silver, copper or golden wires across the fields and which, when you stood and looked at them, made you shut one eye and fall prey to fruitless meditations on the law of perspective.

For Crick, whose life and work seem to be disintegrating about him, these stories offer perhaps a chance to purge the past, to exorcise the childhood demons that continue to haunt him. For the pupils in his classroom, and for *Waterland* readers, Crick's lessons are riveting tales of fenland life. Here in the fictional villages of 'Hockwell' and 'Wansham', by 'Stump Corner' and 'Polt Fen' families of farmers, fishermen, eel trappers, brewers and barley-growers living 'like water-rats', are stubbornly struggling to survive in an ambiguous, water-logged landscape.

In the best tradition of novelists, Swift merges fact with fiction as he plots the history of Crick's family alongside the progression of fenland engineering: the digging of the New Bedford river (Hundred Foot

The 'low and liquid world' of the fens at dusk

A lock-keeper's cottage near Upwell – Tom Crick, the narrator of *Waterland*, was raised in a similar home close to the 'salty, unparochial tang' of the Great Ouse.

Drain), the formation of **Denver Sluice** and the terrible flooding of 1713 where 'thousands of acres were submerged'.

Beyond the fens, *Waterland* also travels around other parts of Norfolk: boating along the Great Ouse river with its 'salty, unparochial tang', on board with the Great Eastern Railway to nearby **Downham Market**, and further out to the industrial towns of **Swaffham***, **Thetford*** and **Norwich***, where the 'Atkinson' breweries of Crick's ancestors are located. Swift's fenfolk are an independent and introspective people, resigned to hardship, used to contemplating the exposure and loneliness of life under wide open skies and nothing much beyond.

Waterland is a tragic, sometimes terrible tale of adolescent desire, emerging sexuality, confused identities, inner turmoil and mental anguish. And throughout Swift's 'low and liquid world, a scarcely substantial world', the churning, flowing, watery landscape is of overriding importance – determining moods, reflecting emotions, guiding destinies. It is a continual process of creation and destruction, as Tom Crick confirms: 'It's progress if you can stop the world slipping away. My humble model for progress is the reclamation of land. Which is repeatedly, never-endingly retrieving what is lost.'

In a slightly different vein, **Fay Weldon** (1933–) sets her novel *Growing Rich* (1992) in 'Fenedge', an unspecified new Fenland town near **King's Lynn*** which explores the lives of Laura, Annie and Carmen as they leave school. In a summer of dusty roads and failed exams, the girls look for ways to extract themselves from 'Dullsville' while the narrator, a handicapped elderly lady who has sat at her window overlooking the beet fields for seventeen years, muses: 'perhaps Fenedge is in some way pivotal to the great cosmic conflicts of good and evil'.

Typically witty and ironic, and full of realistic dialogue, *Growing Rich* is a blend of fantasy and gritty reality, with the girls 'waiting for the Employment Exchange to open', and waiting for the right man. In fact, 'they'd been waiting for one thing or another all summer, while the mock yellow irises ... and the marsh marigolds ... turned the fen woodland bright, and the dragonflies and the damselflies hatched ... and the skuas turned up on the beach to make the life of the common tern wretched for the season, and the slipper limpets changed sex.'

The girls' job-seeking leads the trio to a poultry factory at 'Peckham', to 'Bellamy Airspace outside **Fakenham**' and to a grandiose new hotel conversion outside Fenedge on the long straight road towards 'Winterwart', which:

Fay Weldon

She explores the 'Fenedge' of the Norfolk flatlands in *Growing Rich.*

> ... passes first through the beet fields, interrupting the long straight lines of low foliage which run sternly on either side to meet the horizon, allowing all the space in the world to the sky and the winds ... then crosses a patch of the old wood, where the oak, the ash, the maple and the beech stretch above the road to form a dappling canopy, before coming to the straight and boring conifers of the Forestry Commission – at least the crossbills love the conifers, if nobody else does.

'Around here the land is flat and drained ... The people of Fenedge ... will say, "The sea? A couple of miles away." Or "five miles away" or "just down the road", depending on what they think you want to hear, and because they are themselves unsure. The margins between sea and land are unclear ... in Dullsville, Somewhere-Near-The-Sea.'

Fay Weldon, *Growing Rich*, 1992

When the girls head their separate ways, Carmen goes job-hunting in **Walsingham*** and falls in love with Ronnie, assistant at Pious Artefacts. But at Fenedge she remains under the close supervision of 'Driver' – the Devil's agent, who allows her glimpses of a new identity in return for accepting the advances of Sir Bernard Bellamy, son of a local farm boy turned boiling-fowl breeder, who has already sold his soul.

In passing, Weldon explores the constant battle between the need for new development and the preservation of the past: 'What we want round here is work and housing and medical care, forget the spotted redshank, forget ancient graveyards and the bones of the dead. What about our living ones, our hips that need replacing?' But the ancient graveyard discovered under the sand dunes near by changes the fortunes of both Carmen and the town of Fenedge.

Arguably the most poetic prose to have come from the fens stems from the pen of **Edward Storey** (1930–), who has carved a niche for himself as literary ambassador of the fenland region. Epitomising his intimate and thought-provoking style is *Spirit of the Fens* (1985), both a personal and anecdotal exploration of fenland history – a collection of 'interviews, essays and reflections' cross-referencing other writer's impressions of this beguiling landscape.

Edward Storey

'I was but a figure in a landscape' – the fenland 'ambassador' writing in *Spirit of the Fens.*

' ... there is something more than space or light, something more than weather or seasons. There is history as well as geography ... Every field, bridge, tree, house and church has its own history. Everything the eye can see is there for a reason.'

Edward Storey, *Spirit of the Fens*, 1985

Though he cites **Hilaire Belloc**, for whom the dykes were 'accursed things ... the separation of friends and lovers', Storey himself never seems to tire of the 'great distances' of an 'elusive' landscape which has possessed him for so long. In *Spirit of the Fens*, even his description of a passing storm takes on an almost surreal sense:

> And then, I thought I saw the fields shrink back into themselves, tremble a little, shudder from their shoulders down to their buried toes, as if the change of wind told them something only they could know ... I felt the air put on weight and become sultry. It was as if some invisible tide had turned. The horizon's clouds grew dark and heavy as rocks. The light in the fields went out. A minute later and it began to rain.

As Graham Swift's *Waterland* shows, the very unobtrusiveness of the Fens can be successfully used in fiction as a stage for human passion and history. Looking for an explanation for the Fenlanders' reputation for stubbornness and cunning leads Storey to explore the struggle against water that has been instrumental in shaping the spirit of a man-made landscape which bears all the marks of struggle and human determination.

Dame Barbara Cartland

'Pink helps you to be clever and helps you to be bright.'

In the early summer of 1998, the owner of Hermitage Hall here at **Downham Market** opened a museum on the grounds of his farm to celebrate the world's most famous romantic novelist, **Dame Barbara Cartland** (1901–). Dame Barbara, whose 600-plus books have sold over 600 million copies all over the world, met Eric St John-Foti in the early eighties, when he was producing Norfolk Punch following a Tudor copy of a medieval recipe found in his former home in **Upwell***. Cartland also shares a common concern with **George Borrow*** – a commitment to gypsy issues – and in 1962 successfully campaigned for a change in the law, forcing local authorities to provide a site for their gypsies, enabling them to send their children to school.

East Winch

Best-remembered perhaps as the long-serving cartoonist for the *Daily Express*, **Osbert Lancaster** (1908–86) was also a witty and talented writer with Norfolk roots. His two autobiographical volumes, *All Done From Memory* (1953) and *With an Eye to the Future* (1967), are humorous, acutely observed and more valuable as records of Britain's transition through the trauma of the First World War than insightful into the very private character of a very public man. *All Done From Memory* does, however, reference Osbert's extended Norfolk family connections and his childhood holidays spent at East Winch Hall – the imposing late-Georgian residence of Osbert's grandfather, Sir William Lancaster.

Osbert was to rely upon the support of his family after his father was killed on the Somme in the early action of the First World War and made many visits to his grandfather's village. Arriving at East Winch station, 'lost amidst the un-by-passed fields of my Edwardian childhood', even the railway platform appeared to be a 'raised island' in the flat 'elm-broken cornlands'. From here, it was a short walk down Station Road and along the Lynn-Swaffham road towards the globe-topped entrance gates of East Winch Hall, today screened from view of the thundering traffic by copper beeches.

Here, adjoining the vast gabled porch, Osbert played tennis and croquet with his cousins and listened to tales of his eccentric relatives, in particular the 'Grateful Hearts' – an exclusively female group of 'extraordinary survivals from a long-vanished Norfolk of gloomy farmers and manic-depressive yeomen'. One such character, described in *All Done From Memory*, is Osbert's Great-Aunt Martha:

Osbert Lancaster

In his own inimitable style, the writer and cartoonist traces his Norfolk ancestry at East Winch Hall.

The remains of East Winch station today

> She appeared, and indeed she was, exceedingly robust and just about as fragile as well-seasoned teak ... Her features were strong and masculine and bore a close resemblance to those of Sir Robert Walpole ... and she retained a marked Norfolk accent ... alone of all the Lancasters she professed a keen interest in food and was reputed to be the finest hand with a dumpling between King's Lynn and Norwich. In addition she was never at any pains to conceal an earthy relish for scandal which, linked to a prodigous memory, made her a far more entertaining, and quite possibly a more accurate, authority on the genealogies of most Norfolk families than Burke.

There is a strong flavour of **P G Wodehouse*** in Osbert's light-hearted style and keen eye for detail – essential qualities for the successful cartoonist. The entrance gates to his grandfather's home are described as being 'generally felt to be an overstatement', while the house itself, built by some 'modest nabob who had done well in the tea trade', appears to have been 'deliberately designed on the model of a tea-caddy'.

Osbert would probably smile to find a row of smart new executive homes sitting on Lancaster Way at the entrance to the village, while the Carpenter's Arms appears to be the sole survivor of the four pubs from his day. Meanwhile, the retreat of the railway has left East Winch station sitting forlornly at the end of the disused railway siding that is now private property belonging to the Old Station House. Where Osbert once approached is now a muddy, trammelled path, lined with brambles and hawthorn, with a firmly closed gateway blocking further access.

> 'There is no silence in the world so overwhelming as that which prevails on a small country station when a train has just left. The fact that it is by no means complete, that the fading echoes of the engine are still clearly audible from beyond the signal-box behind which the guard's van is finally disappearing, that one now hears for the first time the cawing of rooks, a distant dog's bark, the hum of bees in the station-master's garden, in no way detracts from its quality. The rattling world of points and sleepers, of gossiping fellow-passengers and sepia views of Cromer beach has been whirled away leaving a void which, for some moments yet, the sounds and smells of the countryside will be powerless to fill.'
>
> *All Done From Memory*, 1953

Osbert became particularly close friends with **John Betjeman***. The two men shared a passion for architecture and an ability to find humour in the strangest of places, and Osbert became the perfect illustrator for the poet laureate's work. When he died in July 1986, Osbert Lancaster was buried in **West Winch** church where he lies today alongside the tombs of his ancestors.

Fincham

For those interested in the preservation of Norfolk's distinctive dialect, one work is increasingly sought-after: *The Vocabulary of East Anglia*. Written by **Robert Forby** (1759–1825) and published posthumously in 1830, it was re-issued in 1970.

Born at nearby **Stoke Ferry** and educated at the free school of Lynn Regis (as **King's Lynn*** was then known), Forby was rector of St Martin's, Fincham for twenty-five years. Forby's notes 'often reveal that words and expressions used by **Shakespeare*** ... and sufficiently obsolete to puzzle **Doctor Johnson** and the other great commentators of the eighteenth century, were still in active use in rural Norfolk in the reign of George IV ... a few minutes' talk with one of Forby's parishioners would have explained to them what Puck meant by a "minnock" and King Lear by a "crow-keeper"', comments **Robert Wyndham Ketton-Cremer***. However, as **Arnold Wesker*** was to discover with his play *Roots* (1959), few 'furriners' can successfully master the dialect.

Phineas Fletcher (1582–1650), the one-time rector of All Saints Church, **Hilgay** owes his place in literary history to *The Purple Island or the Isle of Man* (1633): an allegorical poem of the human body and mind in ten books in imitation of **Spenser**'s *Faerie Queene* (1590).

Northwold

In his widely acclaimed *Autobiography* (1934), **John Cowper Powys*** (1872–1963) acknowledges the influence of the Norfolk countryside during his 'intensely happy' visits to his maternal grandfather's rectory, here where the fenlands and brecklands merge. Once, Powys himself had entertained thoughts of becoming a country curate 'near some river like the Wissey', but instead he went on to tour the American lecture circuit for many years before devoting himself to his poetry and novels.

John Cowper Powys

His *Autobiography* (1932) recalls the 'flawless felicity' of childhood stays here.

The 'intermittent fragments of flawless felicity' Powys experienced at Northwold were never to be forgotten and forty years later Powys returned with his brother Littleton – 'stirred to the soul' – to spend a week at the old rectory, walking the grounds, retracing their childhood footsteps along the Wissey. Powys talks of exchanging 'wordless signals' with the two little boys that they once had been, until the ghosts of the past recede 'hand-in-hand ... faded into the branches of the cedar on the lawn, into the bushes by the fish-pond, into the poplars along the river, into the alders of Alder Dyke.' In a typically philosophical reflection, Powys wonders 'Shall we ever be able to summon them back again, those little wraiths of the past?'

In *A Glastonbury Romance* (1932), written some two years earlier, Powys achieves exactly this – weaving the 'wraiths' of his childhood into the fabric of a historical masterpiece. The novel opens with John Crow, a 'frail, thin, loosely built man of thirty-five', stepping off the train at Brandon station and setting out on foot towards Northwold for the funeral of his grandfather. With only the 'cold blue sky and biting east wind' for companions, Crow is disturbed from his reverie by a passing car, whose driver enquires 'Canon Crow's funeral Sir?', as it draws to a halt beside him.

John Crow accepts a lift, already searching 'the far grey horizon' for childhood visions such as 'the great towers of Ely Cathedral, visible across leagues and leagues of level fens', before looking up to find himself face to face with his beautiful and passionate cousin Mary. Thus the romance begins, not in Glastonbury, but here in the flatlands of Norfolk.

Powys' sixth novel, *A Glastonbury Romance* is an extraordinary tale. Over a thousand pages of lyrical and often profound prose, it combines a Norfolk-born romance with the mythology of Glastonbury and King Arthur's Holy Grail, and the storytelling tradition of **Hardy** or **Dickens***:

The Old Rectory and its 'great lawns' – where John Cowper Powys summons the 'wraiths of the past' in *A Glastonbury Romance* (1932)

The only sound that reached his ears was the sound of a faint trickle of water which came from some infinitesimal ledge in the bank above his head and fell down drop by drop into the ditch. Not a breath of wind stirred. Not a leaf-bud quivered. Not a grass-blade swayed. There was only that elfin waterfall and, except for that, the very earth herself seemed to have fallen asleep. 'This is Norfolk,' he said to himself, and in that intense, indrawn silence some old atavistic affiliation with fen-ditches and fen water and fen-peat tugged at his soul and pulled it earthward.

Powys' observations of Norfolk are adept, describing the local tongue as that 'peculiar up-drawing, up-tilting, devil-may-care intonation, no doubt derived from a long line of Danish ancestors', while lovingly recreating the local landscape. Beside the 'queer blind face' of the windowless 'Harrod's Mill', John Crow scents the 'faint fragrance of sap-filled grass' as his head fills with boyhood memories of fishing, and for a moment John Crow and the author become one. The 'tolling of the bell in the flint tower of the high-roofed Northwold Church' then summons John Crow to the churchyard, to the scene of his grandfather's burial.

Later, in an atmosphere of 'strained expectancy', in the creaking rooms of the rectory, his grandfather's will is read – but who has inherited his wealth? Everyone assumes it will be the rector's son, Philip. But it isn't. Nor is it John Crow, who, still heady with his sudden passion for Mary, observes the reading of the will and the shocked reactions of his relatives with a curious detachment. John holds no great affection for his Uncle Philip, but soon he will be drawn away from Norfolk, towards his uncle's home in Glastonbury.

John overnights at the New Inn (also known as the Northwold Arms) and the next day the young lovers walk out, over **Foulden Bridge** and across the fields, turning left to follow the river bank before finding their boat at Alder Dyke. From here they row downstream, make love, and lose themselves in the serenity of the Norfolk landscape. The intensity of their passion is conveyed through John Crow's heightened sense of the landscape around him; its sights, sounds – and smells:

And there came to his nostrils, as he lay with his eyes shut, a far-flung, acrid, aromatic smell. It was not the smell of mud, or leaf-buds, or grass-roots, or cattle-droppings, or ditch-water. It was not the smell of last night's rain, or of the sleeping south wind. It reached him independent of the eel slime that still clung to the bottom of the boat. It was the smell of East Anglia itself.

But romance, of course, is never straightforward, and even as they cling to each other, the crowding in of events from John's and Mary's pasts, the 'revival of local memories', begin to complicate matters. Before John Crow follows Mary to Glastonbury, he makes a wish: 'With the smell of

Alder Dyke in our souls we'll defy Glastonbury and Philip together! Our ancestors got their bread from the fens and we'll get our bread from Glastonbury and then come home, home to Alder Dyke!' Needless to say, things don't quite work out the way he intends.

Today, a short walk from the churchyard of the copper-roofed St Andrew's, down the chestnut-lined Riverside Lane, is a footpath towards the village of Foulden, through low-lying fields dotted with sheep. A small wooden bridge marks the crossing-point of the Wissey, which John Crow himself steps across in *A Glastonbury Romance*.

Though only a short distance from the village, with the church tower still tall on the horizon, it is quite possible to picture John Crow and Mary pausing for a moment at this tranquil spot and breathing the sweet-scented air, before walking on to take their boat moored at 'Alder Dyke' out along the clear waters of the Wissey. And on the return to the village, the 'Northwold Arms' inn – today called The Crown – awaits the thirsty traveller.

Opposite: The River Wissey at Foulden Bridge – in *A Glastonbury Romance*, it is from here John Crow and his cousin Mary boat with the 'smell of East Anglia' in the air.

Upwell

One author perfectly at home with the mysterious qualities of the fens is detective writer **Dorothy L Sayers** (1893–1957), who lived for some twenty years in the area. Her grandfather had been curate of **Tittleshall** for a decade, while her Norfolk-born father was a vicar who had attended Magdalen College, Oxford with **Oscar Wilde***.

When Dorothy was four years old, the family moved to take up the living at Bluntisham Rectory on the southern edge of the Cambridgeshire fens where, some years later, her father had the bells of St Mary's church restored.

This was Sayers' first close contact with bells, which are so integral to her detective fiction classic, *The Nine Tailors* (1934), written twenty-five years later. This intricately planned and absorbing tale is set in the heart of fen country close to the Norfolk/Cambridgeshire border and over towards **Denver Sluice**.

In the summer of 1921, Sayers was completing work on her first novel *Whose Body* (1923) where she introduced her famous detective character Lord Peter Wimsey. During this summer, Sayers also worked as a French tutor at the rectory here in Upwell, which provides part of the setting for *The Nine Tailors*.

This mystery opens with Lord Peter Wimsey stranded in Fen country in an easterly snowstorm, after landing his car in a ditch coming over 'Frog's Bridge'. In the distance, the sound of church bells is heard, muffled by the snow. Lord Wimsey, even in these conditions, is not abandoned by his upper-class education and literary associations:

> 'Thank God!' said Wimsey. 'Where there is a church, there is civilization. We'll have to walk it. Never mind the suitcases; we

Dorothy L Sayers

The Nine Tailors finds the mystery writer perfectly at home in the fens.

Dorothy Sayers' early connections with Norfolk were consolidated through her work as a copywriter with the London advertising company Benson's (1922–31) where she was instrumental in the creation of culinary detective stories and the 'Mustard Club' as part of the campaign for Norfolk mustard with J & J Colman of Norwich.

can send somebody for them. Br'rh! It's cold. I bet that when Kingsley welcomed the wild northeaster he was sitting indoors by a good fire, eating muffins. I could do with a muffin myself. Next time I accept hospitality in the Fen-country, I'll take care it's at midsummer.

Thus Wimsey and his man-servant Bunter follow the signs to Fenchurch St Paul: 'There was no other direction; ahead, road and dyke marched on side by side into an eternity of winter.' When they reach the village, Wimsey finds himself not only dragged into a nine-hour-long session of change-ringing, but unwittingly becomes an agent in the violent death of a man by doing so.

Of her meticulous treatment of change-ringing, in a book which took her two years to write, Sayers was justly proud. Apparently, experienced bell-ringers were only able to find three tiny technical errors, even though she had never pulled a rope in her life! Her grasp of such a difficult craft, the 'rope-sight' she demonstrated, led to her being made Vice-President of the Campanological Society of Great Britain, of which she felt 'sinfully proud'.

The neatly constructed plot of *The Nine Tailors* includes a dramatic flood, based upon real events in 1713, and is certainly influenced by

St Peter and St Paul's Church – 'Reader! Why hast thou been spared? To what purpose hast thou been left until now?' – this inscription is not directed to readers of *The Nine Tailors*, but commemorates cholera victims who died here in 1832.

Norfolk bell-ringers *c.*1950 – D L Sayers displays admirable 'rope-sight' in *The Nine Tailors.*

Sayers' admiration of **John Meade Falkner**'s *The Nebuly Coat* (1903) – 'that remarkable book', as she termed it – which too displays an intimate knowledge of ecclesiastical architecture. Sayers also creates the 'Duke of Denver' as 'the owner of all this part of Norfolk from **Denver Sluice** to **King's Lynn***'.

Wimsey and Bunter are less than enthusiastic about the scenery here, noting the ugly little brick house at 'Van Leyden's Sluice' 'standing up like a pricked ear, between the two sides of the Sluice' and wishing that 'everything wasn't so rectangular in this part of the world'. Nevertheless, when a late spring arrives at Fenchurch St Paul, the waterlands reveal themselves in a different, and certainly more flattering, light:

> In its own limited, austere and almost grudging fashion, the Fen acknowledged the return of the sun. The floods withdrew from the pastures; the wheat lifted its pale green spears more sturdily from the black soil; the stiff thorns bordering dyke and grass verge budded to a softer outline; on the willows, the yellow catkins danced like little bell-rope sallies, and the silvery pussies plumped themselves for the children to carry to church on Palm Sunday; wherever the grim banks were hedge-sheltered, the shivering dog-violets huddled from the wind.

Lord Peter Wimsey's eccentric forbears and the Wimsey family seat in Norfolk ('Bredon Hall', near 'Duke's Denver') feature in *Busman's Honeymoon* (1937), an adaptation of her 1936 play and Sayers' last full-length crime novel. Here Sayers presents an ancestor of Lord Peter, the eccentric Lord Mortimer Wimsey, who, in the early nineteenth century 'conceived himself to be one of the fish netted by St Peter the Apostle', and lived the life of a hermit for many years in a hut on the marshes to the east of the Wash, 'wholly mute and eating nothing but shrimps and seaweed'.

It is to Bredon Hall that Lord Peter and his bride Harriet Vane embark towards the end of *Busman's Honeymoon*. Their drive takes them through **Downham Market*** and 'the original' **Denver**, and after a further drive eastwards ('Duke's Denver is about fifteen miles further on') effectively ends at the village of **Narborough**, where 'the fen lay behind them now and the country was growing more wooded'.

Two of Sayers' short stories also reference Norfolk: 'The Dragon's Head' takes place in the decayed stately home of 'Yelsall Manor', while 'The Cyprian Cat' mentions a rectory garden party in the wilds of Norfolk. Always a prolific writer, D L Sayers devoted her later life to translations and to radio and stage plays, with the Tour production of her play *The Zeal of Thy House* taking place in **Norwich*** in 1938.

West Acre

This village in the Nar Valley, whose Augustinian priory used to be larger than that of its more famous neighbour **Castle Acre**, is the birthplace of the writer and schoolteacher **Anthony C Wilson** (1916–86), creator of the enormously popular boy detectives Norman and Henry Bones. Wilson was born on his father's tenant farm and **Adrian Wright***, in 'Heroes of a Forgotten England', relates Wilson's early passion for the surrounding countryside and wildlife – and also for the wireless. Every night Anthony and his brother would walk the two miles to their aunt's house in the village to listen to the BBC's Children's Hour.

The Norman and Henry Bones detective stories Wilson wrote (initially for radio) while working as a teacher are mainly set around the fictitious, slumbering fenland hamlet called 'Sedgewick' near 'Lagdon', where dark rain clouds are 'sweeping low over the sombre fields, and the tops of the bulrushes swayed like metronomes above the bank of the river', measuring 'the music of the fens'.

Norman, at sixteen the elder of the two, is endowed with a sleuth's wisdom, a knowing smile to match, and a Sherlock Holmes-like authority over his fourteen-year-old cousin, the faithful Henry. Being called in when the adults and the police get stuck must surely be every boy's dream, and once the two of them have got hold of a mystery, they hold on 'like veritable leeches'. In *Norman and Henry Bones* (1959), our sleuths tackle the mysteries of the 'Railway Copse' poachers, the 'Deadly Nightshade' burglaries and the suspicious lodger in the Fen windmill with panache.

Anthony C Wilson

Pictured with typewriter and pet monkey, the writer sets his boy detectives to work with 'the music of the fens' in their ears.

Moving with his family to The White House in **Swaffham*** in the mid-fifties, Wilson expanded the Bones' exploits to include books that were subsequently translated into several languages. After retiring from teaching, Wilson returned to his childhood haunts, settling in a cottage on **East Walton Common**, two miles from Westacre. He took to drawing wild flowers, among other things, and died sitting at his sister's kitchen table in Swaffham, 'painting some pussy willow'.

Wiggenhall St Mary Magdalen

For the novelist and traveller **Lisa St Aubin de Terán** (1953–) fenland life here amidst the beet fields and flatlands of west Norfolk was to hold little appeal. Home was the splendid isolation of St Mary's Hall – an imposing, castellated presence, shrouded by trees on the outskirts of the village at the end of a 'winding blustery lane which seemed to lead nowhere'. Already her marriage to the poet **George MacBeth** (1932–92) was close to collapse, and their move here in 1983 was tinged with desperation.

The couple had expended considerable energy restoring the spacious old rectory in **Oby***, but after the 'traumatic' birth of their son

Lisa St Aubin de Terán

'Behind the crenellations I was growing out of touch with the world. When I looked through the thick windows across the dank black mud of the Fens, I just kept thinking I didn't want to be there.'

Off The Rails, 1989

St Mary's Hall – 'Our passion for pretty ruins consumed us,' writes Lisa St Aubin de Terán in *Off The Rails*, after her arrival here with her husband, George MacBeth, in 1983.

Alexander, the normally indefatigable St Aubin saw St Mary's Hall more as a burden than a challenge. Nor did the landscape here inspire her, their nearest neighbour being the 'squat tower and grotesque gargoyles' of Wiggenhall St Mary the Virgin church.

The itinerant and often incredible life that St Aubin had lived before arriving in Norfolk is detailed in her fascinating first volume of memoirs *Off The Rails* (1989), though her writings of Wiggenhall speak only of the 'bleak dark nothingness that is all the Fens can mirror to a sick mind'.

Nevertheless, St Aubin continued to write and her third novel *The Tiger* was published in 1984, following on from the success of her autobiographical fiction in *The Slow Train To Milan* (1983). The couple also continued to enjoy social gatherings in the splendid surroundings of their new home. **Malcolm Bradbury*** remembers the 'state of extraordinary creative disorder' of the house, which was 'regularly filled with large numbers of people' – with a bagpiper friend of George MacBeth's often present to regale their guests. But St Aubin could still feel 'the grey mould of the Fens settle on my mind' and after two years at Wiggenhall, she was more desperate than ever to reach her beloved Italy:

George MacBeth

'There had been a dream, and you had been in the dream, and we had been happy, and then there were only reminders, material things with echoes in them.'

Another Love Story, 1991

> For almost two years I had looked out across the bleak flatlands of the Fens, watching the bare treeless expanses of clay mud peppered only by scattered bungalows and the distant glint of the sugar factory chimney. It seemed ironic that I, who had once been the Queen of the Andes, with my endless miles of sugar-cane and the tallest chimney in the state, should have come to fester in the long shadow of a steel sugar-beet plant.

Lisa St Aubin de Terán, *Off The Rails*, 1989

St Aubin was not destined to 'fester' at St Mary's for much longer and her departure for the sun-drenched Umbrian landscape sounded the final death knell for her marriage to MacBeth. Sadly, her fondest memories of Wiggenhall will probably remain the train journeys from the nearby Magdalen Road Station, bound for 'another world' that was London.

George MacBeth remarried, although his creative and often chaotic life ended soon afterwards in 1992, the same year that *The Patient* was published. He is remembered in **Anthony Thwaite**'s* intensely moving tribute 'For George MacBeth': 'Last words are right: / You whispered them / That last intolerable night, / Darkness itself, deep / Gathering of choked phlegm – / 'How long will I sleep?"

CHAPTER TEN

Breckland

Rev. Francis Blomefield, Brian Cooper, George MacDonald Fraser,
Michael Home, Charles Kingsley, Mary Mann, Hilary Mantel,
Colin Middleton Murry, John Middleton Murry, Thomas Nashe,
Thomas Paine, Thomas Shadwell, Barbara Vine, Virginia Woolf

Blo' Norton

Virginia Woolf, 1902

The Bloomsbury icon found herself 'making out beautiful stories every step of the way' during her time at Blo' Norton Hall.

Admirers of **Virginia Woolf** (1882–1941) might be surprised to learn that Norfolk can lay claim to a significant connection with the Bloomsbury figure and feminist icon. During the month of August 1906, Virginia Stephen, as she was then, and her sister Vanessa rented Blo' Norton Hall, a moated Elizabethan manor on the Little Ouse: '300 years old, striped with oak bars inside, old staircases, ancestral vats, and portraits':

> We seem to be in the middle of what in geography is called an 'undulating plain' well cultivated but, apparently, almost deserted. The corn brims the fields; but no one is there to cut it; the churches hold up broad gray fingers all over the landscape, but no one, save perhaps the dead at their feet, attend to their commands; the windmills sail round & round, but no one trims their sails; it is very characteristic that the only sign of life in the land should be that produced by the wind of Heaven.

> Virginia Woolf, *A Passionate Apprentice – The Early Journals, 1897–1909*

The Modernist in Woolf rejects the overt charm and 'depths of age' of a house 'too remote & solitary and ancestral' for her liking. The sense of isolation for the twenty-four-year-old writer is palpable; being some seven miles from the railway at **Diss***, 'every mile seems to draw a thicker curtain than the last between you & the world ... no sound what ever reaches your ear; the very light seems to filter through deep layers'. But Woolf resists the inertia Blo' Norton seems to represent; walking for

Blo' Norton Hall, *c*.1930 – the month Virginia Woolf spent here in the summer of 1906 inspired 'The Journal of Mistress Joan Martyn'.

hours through this 'charming' and 'lovely old country', leaping ditches, wading rivers, falling into the mud where the 'fen plays you false at every step' – and always, 'making out beautiful stories every step of the way'.

Although she mentions the many 'difficulties of writing in this place', the old hall, awash with the deep blue of the summer sky, and its walls the colour of an 'apricot in the sun; with touches of red upon it', proved beneficial to her work. In four weeks she revised two short stories, 'Phyllis and Rosamond' and 'The mysterious Case of Miss V', while another short story, 'The Journal of Mistress Joan Martyn' was certainly inspired by her stay here.

In 'The Journal', medievalist Rosamond Merridew is researching into England's ancient land-tenure system. The story explores different concepts of history as Merridew's hunt for medieval documents results in her finding an old journal at 'Martyn Hall'. This is Joan Martyn's diary; a document of the late fifteenth century which, in contrast to the **Paston*** letters, details a year in the life of an obscure woman during the Wars of the Roses.

Joan Martyn's everyday experience, lacking the adventure and drama of 'real' (i.e. male) history, is dismissed both by herself and by her twentieth-century descendant, John. 'If I ever write again, it shall not be of Norfolk and myself, but of Knights and Ladies and of adventures in strange lands', says Mistress Martyn, enthralled by the romances of an anonymous singer who spends one night at Martyn Hall. Throughout 'The Journal', Woolf questions assumptions about the roles women have played in English history and the way 'history' itself is recorded.

Although every day appears much like the next at Blo' Norton, Woolf finds it 'not in the least dull' as she scrambles beneath the barbed wire guarding the tributaries of the Little Ouse or lies on the Norfolk turf staring up at the huge skies above her. With her usual wit and

Opposite: A glimpse of the 'lovely old country' of Breckland that prompted Virginia Woolf to describe Norfolk as 'one of the most beautiful of counties'

perception, Woolf also observes that 'though a walk in the fen has a singular charm, it is not to be undertaken as a way of getting to places'.

Two miles west of the Hall, she comes across the twin sources of the Little Ouse and the Waveney, a location that plays an important part in **Barbara Vine**'s* 1996 novel *The Brimstone Wedding*. Woolf also journeys to **Thetford*** and to nearby **Kenninghall** cemetery, following in the footsteps of nineteenth-century nature writer and novelist **Richard Jefferies**, and is intrigued by the 'surface oddity' of the stumbling epitaphs on the headstones. In her diary entry for that day, Woolf ponders the 'paradox' of Norfolk, and is half surprised to find her urban eye discern it as 'one of the most beautiful of counties' – an observation echoed by many writers since.

In her *Early Journals*, Virginia Woolf describes Norfolk as a 'strange, grey green, undulating, dreaming, philosophising & remembering land ... so soft, so melancholy, so wild & yet willing to be gentle: like some noble untamed woman conscious that she has no beauty to vaunt'.

The influential antiquary and author of the unfinished *Essay towards a Topographical History of the County of Norfolk*, **Reverend Francis Blomefield** (1705–52), is buried in the chancel of the thirteenth-century church of nearby **Fersfield**. Probably born in the hall next to the church, Blomefield was rector of Fersfield for twenty-three years and set up his own printing press, which was tragically destroyed by fire together with the first edition of his work. Having caught smallpox, he refused inoculation, believing it 'wrong to attempt to avoid evils sent by his Creator' and died in debt, 'Snatched away in the midst of his Labors', in 1752.

East Harling

The novels of **George MacDonald Fraser** (1925–), creator of 'The Flashman Papers', are renowned for their historical detail and parodying of other works: *Mr American* (1980) is skilfully set in the leafy backwaters of early twentieth-century Breckland. This ripping yarn is the tale of Mark J Franklin, who in 1909 leaves the silver mines of Nevada for the place from whence his ancestors, the Franklins of 'Castle Lancing', emigrated to America back in 1642.

The exact location of Castle Lancing is never disclosed, but this drowsy village is situated a short distance from **Harling Road Station**, where Mark Franklin – referred to throughout as 'Mr' Franklin – steps off the train one beautiful autumn day:

George MacDonald Fraser

His wartime experiences here inspire the setting of his 'Norfolk' novel, *Mr American*.

... if Mr Franklin was now disposed to haste, he soon discovered that Norfolk was not. The station was a tiny one, and it took half an hour to summon an ancient gig, driven by an urchin of perhaps nine years, and drawn by a horse possibly twice as old. Mr Franklin gave the lad his destination, and resigned himself to patience as they creaked off at a slow walk.

'Marching over most of the county, I conceived a great affection for [Norfolk] and its people – I remember especially ... the friendliness of the folk, particularly in the remote areas where they spoke (and possibly still do) with the soft drawl that is so plainly the parent of the American accent.'

George MacDonald Fraser, 1998

Travelling like this, it takes them two hours to reach 'Cassel Lancin' village, 'nestled among woods in the hazy afternoon' and equipped with 'a scatter of cottages round a little triangular green; a dusty street winding in front of a small inn; a pond, mud-fringed, a pump and a horse-trough; on the farther side, a lych-gate and the square tower of a Norman church rising among elms and yews.'

Mr Franklin, while not exactly in hiding, is nevertheless keen to settle into a quiet existence in his newly acquired property, Castle Lancing Manor. Understandably, Edwardian Norfolk is somewhat suspicious of this charming and handsome 'furriner'. As Franklin enters the gloom of his local tavern for a pint and some technical assistance with the manor's water supply, the 'Apple Tree' is 'stricken to silence' until the newcomer makes a totally unheard-of offer – a free round of drinks.

After much muttering and confusion, everything gets sorted out and in no time at all, Mr Franklin's directness, heart of gold and heroic actions earn him the respect of his fellow villagers and transform him into the respected 'Yankee Squire'. Assisted by the elucidations of eccentric local historian Geoffrey Thornhill, Franklin feels that he has come home at last. On Castle Lancing churchyard this rough diamond, 'the miner, the ranchhand, the wanderer', realises that this Norfolk village is

> ... old, and whether he stayed or whether he went away, it would remain, in his mind, and there would remain, too, the sense of belonging to it – where did he belong, if not here? ... within a few yards of him, under the grass, there were the bones of people who, if they could have come back to life, and could have known all that had happened in three hundred years, would have looked at him and thought, why, that is the son of Luke, who was the son of John, who was the child of Matthew's people who went to the New World in the time of the Great Rebellion, the King's War ... Johannes Franklinus had walked down this same road where he was walking now, with Thornhill prattling at his elbow.

Fraser's plot borrows from both English and American literary legend and includes the classic scene where, during a drive to 'West Walsham', a fox hunted by local aristocrats jumps into Franklin's picnic basket. In the ensuing confrontation with the hunting pack, the King of England himself comes along to lend a helping hand. The subsequent invitation up to **Sandringham** for Christmas has got to be one of the highlights of Mr Franklin's spell in Norfolk, as he helps a slightly deaf Queen Alexandra to complete a jigsaw and is thrown in at the deep end as the bridge partner of a droning Edward VII.

It is at this stage of his pacy historical romance that Fraser manages to introduce his now ageing 'Flashman' character. General Harry Paget Flashman, Fraser's fictional development of the school bully featuring in **Thomas Hughes**' influential novel *Tom Brown's School Days* (1857),

is by now nearing ninety and still behaving badly with admirable aplomb, chasing Sandringham chambermaids and irreverently slandering his royal host.

Sunset over the pines of East Harling

As for Franklin, he soon finds himself married to the charming and attractive socialite Peggy Clayton of 'Oxton Hall'. However, the antics of her social circle hold little appeal for Franklin, who prefers instead to focus on the rural pleasures of his manor and his plans for converting the impoverished Oxton Hall into a stud.

Norfolk, where everyone knows their place in the squirarchy, represents continuity and serenity; free from the triteness of Peggy's frantic social life and the upheavals of the suffragette movement and ragtime in faraway London. But, as a long-presumed-dead acquaintance from his mining days suddenly turns up in Norfolk, the shadowy past catches up with the roaming spirit of Mr Franklin. For the space of one night and one shoot-out, slumbering Castle Lancing is transformed into the genuine American Wild West. Riddled with suspense and humour, *Mr American* is a great read – and features one of the most unlikely literary characters ever to have haunted the lanes of Breckland.

Fraser discovered 'Oxton Hall' by accident during his Second World War cross-country exercises in Norfolk: 'I've no idea where it is, but I spent a night in a ditch under one of its hedges, and in the morning encountered a splendid old aristocrat who was plainly the owner ... he became Sir Charles Clayton, and his stately home became Oxton.'

Great Hockham

For prolific writer **Michael Home** (1885–19??), the beauty of Breckland was 'something unique and curiously intimate'. Born on Christmas Day 1885 in a village he describes as standing 'with its shoulders humped, as it were, into and against the oncoming bracken', Home went on to write military adventures and over fifty detective novels under his real name **Christopher Bush**. But it is through his memoirs and novels on Norfolk life that Home conveys his deep attachment to the land and the community life it represents.

In Autumn Fields (1944), Michael Home notes that whereas Norfolk 'has always been a lonely and somewhat neglected corner of England,' Breckland remains, 'even to the rest of the county's inhabitants, an unknown part of it.'

Flints 'growing' in the fields of Breckland's 'arid land' – with a rainfall of less than twenty-five inches per year this is the driest part of the British Isles.

Home was adopted as an infant by his aunt and taken to live in London, but as an eight-year-old Michael returns to Norfolk with his father, wondering at the 'vast region of heather and waving bracken interspersed with woods, and in the distances the faint blue of low hills'. As the bracken brushes against the wheels of the cart he travels in with his father, Michael remarks upon the 'lovely ferns'. 'They're not ferns', laughs his father. 'Brakes. That's what we call them. Brakes.'

Throughout his Norfolk novels and memoirs, Home describes the Breckland landscape in loving detail; oak, pine, spruce and fir woods, the 'arid land' of the brecks, 'dry, sandy and stony', and the bracken-covered heaths with their richly coloured moss pools, low-lying heather and elegant silver birches. Although the land 'all lies strangely open to air and sky', life here in this closed corner of Edwardian Norfolk is linked to centuries-old village customs, to the fortunes of the local squire, and, inextricably, to the harvest drawn from the 'light and flint-strewn' land:

> Pick up a handful of our soil in dry weather and it would slip through your fingers before you could examine it. After rain the flints would be clean and visible which was doubtless why men would cling to the old belief that stones actually grew. When a high wind rose on a cultivated breck the air would be thick with the fine soil and when it subsided the stones would again lie clear.

The religious tensions between the largely Methodist labourers and the High Church squire are explored in Home's early novels: *God and the*

Osbert Lancaster* (1908–1986), writing at the same time as Michael Home in *All Done From Memory* (1953), describes Breckland rather unfavourably as 'that scruffy, sandy waste which runs like some horrid birthmark across the homely face of East Anglia'.

Rabbit (1934) follows the fortunes of local lad 'Harry Francis' who, like Home, wins a scholarship to the local grammar school, while *In This Valley* (1934) looks at religious prejudice and social inequality within a small farming community.

In Home's day many people still lived in or on the edge of poverty, inhabiting the 'pitifully small', low-ceilinged cottages with primitive sanitation that had 'changed little since **Cobbett**'s time'. Although discipline is harsh for the youth of the village – Home's 'Risin' Generation' – life on the land is still full of simple pleasures; rabbiting day and night, hunting for wild-fowl eggs, gathering chestnuts, carving whistles from sycamore or hazel, bathing or wading in the mud-lined farm pools.

In his evocative and unsentimental volumes of reminiscences, *Autumn Fields* (1944) and *Spring Sowing* (1946) – collected and re-issued in a later work *Winter Harvest* (1967) – Home relates numerous anecdotes of village life and its colourful characters; tales of poaching and gamekeeping, harvesting, village cricket matches and of walking the ancient Peddar's Way. He fondly remembers the village roads, lined with thick hedgerows and arched over into 'great avenues' by the rich foliage of oaks and elms. But as he observes in *Spring Sowing*:

Rabbiting at Hockham, 1906

Some of Michael Home's 'Risin' Generation' display their wares.

Henry Howard, Earl of Surrey

As a poet he pioneered the 'English' sonnet before being executed for plotting against the throne.

'Heathley [Great Hockham] was a farming village with no crafts or industries. It lived or died by the land.'

In his later years, Home sees that the signs of decay, the 'last hectic flush on the face of a consumptive' as he describes it, are already here. The 'once shadowy lanes' have been denuded of their oaks and the 'music of the forge' has long since fallen silent. The outlying fields, once thick with haystacks, are being 'devoured by the onward surge of bracken and the rabbit', while the 'beauty of new-turned earth' and the 'poignant melancholy of an autumn stubble' have been replaced by the 'impersonal rigidity' of the vast Forestry Commission plantations – 'unreal and unnatural'. Few visitors today would be aware of how much Breckland has altered over the past century, but through the pages of his books, Michael Home preserves not only lost landscapes but the lost communities that depended upon them.

Kenninghall Place, a farm some two miles past St Mary's Church, **Kenninghall**, is the remaining wing of the palace built by Thomas Howard, third Duke of Norfolk, and the birthplace of his son, the poet and soldier **Henry Howard, Earl of Surrey** (?1517–47). Henry Howard was the first to use the 'English' sonnet form with its 'heroic couplet' (later used by **Shakespeare***) and was innovative in his use of blank verse in his translation of two books of the *Aeneid*. His poems are collected in *Tottel's Miscellany* (1557) but his writing career was cut short ten years before that, when he was executed on a charge of treasonably quartering the royal arms.

Larling

John Middleton Murry

His stormy marriage turned a move to the country into the 'hell of Larling'.

John Middleton Murry (1889–1957) is remembered as an influential and highly respected writer, critic and intellectual, and also for his marriage to short-story writer **Katherine Mansfield** (1888–1923). Murry never truly recovered from her death from tuberculosis, and her spirit was to haunt him for the rest of his life – more so when his second wife, Violet le Maistre, died from the same disease at an even younger age. To add to this trying time, Violet's death came soon after that of **D H Lawrence** (1885–1930), with whom Murry had experienced an intense though often difficult friendship.

In his grief, Murry turned to his housekeeper, Elizabeth 'Betty' Cockbayne, a farmer's daughter. They were anything but well-suited and with Betty's relatives warning of her unpredictable and fierce temper, Murry's horrified friends advised strongly against the match. Nevertheless, the marriage went ahead, and the stormy years that followed their move to Norfolk were characterised by furious arguments and almost constant strife.

The Old Rectory at Larling – a spacious and 'wholly beautiful' home, it held powerful and contrasting emotions for the members of the Middleton Murry family.

In spite of Betty's frequent and often violent rages, Murry continued to write, producing a controversial study of Lawrence in *Son of Woman* (1931), a biography of *William Blake* (1933) and his own autobiography *Between Two Worlds* (1935). Eventually, the travesty of his marriage to Betty became all too apparent to Murry, and he left both her and Larling in October 1941, returning only once, in 1950, shortly before the Old Rectory was sold.

The walled garden, potting sheds and stables, sweeping lawns, wide paddocks and beech plantations of Larling should have been a paradise for children. But in *Beloved Quixote* (1986), **Katherine Middleton Murry** (1925–), the first child of John and Violet, writes largely of the traumas of a childhood spent under Betty's tyrannical reign. While the countryside and nature surrounding the 'terrible' rectory are tranquil and beautiful, fear is a constant companion, and it is the 'perpetual storm, perpetually oncoming, perpetually menacing' that she dreads most.

Memories of Larling are less traumatic for '**Colin**' **John Middleton Murry*** (1926–) who experienced a genuine sense of belonging here. 'All my deepest roots were there ... in the sheer familiar beauty of the house set amidst its golden Norfolk landscape', he writes in *Shadows on the Grass* (1977), the second volume of his moving autobiographical account, following *One Hand Clapping* (1975).

Moving to the Old Rectory when he was just five years old, Colin immediately felt at home, 'as if the house and garden were opening invisible arms and enfolding me'. More striking than the towering trees and views across the meadows to the winding River Thet was the abundance of unfamiliar smells assailing young Colin's nose:

Colin Middleton Murry

As a child he thrived on the 'sheer familiar beauty' of Larling.

They broke over me like waves. Fresh distemper and moist, scrubbed bricks in echoing sculleries and dairies; the intoxicating perfume of clove carnations in the walled garden; fizzing acid in the glass accumulator cells in the battery house; last year's rotting conker leaves drifted in the shrubberies; musty, sparrow-riddled reed thatch on the ancient summer-house; piles of spiralled pinewood shavings where the carpenter had been constructing dozens of new bookshelves. And everywhere, pervading every corner of the house, the delicious fragrance of freshly applied linseed-oil paint. So firmly did these scents imprint themselves upon my five year old memory that I have only to catch a whiff of one of them today and I am at once transported back in time to that first dreamlike encounter.

Colin Middleton Murry, *One Hand Clapping*, 1975

Colin remained more capable than most of steering clear of Betty's 'awe-inspiring' and 'almost supernatural' fits of temper and although her 'truly elemental fury' kept his schoolfriends away – loneliness was never really a problem for Colin: 'beneath those limitless Norfolk skies, I needed no one'.

His Norfolk roots provide the inspiration for several of Colin Middleton Murry's works – including *The Golden Valley* (1958), a semi-autobiographical story of adolescent love set in Larling – while many more books were to follow under the pen name of **Richard Cowper**. But nothing displays the strength of his attachment to Larling and the Old Rectory better than the flood of emotions which threaten to overwhelm him when, in September 1949, Colin visits here for one last time:

I felt like a ghost as I wandered through the empty rooms furnishing them all from memory. Mellow afternoon sunlight streamed through the uncurtained windows and splashed upon the bare board floors ... Bluebottles buzzed against the window-panes, and upstairs, in what had been my own bedroom, a tortoise-shell butterfly fluttered. I opened the window and let it out. When I closed the sash again the silence was almost palpable ... I knew every corner of this house and garden, had made them so much a part of myself that even today if I needed to visualise a landscape or even a mere room it is these that claim me first, importuning me, demanding me their rights. It is as though I have first to pass through them and acknowledge them, before I can go beyond. They belong to me as I to them. And when my time comes I shall surely return to haunt them.

Colin Middleton Murry, *Shadows on the Grass*, 1977

Opposite: South Lopham Fen, close to the source of the Waveney and the Little Ouse

'The fen has big trees in it but mostly it's like a forest of bushes, the water not far below the surface.'

(Ruth Rendell, *The Brimstone Wedding*, 1996)

South Lopham

Ruth Rendell

She draws a veil of mystery 'across the meadows and the fen' in *The Brimstone Wedding*.

The source of both the Little Ouse and the Waveney rivers lies at **Lopham Gate**, just below the village of South Lopham. The exact site of the rising is not really visible, but from here the Ouse continues west via **Thetford*** towards **King's Lynn***, while the Waveney wanders eastwards, tracking the ancient Angles Way and marking the Norfolk/ Suffolk border all the way up to the coast. In fact, this is the only place you can cross into Norfolk from Suffolk without bridging a river.

On the Norfolk side of the Waveney lie a group of boggy fens surrounded by wide, flat fields and the blue waters of reed-rimmed meres. It is into the 'great empty spaces' of this landscape that **Ruth Rendell*** (1930–), writing as **Barbara Vine***, places the characters of her compelling mystery *The Brimstone Wedding* (1996). Set largely in 'Middleton Hall', a residential home for the elderly, the drama parallels the past and present love affairs of two women: Stella Newland, a wealthy patient at the home who is dying, and Genevieve ('Jenny'), her nurse.

The lives of the women are inextricably linked by past events and by the mysterious disappearance of Stella's actress friend Gilda Brent. From the upstairs lounge window of Middleton Hall, just visible 'across the meadows and the fen', stands the key to the past – in the form of the bricks and mortar of Stella's red-roofed cottage. Here, when 'Breckland was still a wild, strange place and the fens lonely and silent', she used to meet with her lover, until tragedy occurred. Now, the cottage offers similar opportunities and risks for Jenny – a hiding place for her and the married man she loves.

Always keeping the reader guessing, the tale winds its way through the back roads, ploughed fields and villages ('Thelmarsh', 'Breckenhall' and 'Tivetshall St Michael') of Rendell's fictional but entirely believable Norfolk landscape. And the countryside here, where 'you're a prisoner without a car', is not always a scene of pastoral bliss:

> People talk about the country as if it's always beautiful. The ones who don't live in it, that is. There's something awful about an East Anglian village on a Sunday afternoon in winter, something grim. The surrounding land is grey and shrouded in mist. The village street is long and straight, the houses are low and the trees are low while the sky is a huge lid, dull and dimpled like pewter.

Ruth Rendell started out in journalism before turning her hand to fiction, and it was her first crime novel, *From Doon with Death* (1964), that introduced Detective Inspector Wexford to the literary world. Since the 1980s, Rendell – who prefers to avoid the label 'Queen of Crime' – has also written more mainstream fiction as Barbara Vine, adding to her reputation as one of Britain's leading authors.

In *The Brimstone Wedding*, the future of Norfolk born-and-bred Jenny ('I've lived at Stoke Tharby all my life') is far less certain. Jenny's marriage is a stale and meaningless mess and through her character Rendell cleverly presents opposing elements of rural life – the stifling atmosphere of small village seclusion and the natural beauty of the murmuring landscape:

> It was a dull, warm evening. The sun had quite gone. I drove the car a little way up the thistly path to get off the road. It's very silent around here when all the birds have gone to roost and even the cackling of geese has stopped. If you know our countryside you'll understand how still it can be in the evenings, how soft and hushed, almost as if it were listening for something. The fen has big trees in it but mostly it's like a forest of bushes, the water not far below the surface, and all the reeds and rushes, the hazel and the dogwood, moving very faintly, whispering and shuffling. When all else is quiet you can still hear the trickle of water.

Through her detailed and carefully structured mystery, Rendell successfully captures the essence of Norfolk; its lifestyle, pace and scenery. And even as Stella unburdens her secret on to the cassette tapes that she bequeaths to Jenny ('something that no one knows but me and which should be known'), the reader is kept guessing to the last. Finally, as Jenny wanders through the silence of the fen behind her house, spotting a rare swallowtail butterfly, she places the tapes into her Walkman. Here, 'among the willows and the alders and the meadow-sweet', the tragic and awful past meets the emotional turmoil of the present as all the strands of the story are pulled neatly together.

Shropham

On 20 May 1929, the *Eastern Daily Press* carried a small obituary to a 'Norfolk novelist ... a lady whose fame has travelled far beyond her native county'. The funeral took place here in Shropham, two days later, and the body of **Mary Mann** (1848–1929) was lain beside that of her husband in the village graveyard.

Mary Mann

Her stories paint an honest and uncompromising picture of rural hardship.

Born in **Norwich*** as Mary Rackham, a merchant's daughter, Mary Mann lived all of her life in Norfolk. After her marriage to Fairman J Mann in 1871, she lived with him first at Church Farm (situated just to the east of St Peter's Church), before the couple relocated to Shropham Manor where several generations of the Mann family had lived. The move from a thriving city to an isolated village already afflicted by agricultural recession cannot have been easy for the lively and sociable writer. Yet, stirred by the lives of those around her, and by the rural hardship she witnessed first-hand, Mary Mann produced a string of fine novels, starting with *The Parish of Hilby* (1883).

Mary Mann's writing is characterised by its use of local dialect and its unflinching portrayal of the harshness of country life. Her work is perhaps best represented by *The Fields of Dulditch* (1902), a marvellous

Shropham Manor – where
Mary Mann combined
farming with writing for
many years.

collection of acutely observed short stories charting the cruellest of life's
injustices with a strong, if bleak, humour.

In 'A Dulditch Angel' she describes life for Angel, a widower
struggling to cope with the recent loss of his dearest wife Mary
('Meery'). To add to his troubles, Angel is persuaded by a local woman
that the strange noises which disturb his sleep are actually caused
by the restless spirit of his dead wife. Leaving his window open each
night to enable 'Meery's' spirit to move freely, poor Angel lies in a
freezing draught, catches a severe chill and dies. The cause of the
nightly fluttering is then revealed to have been a bat, though the local
woman remains adamant: 'Bat or no bat, 'twere Meery', she declares,
adding ''twere old Meery, safe enough. And I jemmed my foot on 'er,
thank the Lord!'

Mann's work employs many Norfolk locales, but much of her best
writing uses her close acquaintance with village life at Shropham.
Although she entered community life to the full (teaching at the local
school, visiting labourers' homes) Mary Mann was never able to shake
off her urban origins, and, as an 'outsider' herself, empathises strongly
with the solitary and often lonely characters within her writing. Mann
also uses her stories to relate the often brutal conditions faced by women
and children in the shadow of the agricultural depression. In 'Wolf
Charlie', again from *The Fields of Dulditch*, 'Wolf' is an impoverished
labourer who takes on an abandoned wife with a wooden leg and five
children. Working one day in the fields, Wolf spies the woman's husband
passing by in a donkey-cart:

'I ha' got yar wife an child'un', the Wolf shouted aloud to him. The driver gazed for a moment at his wretched-looking rival, then turning back to his donkey, belaboured it with a heavy stroke across its ribs.

'I don't keer whu th' devil ha' got 'em so long as I ha'nt', he called out. And so, master of the situation, drove off.

Admired as an 'East Anglian' novelist, Mary Mann deals skilfully with universal themes. *A Lost Estate* (1889) is a complex tale of heady and dangerous passions, *The Patten Experiment* (1899) has an amusing 'trading places' plot as a clergyman attempts to experience the life of an agricultural labourer, while in *Rose at Honeypot* (1906), Mann tells the tale of a young naval officer's wife meeting a handsome young gamekeeper. No wonder **D H Lawrence** (writing to **Katherine Mansfield** in 1919) mentions reading and enjoying Mann's work.

After the death of her husband in 1913, Mary Mann moved away from the village, first to **Winterton*** and later to **Sheringham***, but, as the papers at the time of her death reveal, she remained 'held in high esteem by the older residents in Shropham and the adjacent parishes, many of whom assembled to pay their last respects'. Recently, her work seems to have enjoyed a deserved revival – a new edition of Mann's stories was published as *Tales of Victorian Norfolk* in 1992, and her tale 'Little Brother' (described as a 'grim little Norfolk tale of rural poverty ... spiky with morals and the inadequacy of morals') is included within *The Oxford Book of English Short Stories* (1998), edited by **A S Byatt**.

The author **Edward FitzGerald*** (1809–83) died a few miles north of here at **Merton** after being taken ill during a visit to his friend George Crabbe (grandson of the poet of the same name). The Old Rectory here was often visited by 'Old Fitz' while Crabbe was incumbent.

Swaffham

According to crime writer **Brian Cooper** (1919–) this historical market town was 'one of the social centres of England' in Regency times. In the market place the town sign displays the famous legend of 'The Tinker of Swaffham who did by a dream find a great treasure' and the fifteenth-century church of St Peter and St Paul contains a display of ancient books including *The Black Book of Swaffham* – an inventory of church rents, donations and possessions for the period 1435–74.

No doubt this would all be familiar territory to Cooper – a retired Head of History who uses the Breckland area as the setting for *The Travelling Dead* (1997), featuring his double-act of Detective Chief Inspector Mike Tench and his mentor, retired Chief Inspector John Lubbock. 'Most of my plots begin with seeing a place that intrigues me,

Brian Cooper

'... the perception that the Breckland was a unique part of Norfolk ... led me to weave a story around the old flint industry.'

The 'Butter Cross' at
Swaffham – with the Goddess
of Plenty on top. The
Assembly Rooms (rear left)
are commandeered by
Detective Chief Inspector
Mike Tench in Brian Cooper's
The Travelling Dead.

and linking it with either a legend or historical fact', says Cooper, whose
last six novels are all set in Norfolk. He first visited the county a quarter
of a century ago, for a short holiday break at **Weybourne** and now
returns every year to wander from village to village, staying mainly on
the north coast.

Cooper's Norfolk novels all have their genesis in local lore: the legend
of **Bylaugh Hall** yielded *The Cross of San Vicente* (1991), introducing
the Lubbock/Tench partnership, Norfolk windmills are the main
inspiration for *The Singing Stones* (1993), while **Salle** and **Cawston***
merge into 'Salleston' in *Covenant with Death* (1994). The latter is a
mystery inspired 'by the legendary theft of the parapet and pinnacles
of Cawston church tower'. Cooper's seventh Norfolk novel, *The
Blacknock Woman* (1998), is 'based on the legend of the cockle woman

who was trapped by the tide and the fog and drowned on the mud flat known as Blacknock'.

In *The Travelling Dead*, it is autumn 1950. Petrol rationing has only just been abolished, and three-wheeler cars cruise the coast road. An attractive young woman is found dead in the bracken of 'Red Lodge Wood', two miles south of Swaffham. Another death soon follows and Detective Chief Inspector Mike Tench quickly establishes his investigation centre in the Assembly Rooms in the centre of Swaffham.

Cooper's whodunit has a classic set-up – a grumpy pathologist, a superior asking for daily updates, a smelly but harmless vagrant – combined with local peculiarities such as the flint knappers who utilise similar techniques to their ancient counterparts in the 'chipping fields' of **Grimes Graves***. In addition, *The Travelling Dead* is littered with as many Norfolk locations as it is bodies and employs a uniquely local murder weapon.

Retired Chief Inspector John Lubbock drags himself away from his hobby of recording each and every one of the county's many windmills to lend a hand, and provides the vital clue in the solving of this mystery. As Cooper generously ladles out motives and opportunities, garnished with an ingenious double-bluff, Lubbock's knowledge of 'the sticks' gives the locals the edge over the 'townies' of Tench's Norwich-based force.

Cooper captures the spirit of the fifties, a time when Breckland was far more isolated than it is now. The inhabitants of 'Handiford' don't bother reading the papers and have no idea that a murder has been committed only eight miles up the road. Finding a witness, 'someone in this God-forsaken place who wasn't exactly moribund', proves difficult. Part of the problem, according to the Handiford publican, is that there are 'more trees ner folk aroun' these parts o' Norfolk. Trees an' rabbits, an' tha's about it'. Worse still, according to Lubbock, the whole of Norfolk is 'a topographical graveyard':

> ... a potential charnel house, ... a dumping ground for bodies. What better place for a murderer to rid himself of his victim? Drive out at night, who's to see you? Who's to hear? Strangle a girl and there are so many lonely places to hide the body it may never be found. Some we find, some we don't. There must be literally hundreds littering the county, hidden under peat or leaves or bracken, weighted down and dropped into fenland or marsh.

After a final dramatic showdown on the disused airfield of 'Tottingley', there is a champagne get-together in Lubbock's black-tarred, white-capped working mill 'on the crest of Kettle Hill between **Morston*** and **Blakeney***' which features in every Tench/Lubbock story. And at least one of Cooper's list of suspects is mightily relieved – the Head of History at a local school!

'Bowed arthritic pines', standing like 'witches at a christening' on the outskirts of Swaffham.

There are lessons to be learned from the past for Ralph Eldred, one of the protagonists of *A Change of Climate* (1994), a truly 'Norfolk' novel by **Hilary Mantel** (1952–). Eldred hails from Swaffham, in a landscape where an 'artefact you drop tonight may be lost by morning, but the plough turns up treasure trove', where 'man's work seems ephemeral, his influence transitory.'

Ralph comes home to the Brecklands after the Second World War to find evidence of the recent military 'occupation' everywhere – 'fences broken, orchards cut down, avenues of trees mutilated'. But he also finds a herald from Breckland's much more distant past – a flint arrow-head, an 'elfshot'. Some years later, when Ralph and his family return from Africa, man's influence seems less 'transitory' and the changes wrought on the landscape by the military far more permanent. Bungalows have also mushroomed in the villages empty at the time Ralph went away, and the power of ancient Breckland is in danger of being usurped:

> Between settlements, there are still tracts of heather and furze, and black pine plantations: barren, monotonous, funereal, like the contents of an East European nightmare. But the bowed arthritic pines that line the roads creep to the edges of the small towns, intruding themselves among the DIY merchants and filling stations and furniture warehouses; they gather round the new housing estates, like witches at a christening.

Hilary Mantel

She explores every inch of Breckland, the 'county's heart', in *A Change of Climate*.

By the summer of 1980 Ralph, a charitable trust worker, and his wife Anna, have reached middle age. Avoiding the demons of the past – traumatic events from the very different 'climate' of Southern Africa decades earlier – has made life liveable for them. But the death of a close relative marks a turning point for the Eldreds. And as their children move away from home, the very fabric of Ralph and Anna's lives starts to unravel, with issues of loss, loyalty and the pent-up memories of an act of gratuitous barbarity demanding confrontation.

The 'Red House', where the Eldreds live is 'a farmhouse that had lost its farm', situated somewhere east of Swaffham, but it has never really succeeded as a family home. Partially, this is due to the overspill of Ralph's social work but more so, it is the Eldreds' discomfort of living with their terrible burden, mirrored by the landscape, by the very soil their house is built on, here 'at the county's heart' among 'the great wheat fields ... denatured, over-fertile, factory fields'. Even the attempts of their son Julian to farm their half-acre of ground appear 'to be an imposition on the natural state of things, as if it were the bicycle sheds that were the work of nature, and the potatoes the work of man'.

In *A Change of Climate*, Hilary Mantel scatters Norfolk references like flints in the Breckland soil; taking tea in **Holt***, shopping in **East Dereham***, chance meetings in **North Walsham**, prayers at the **Walsingham*** Shrine. Thus the tranquillity of the county serves more as a backdrop to Mantel's neatly executed character development, and for her study of how an act of evil can continue to torment a truly good family. As Ralph's carefully constructed concept of world order – and of his place within it – starts to fall apart, there is no holding back the troubled tide of the past. In his dreams, Ralph is transported back to his Swaffham childhood:

> This is the town, the date, the place, to which his dreams return him: Ralph walks on cobblestones, his wrist manacled in his grandfather's hand, his eyes turning upwards to scan the column of his grandfather's body. Ralph is three years old ... This is Ralph's first memory: the cobbles, the deep moaning of the wind, the thick cloth of his grandfather's overcoat sawing against his cheek.

As this moving and deeply psychological story approaches its climax, it becomes clear that before the Eldred's transition into today's 'climate' can be successfully completed, a remembrance of the past is required, and another young life must be acknowledged.

'The house itself was built of red brick, and stood side-on to the road. It had a tiled roof, steeply pitched; in season, the crop-spraying plane buzzed its chimney-stacks and complicated arrangements of television aerials. There were a number of small windows under the eaves, and these gave the house a restless look: as if it would just as soon wander across the land and put down its foundations in a different field.'

Hilary Mantel, *A Change of Climate*, 1994.

Thetford

Thetford, the eighth-century settlement of 'Theodford' (The People's Ford), may once have been able to lay claim to the title of 'City in the East', but by the time the writer and political reformer **Thomas Paine** (1737–1809) was born, the fortunes of the town had declined considerably. From his home in White Hart Street (standing on or close to the grounds of today's Thomas Paine Hotel) Paine was able to walk the short distance to the Free Grammar School. Situated just over the bridge across the Little Ouse and dating from 1566, this is one of the oldest schools in England (though no longer free) and

To where of old rich abbeys smil'd
In all the pomp of Gothic taste
By fond tradition proudly styl'd
The mighty 'City in the East'

Robert Bloomfield, from 'Barnham Water', 1890

Thomas Paine

His fiery political writings were preceded by this simple epitaph for his pet crow, penned as an eight-year-old boy:

Here lies the body of
John Crow
Who once was high but
now is low;
Ye brother Crows take
warning all,
For as you rise, so must
you fall.

numbers **Colin Middleton Murry*** and local historians **Francis Blomefield*** and **Tom Martin** among its past pupils.

The family home stood within clear view of Gallows Hill – a low, windswept chalk hill known locally as the Wilderness. Justice was harsh and arbitrary, especially for the poor, and capital offences were ever increasing. The annual ritual, each spring, of condemned prisoners being led up the hill to be hanged before the gathering crowds must have made a lasting impression on the young Thomas Paine.

Paine's father was a skilled staymaker (the thin strips of bone or steel used to stiffen corsets – once a standard feature of female dress) and at the age of thirteen Thomas left school to be apprenticed into his father's trade. Three years later Paine's yearning for adventure led him to contemplate a 'cruise against the French' and, by his own admission 'heated with false heroism', Paine headed for the Thames docks and an ominously named privateer called the Terrible under Captain Death. Fortunately, Paine's father persuaded him to abandon his enterprise, and as Paine turned his back on the ship, the Terrible went on to suffer a bloody defeat that left it 'much shattered' and most of its crew dead or dying.

Paine still set sail – on another privateer – but returned to work as a staymaker before undertaking a new, and potentially dangerous career as an exciseman. Smuggling in Britain was both widespread and largely accepted as a career of its own at this time; **Parson Woodforde*** writes freely in 1777 of receiving tea from 'Andrewes the Smuggler'.

Already writing poetry and extending his learning, Paine was acutely aware of the social injustices and political inequalities around him. Thetford was then a classic 'Rotten Borough' with a population of some two thousand, yet, through the influence of the Dukes of Grafton, it still had two Members of Parliament – the same as the entire county of Yorkshire! Paine later wrote: 'Society is produced by our wants and

The Free Grammar School, 1821 – still in use today, though no longer free, the school counts Thomas Paine and Colin Middleton Murry amongst its literary pupils.

government by our wickedness.' But it was to his new career that Paine first turned his pen in *The Case of the Officers of Excise* (1772) – a concisely argued, forceful pamphlet stating the case for better pay and conditions for excisemen. For his efforts, Paine found himself dismissed from service and searching for new horizons. In 1774 he discovered them when he journeyed across the Atlantic and became embroiled in the American War of Independence.

It was here, a long way from his native Norfolk, that he really made his name, both as a journalist, penning anti-slavery and other articles, and as a writer and political activist. Paine's *Common Sense* (1776) sold many thousands of copies as he attacked the injustice and greed of England's colonial rule over America in a cogent style of writing easily accessible to the masses. As the battle for independence dragged out over an eight-year period (1776–83), Paine's influence (through a series of pamphlets forming *The Crisis*) was significant.

Needless to say, Thomas Paine was not a popular man in England, and when he returned in 1787, he antagonised the authorities further with his famous attack on royalty and hereditary succession in the two-part *Rights of Man* (1791–2). In this work – written in response to **Edmund Burke**'s attack on the French Revolution – Paine pre-empted the rise of trade unions and the development of the welfare state. Paine was subsequently convicted of treason and, in his absence, banished from England.

It was to France, once the object of his 'false heroism' that Paine now turned his attention. Here, imprisoned and under threat of execution during the tumultuous and bloody events of the Revolution, Paine produced his most famous work, *The Age of Reason* (1794–6). No doubt influenced by his own experience as a religious misfit in a Quaker/Anglican household, this brave and coherent attack on the dogma and intolerance of religion distanced Paine still further from many of his previous allies. These were times when an individual's status was still measured as much by their religion as by anything else.

Paine returned to America in 1802, but no longer as a hero, and died there seven years later. In a final bizarre twist to the tale, **William Cobbett***, a late convert to the revolutionary cause, visited Paine's grave in America a decade later and returned to England with the disinterred remains of Thomas Paine in his trunk! Sadly, Paine's bones never made it back to Norfolk and have never been found, though his death mask can be seen in the local museum.

Paine's immense contribution to political and social reform has often been overlooked and his rebellious reputation meant that even the commissioning of his statue aroused much controversy in the local council, although it was finally erected in 1964. The author of *Rights of Man* would probably appreciate the irony of having an impressive gilt statue situated in King Street.

'An office that may be filled by a person without talent or experience, an office that does not require virtue or wisdom ... which is the reward of birth, and which may consequently devolve on a madman, an imbecile or a tyrant, is, in the very nature of things an absurdity.'

Thomas Paine,
Rights of Man Pt II, 1791–2

Thomas Paine's gilt statue standing outside the Council Offices in King Street

Another pupil at the Thetford Grammar School for Boys, some two hundred years after Thomas Paine, was **Colin Middleton Murry** (1926–), whose experiences here contrasted terribly with the fairly benign school atmosphere back home at **Larling***. His father's parting gift was, rather inappropriately, a copy of *Tom Brown's Schooldays* which turned out to be all-too prophetic, 'Col' spending much of his early school life either fleeing from, or being tormented by bullies. But probably his most terrifying experience was on a school trip to the ancient flint workings at nearby **Grimes Graves**.

Taking a wrong turn, the panic-stricken Colin loses sight of his guide and is left to crawl around inside a tunnel, 'like being inside a rabbit warren'. The tunnels were at that time dimly lit by a line of small candles. When a candle is dislodged and extinguished, the walls come crowding in and after screaming for help, a terrified young Middleton Murry emerges to meet his laughing schoolmates. As he writes in *One Hand Clapping* (1975), 'I just couldn't see the funny side of it. But it certainly cured me of any incipient inclinations towards spelaeology [the study of caves]!'

An aerial view of Grimes Graves – these 'Devil's Holes' become terrifyingly familiar to the young Colin Middleton Murry and form the centre of Brian Cooper's 'chipping fields' in *The Travelling Dead*.

In her journal for the summer of 1906, **Virginia Woolf*** (1882–1941) writes of journeying across from nearby **Blo' Norton*** for a memorable day here in Thetford. An hour's bike ride from Blo' Norton Hall, avoiding numerous pheasants and partridges along the way, brings her across Thetford's low stone bridges flanked by anglers and book-browsing nursemaids. Woolf, already working for the *Times Literary Supplement*, but still a decade away from the publication of her first novel, seems to have been quite taken in by the town's quiet charm. 'Often in London shall I think of Thetford, & wonder if it is still alive', she muses after drinking in the tranquil and picturesque scenery, unfolded before her as if 'got up for some benevolent purpose' to please the London tourist: 'No one would notice if the whole town forgot to wake up one morning', she adds.

These same 'chipping fields' also feature in *The Travelling Dead* by **Brian Cooper***. His character Snake Bishop, sporting 'a flat cap, an apron and a leather guard on his thigh', comes from nearby Brandon (at that time half in Norfolk, half in Suffolk) and makes gunflints from the black flints unearthed in Breckland, 'the largest flint extraction site in the country'. Before they were found to be 4000-year-old flint-mining shafts, the 300 or so hollows in the ground at Grimes Graves were known locally as the 'Devil's Holes' (Grim being a Scandanavian word for the Devil). Cooper remembers Grimes Graves well from his days as a student of history and from later trips: 'These connections and the perception that the Breckland was a unique part of Norfolk produced a fascination that led me to weave a story around the old flint industry.'

Weeting

Restoration wit and playwright **Thomas Shadwell** (?1642–1692) was born at Stanton Hall near Weeting, just outside Thetford. Shadwell spent his boyhood at the priory here – a few remains are still visible – and later found success through plays such as *The Sullen Lovers* (1668) in a literary world then dominated by **Dryden**.

Shadwell's acute observation and quick humour lay at the root of his popularity, but his very public dispute with Dryden achieved more prominence for him than his writing ever could. Hearing of Shadwell's objections to some of his work, Dryden ruthlessly dismantled his rival's literary reputation through his poems, describing Shadwell as 'Every inch that is not fool is rogue / A monstrous mass of foul corrupted matter / As all the devils had spewed to make the batter'. Shadwell was so thoroughly castigated that he remained best known for his 'battering' at the hands of Dryden. Nevertheless, Shadwell had the last laugh when he succeeded Dryden as poet laureate in 1689.

Charles Kingsley

He smuggles his hero into
Weeting Castle in *Hereward
the Wake*

The ruins of twelfth-century
Weeting Castle – it is here that
Hereward, 'last of the English'
fools the Norman king and his
entourage.

The ruined castle and moat at Weeting serve as reminders of the Old English heroism written by **Charles Kingsley** (1819–75) into his historical novel *Hereward the Wake* (1866). Set just after the Norman Conquest, when the real Hereward, 'last of the English', became a national figure for his resistance to the Norman invaders, Kingsley's novel is a thoroughly enjoyable open-air romp. Dsespite its uncharacteristically loose interpretation of history, *Hereward* skilfully explores the surrounding fenlands, woods and moors.

It has been said that Kingsley, escaping the fetters of history donship in Cambridge, does take liberties, but his novel remains compulsive reading today as Hereward sets about thwarting the Normans. Weeting's involvement comes when the intrepid Hereward volunteers for a dangerous spying mission against the Normans who are based at the castle.

Cropping his golden locks and beard and browning his skin with walnut, Hereward leaves his refuge on the Isle of Ely. Assuming a potter's disguise and calling 'Pots! pots! good pots and pans!' along the way, Hereward makes for Brandon, 'full of heart and happy'. He enjoys 'the keen fresh air of the warrens; … the ramble out of the isle, in which

he had been cooped up so long; ... the jest of the thing – disguise, stratagem, adventure, danger'.

The now dry moat of William de Warenne's castle can still be seen, though today's ruins date from the mid-twelfth century, when the de Plaiz family became lords of the manor. Hereward's first sighting of Weeting Castle illustrates Kingsley's distinctive blend of historical fact and patriotically tinged imagination:

> And he came to Brandon, to the 'king's court', from which William could command the streams of Wissey and Little Ouse, with all their fens; and saw with a curse the new buildings of Weeting Castle – like the rest, of which Sir F. Palgrave eloquently says – 'New, and strong, and cruel in their strength – how the Englishman must have loathed the damp smell of the fresh mortar, and the sight of the heaps of rubble, and the chippings of the stone, and the blurring of the lime upon the green sward; and how hopeless he must have felt when the great gates opened, and the wains were drewn in, heavily laden with the salted beeves, and the sacks of corn and meal furnished by the Royal demesnes, the manor which had belonged to Edward the Confessor, now the spoil of the stranger: and when he looked into the Castle Court, thronged by the soldiers in bright mail, and heard the carpenters working upon the ordnance, – every blow and stroke, even of the hammer of mallet, speaking the language of defiance'.

Faking a deep sleep in the filthy mud-and-turf cabin where he spends the night, Hereward overhears two witches discuss the Norman king's imminent battle plan, and develops his own strategy. The next day Hereward enters William's castle, where, in spite of his successful disguise, he gets involved in a kitchen brawl and is imprisoned. After the king himself nearly blows Hereward's cover, Kingsley's hero manages to escape with 'one great shout of "A Wake! A Wake!"'. With the Normans in hot pursuit, Hereward rides over 'heath and rabbit-burrow, over rush and fen, sound ground and rotten ... shouting at the rabbits as they scuttled from under his feet, and laughing at the dottrel as they postured and anticked on the mole hills'. Hereward loops around the dangerous 'labyrinth of fens and meres', riding south along the Roman roads, until reaching the safety of his stronghold.

West Harling

Isolated on a grassy clearing among windswept pines, the redundant church of All Saint's serves as a reminder of this once sizeable village. Back in the late sixteenth century, Old Harling Hall, described by **Blomefield*** as 'a fine old embatled stone building, moted round', stood close to the rectory and the nearby church, which itself enjoyed a congregation of more than a hundred at that time.

'Hereward's Way' is now a public footpath running from Weeting to Christchurch (Cambridgeshire) along the Norfolk-Suffolk border.

Thomas Nashe

'Let me but touch a peece of paper, there arise such stormes and tempestes about my ears it is admirable'.

For the six-year-old **Thomas Nashe*** (1567–1601), freshly arrived in 1574 at the rectory where his father was now vicar, the surroundings here 'in the countrey' were very different from the seaside sprawl of Lowestoft he had left. Instead of the plaintive cries of seagulls, there was the 'fearefull croking cry' of ravens who 'fluttred and clasht against the windowes'. Lying in his bed, listening to the night noises: the 'blow and batter' of the wind, the 'dry rusty creeking' of a gate, or the 'lavish blabbing of forbidden secrets' of a screech owl, the Gothic imagination of the young Nashe quickly filled with fears of darkness, witchcraft and lurking demons.

Nashe was later to reproduce the eeriness of his 'countrey' childhood in *Christs Teares* (1593) and *Terrors of the Night* (1594) – the latter written while staying in the mysterious fenlands. His sensitivity as a writer though always leaned away from the agoraphobic spread of wide skies and emptiness of the bleak Harling landscape and towards the rural lives that filled it: the saddler 'knocking in of tackes, iarring on them quaveringly with his hammer a great while together', the 'countrie huswives', reapers, masons, and the 'aged mumping bedlams' – superstitious old women and conveyors of rural lore.

As a satirist and pamphleteer, a writer of extraordinary and lurid prose, Nashe was a literary comet whose trail blazed all too briefly through the last years of the Elizabethan era. Raised in rural Norfolk, but inspired by the squalor and low-life of London, Nashe was frequently impoverished himself and ended up in debtors prison on several occasions. Although he found some wealthy patronage, Nashe was a malcontent for much of his career, living his life as 'Pierce Penniless', the impecunious hero of his influential 1592 work. *Pierce Penniless* was something new and exciting for the Elizabethan public and brought Nashe almost instant success, while *The Unfortunate Traveller* (1594), a thrilling, episodic, action-packed yarn, was closer to the modern novel than works written centuries later.

A small, wiry man with straggly long hair, buck-teeth, and – most unusually for the period – no beard, Nashe revelled in the self-generated publicity of his largely controversial work and few wealthy and influential people were left unaffected by his venomous wit. To succeed as a pamphleteer and writer, Nashe needed to be a literary juggler: his satirical and witty writing was part investigative journalism, part biography, part fiction – and always pure entertainment. Having aroused the ire of the government, and in imminent danger of arrest, Nashe fled to the relative safety of **Great Yarmouth*** – where he arrived in 1597.

Norfolk – a 'liberating vision of being at the edge of things' (Richard Mabey)

APPENDIX 1

Bibliography

Biographies and secondary reading are indicated † and listed under subject (author).
Norfolk and East Anglian Guides and Anthologies, and General Reference are listed under separate headings.
(All London publishers unless otherwise stated)

Aldiss, Brian *Bury My Heart at W H Smith's – A Writing Life* Hodder & Stoughton 1990
— *Life in the West* Weidenfeld & Nicolson 1980
— *Forgotten Life* Victor Gollancz 1988
— *Remembrance Day* HarperCollins 1993
— *Somewhere East of Life* HarperCollins 1994
Ashford, Daisy *The Young Visiters* Chatto & Windus 1989
† Malcomson, R M *Daisy Ashford – Her Life* Chatto & Windus 1984
Auden, W H *Collected Poems* Faber & Faber, 1991
† Carpenter, Humphrey *W H Auden – A Biography* George Allen & Unwin 1981
Austen, Jane *Emma* Penguin Classics, Harmondsworth 1987
Barker, George *Collected Poems* Faber & Faber 1987
— *To Aylsham Fair* Faber & Faber 1970
Barker, Raffaella *Come and Tell Me Some Lies* Hamish Hamilton 1994
— *The Hook* Bloomsbury 1996
Benson, E F *More Spook Stories* Hutchinson 1934
— *Final Edition* Longmans 1940
— *The Collected Ghost Stories* Robinson 1992
† Masters, Brian *The Life of E F Benson* Chatto & Windus 1991
Betjeman, John *Collected Poems* John Murray 1984
— *Letters, Volume Two 1951–1984* ed. Lycett Green, Candida, Methuen 1995
† Taylor-Martin, Patrick *John Betjeman – His Life and Work* Allen Lane 1983
Bigsby, Christopher *Hester – A Romance* Weidenfeld & Nicolson 1994
— *Pearl – A Romance* Weidenfeld & Nicolson 1995
Blacker, Terence *Revenance* Bloomsbury 1996
Blyth, James *Juicy Joe – A Romance of the Norfolk Marshlands* Grant Richards 1903
— *Celibate Sarah* Grant Richards 1904
— *Rubina* John Long 1908
— *The Smallholder* John Long 1908
Borrow, George *Lavengro* John Murray 1925
— *The Romany Rye* Cresset Press 1948

† Collie, Michael *George Borrow Eccentric* Cambridge University Press, Cambridge 1982
† Walling, R A J *George Borrow. The Man and his Work* Cassell 1908
† Williams, David *A World of His Own. The Double Life of George Borrow* Oxford University Press, Oxford 1982
Bradbury, Malcolm *Doctor Criminale* Secker & Warburg 1992
Brock, Edwin *The River and the Train* Secker & Warburg 1979
— *Five Ways to Kill a Man – New and Selected Poems* Enitharmon Press, Petersfield 1990
— *And Another Thing* Enitharmon Press, Petersfield 1998
Browne, Sir Thomas *Sir Thomas Browne's Norfolk. Extracts from the writings of Sir Thomas Browne relating to the natural history and archaeology of Norfolk in the seventeenth century* The Larks Press, Dereham 1989
† Shaw, Anthony Batty *Sir Thomas Browne of Norwich* Browne 300 Committee and Jarrold, Norwich 1982
Brownjohn, Alan *In the Cruel Arcade* Sinclair-Stevenson 1994
— *Collected Poems, 1952–1986* Hutchinson 1988
Bryan, Lynne *Envy at the Cheese Handout* Faber & Faber 1995
Bulwer-Lytton, Edward *Eugene Aram*
Burney, Fanny *The Early Diary, 1768–1778 Volume II* George Bell & Sons 1889
— *Journals & Letters, Volumes I & II 1778–1840* ed. Hemlow, Joyce, Oxford University Press, Oxford 1972
— *Selected Letters and Journals* ed. Hemlow, Joyce, Clarendon Press, Oxford 1986
— *Evelina* Oxford University Press, Oxford 1988
† Kilpatrick, Sarah *Fanny Burney* David & Charles 1980
Cartland, Barbara *I Reach for the Stars* Robson Books 1994
Charles, Kate *A Drink of Deadly Wine* Headline 1991
— *The Snares of Death* Headline 1992
— *Evil Angels Among Them* Headline 1995
Clarke, Lindsay *The Chymical Wedding* Picador 1990

Collins, Wilkie *Armadale* Smith Elder & Co 1877
† Peters, Catherine *Wilkie Collins – The King of Inventors* Minerva 1992
Cooper, Brian *The Travelling Dead* Constable 1997
Cowan, Andrew *Pig* Michael Joseph 1994
Cowper, William *Verse and Letters* ed. Spiller, Brian, The Reynard Library 1968
† Newey, Vincent *Cowper's Poetry. A Critical Study and Reassessment* Liverpool University Press, Liverpool 1982
† Thomas, Gilbert *William Cowper and the Eighteenth Century* George Allen & Unwin 1948
Crossley-Holland, Kevin *Waterslain* Hutchinson 1986
— *East Anglian Poems* Jardine Press, Stoke by Nayland 1988
— *Pieces of Land: A Journey to Eight Islands* Jardine Press, Stoke-by-Nayland 1988
— *New and Selected Poems 1965–1990* Hutchinson 1991
— *Norfolk Poems* Academy 1970
— Autobiographical entry in *Something About the Author – Autobiography Series Volume 20* eds. Nakamura, Joyce and Senock, Gerard J, Gale Research Inc., Detroit, USA 1995
Dalton, Amanda *Room of Leaves* Jackson's Arm – Sunk Island Publishing, Lincoln 1996
Defoe, Daniel *A Tour through the Whole Island of Great Britain in Two Volumes* J M Dent, Everyman's 1966
— *Robinson Crusoe* J M Dent, Everyman's 1992
Dickens, Charles *David Copperfield* J M Dent, Everyman's 1991
† Ackroyd, Peter *Dickens* Sinclair-Stevenson 1990
† Kaplan, Fred *Dickens – A Biography* Hodder & Stoughton 1988
Doyle, Arthur Conan *The Hound of the Baskervilles* Oxford University Press, Oxford 1994
— *Sherlock Holmes, The Major Stories with Contemporary Critical Essays,* MacMillan Press Ltd, Basingstoke 1994
† Coren, Michael *Conan Doyle* Bloomsbury 1995

Evans, George Ewart *The Farm and the Village* The Country Book Club, Newton Abbot 1971
— *The Days That We Have Seen* Faber & Faber 1975
— *Where Beards Wag All* Faber & Faber 1977
— *Horse Power and Magic* Faber & Faber 1979
— *The Crooked Scythe – An anthology of oral history* Faber & Faber 1979
— *The Strength of the Hills. An Autobiography* Faber and Faber 1985
Evelyn, John *The Diary of John Evelyn* ed. Bowle, John, Oxford University Press, Oxford 1983
Fiennes, Celia *The Illustrated Journeys 1685–1712* ed. Morris, Christopher, MacDonald 1982
FitzGerald, Edward
  † Ganz, Charles *A Fitzgerald Medley*. London Methuen 1933
  † Martin, Robert Bernard *With Friends Possessed – A Life of Edward FitzGerald* Faber & Faber 1985
Forby, Richard *The Vocabulary of East Anglia* David & Charles, Devon 1970
Fountaine, Margaret *Love among the Butterflies* Penguin 1982
Fraser, George MacDonald *Mr American* Pan 1983
Fuller, Thomas *The Worthies of England* George Allen & Unwin 1952
Gaskell, Elizabeth *North and South* Penguin 1996
Goffin, Magdalen *Maria Pasqua* Oxford University Press, Oxford 1979
Haggard, H Rider *Montezuma's Daughter* MacDonald 1965
— *Red Eve* Tom Stacey Ltd 1971
— *The Private Diaries 1914–25* ed. Higgins D S, Cassell 1980
  † Pocock, Tom *Rider Haggard and the lost Empire* Weidenfeld & Nicolson 1993
  † Ellis, Peter Berresford *H Rider Haggard: a voice from the infinite* Routledge & Kegan Paul 1978
Haggard, Lilias Rider *Country Scrapbook* Faber & Faber 1950
— *The Cloak That I Left* Hodder & Stoughton 1951
— ed. *I Walked By Night* Boydell Press Ipswich 1974
— ed. *Rabbit Skin Cap: a tale of a Norfolk Countryman's Youth* Boydell, Ipswich 1974
— *Norfolk Notebook* Alan Sutton, Stroud 1983
— *Norfolk Life* ed. Williamson, Henry, Alan Sutton, Stroud 1983
Hamilton, Patrick
  † French, Sean *Patrick Hamilton – A Life* Faber & Faber 1993

Hartley, L P *The Shrimp and the Anemone* Putnam 1951
— *The Go-Between* Penguin 1958
— *Eustace and Hilda Trilogy* Putnam 1966
  † Wright, Adrian *Foreign Country – The Life of L P Hartley* André Deutsch 1996
Haymon, Sylvia (*see also* Haymon, S T) *Opposite the Cross Keys* Sphere Books 1989
— *The Quivering Tree* Sphere Books 1991
— *Norwich* Longman Young Books, Harmondsworth 1973
Haymon, S T (*see also* Haymon, Sylvia) *Death of a god* Constable 1987
— *A beautiful death* Constable 1993
— *Death and the Pregnant Virgin* Constable 1996
— *Death of a hero* Constable 1996
Higgins, Jack *The Eagle Has Landed* Pan Books 1983
Holbrook, David *Lights in the Sky Country* Putnam 1962
— *A Play of Passion* Allen 1978
— *Nothing Larger than Life* Robert Hale 1987
— *Worlds Apart* Robert Hale 1988
— *A Little Athens* Robert Hale 1990
— *The Gold in Father's Heart* Robert Hale 1992
— *Getting it Wrong with Uncle Tom* Mousehold Press, Norwich 1998
Home, Michael *Autumn Fields* Methuen 1946
— *Spring Sowing* Methuen 1946
— *Winter Harvest* MacDonald 1967
Hunter, Alan *Gently Scandalous* Constable 1990
— *Gently Does It* Chivers, Bath 1997
Huth, Angela *Nowhere Girl* Collins 1970
— *Wanting* Harvill Press 1984
— *Such Visitors* Heinemann 1989
— *Invitation to The Married Life* Sinclair-Stevenson 1991
James, P D *Devices and Desires* Faber & Faber 1989
Jessopp, Rev. Augustus *The Coming of the Friars and other historical essays* T Fisher Unwin 1905
— *One Generation of a Norfolk House* T Fisher Unwin 1913
Julian of Norwich *The Revelations of Divine Love* Burns & Oates, Tunbridge Wells 1994
Kempe, Margery *The Book of Margery Kempe* Burns & Oates, Tunbridge Wells 1995
  † Gallyon, Margaret *Margery Kempe of Lynn and Medieval England* The Canterbury Press, Norwich 1995
Kingsley, Charles *Hereward the Wake* J M Dent, Everyman's 1966
Lancaster, Osbert *All Done From Memory* John Murray 1963

  † Boston, Richard *Osbert – A Portrait of Osbert Lancaster* Fontana 1990
  † Lucie-Smith, Edward *The Essential Osbert Lancaster – An Anthology in Brush and Pen* Barrie & Jenkins 1988
Lanchester, John *The Debt to Pleasure* Picador 1996
Lear, Edward *The Complete Nonsense of Edward Lear* Faber & Faber 1965
Lubbock, Percy *Earlham* Jonathan Cape 1929
MacBeth, George *Poems from Oby* Secker & Warburg 1982
— *The Rectory Mice* Hutchinson 1982
— *Another Love Story* Bloomsbury 1991
Mackenzie, Compton *My Life and Times, Octave One 1883–1891* and *Octave Two 1891–1900* Chatto & Windus 1963
Mabey, Richard *Home Country* Century 1990
Mann, Mary *The Fields of Dulditch* Boydell Press, Ipswich 1976
— *Tales of Victorian Norfolk* Morrow & Co., Bungay 1992
Mantel, Hilary *A Change of Climate* Viking 1994
Mark, Jan *Thunder and Lightnings* Viking 1976
— *Handles* Puffin 1983
Marryat, Captain Frederick *Children of the New Forest* Hodder Children's 1997
  † Warner, Oliver *Captain Marryat – a rediscovery* Constable 1953
Martineau, Harriet *Biographical Sketches* Macmillan & Co. 1869
— *Deerbrook – A Novel* Smith Elder & Co. 1892
Mitchell, Gladys *Wraiths and Changelings* Michael Joseph 1978
Mottram, Ralph Hale *The Banquet* Chatto & Windus 1934
— *Autobiography with a Difference* Robert Hale 1938
— *The Twentieth Century. A Personal Record* Hutchinson 1969
Murry, Colin Middleton *One Hand Clapping* Victor Gollancz 1975
— *Shadows on the Grass* Victor Gollancz 1977
Murry, Katherine Middleton *Beloved Quixote* Souvenir Press 1986
Nashe, Thomas *Works of Thomas Nashe, Vol. I* ed. McKerrow, R B, Sidgwick & Jackson 1910
  † Nicholl, Charles *A Cup of News – The Life of Thomas Nashe* Routledge & Kegan Paul 1984
Opie, Amelia *Adeline Mowbray – The Mother and Daughter* Pandora 1986
  † Menzies-Wilson, Jacobine *Amelia – The Tale of a Plain Friend* Oxford University Press, Oxford 1940
Paine, Thomas *Rights of Man, Common Sense* J M Dent, Everyman's 1994

† Keane, John *Tom Paine – A Political Life* Bloomsbury 1995

† Philip, Mark *Paine – Past Masters* Oxford University Press, Oxford 1989

† Williamson, Audrey *Thomas Paine – His Life, Work and Times* George Allen & Unwin 1973

Paston family

† Virgoe, Robert *The Illustrated Letters of the Paston Family* Macmillan 1989

Pierpoint, Katherine *Truffle Beds* Faber & Faber 1995

Pocahontas

† Mossiker, Frances *Pocahontas – the Life and Legend* Da Capo Press, New York, USA 1996

Powys, John Cowper *A Glastonbury Romance* MacDonald 1966

— *Autobiography* MacDonald 1967

Priestley, J B *English Journey* Mandarin 1994

Ransome, Arthur *The Coot Club* Puffin Books 1969

† Wardale, Roger *Arthur Ransome's East Anglia* Poppyland, North Walsham 1988

Ready, Oliver G *Countryman on the Broads* MacGibbon & Kee 1967

Rendell, Ruth (*see also* Vine, Barbara) *The Copper Peacock – Short Stories* Hutchinson 1991

Rivière, William *Watercolour Sky* Hodder & Stoughton 1990

— *Echoes of War* Hodder & Stoughton 1997

Roberts, Michèle *The Mirror of the Mother. Selected Poems 1975–1985* Methuen 1986

— *All the Selves I was* Virago 1995

St Aubin de Terán, Lisa *Off the Rails, Memoirs of a Train Addict* Sceptre 1990

Saxton, Judith (*see also* Turner, Judy) *Chasing Rainbows* Sphere 1989

— *Still Waters* Mandarin 1997

Sayers, Dorothy L *The Nine Tailors* Harbrace Modern Classics, New York, USA 1962

— *Busman's Honeymoon* Hodder & Stoughton 1988

— *The Letters of Dorothy L Sayers* ed. Reynolds, Barbara, Hodder & Stoughton 1995

† Hitchman, Janet *Such a Strange Lady – A biography of Dorothy L Sayers* New English Library 1975

† Reynolds, Barbara *Dorothy L Sayers – Her Life and Soul* Hodder & Stoughton 1993

Scott, Clement *Poppy-Land – Papers Descriptive of Scenery on the East Coast* Jarrold 1899

Scupham, Peter *The Ark* Oxford University Press, Oxford 1994

Sebald, W G *The Emigrants* The Harvill Press 1997

— *The Rings of Saturn* The Harvill Press 1998

Sewell, Anna *Black Beauty* Victor Gollancz 1988

† Chitty, Susan *The woman who wrote Black Beauty* Hodder and Stoughton 1971

Shakespeare, William *Henry IV Part I* Penguin 1984

— *Henry IV Part II* Penguin 1965

— *Henry V* Longman 1998

† Crosland, Jessie *Sir John Fastolfe – A Medieval 'Man of Property'* Peter Owen 1970

Skelton, John *Poems* Oxford at the Clarendon Press, Oxford 1969

† Edwards, Anthony S G *Skelton – The Critical Heritage* Routledge & Kegan Paul 1981

Pollet, Maurice *John Skelton, Poet of Tudor England* J M Dent 1971

Smith, Stevie *The Collected Poems* Penguin 1985

— *Me Again – The Uncollected Writings* Virago 1984

† Barbera, Jack *Stevie: a Biography of Stevie Smith* Heinemann 1985

† Spalding, Frances *Stevie Smith – A Critical Biography* Faber & Faber 1988

Snow, C P *Death Under Sail* Penguin 1963

Southey, Robert

† Storey, Mark *Robert Southey – A Life* Oxford University Press Oxford 1997

Spender, Stephen *Collected Poems 1928–1985* Faber & Faber 1986

— *World Within World* Faber & Faber 1991

† David, Hugh *Stephen Spender – A portrait with background* Heinemann 1992

Storey, Edward *Spirit of the Fens* Robert Hale 1985

— *In Fen Country Heaven* Robert Hale 1996

Sugden, Chris and Kipper, Sid *Prewd and Prejudice* Mousehold Press, Norwich 1994

— *The Ballad of Sid Kipper* Mousehold Press, Norwich 1996

Sutton, Henry *Gorleston* Sceptre 1995

— *Bank Holiday Monday* Sceptre 1996

Swift, Graham *Waterland* Heinemann 1983

Swinburne, Algernon Charles *A Midsummer Holiday* Chatto & Windus 1884

— *The Swinburne Letters – Volume 5, 1883–90* ed. Lang, Cecil Y, Oxford University Press, Oxford 1962

† Henderson, Philip *Swinburne – The Portrait of a Poet* Routledge & Kegan Paul 1974

Szirtes, George *Bridge Passages* Oxford University Press, Oxford 1991

— *Portrait of my Father in an English Landscape* Oxford University Press, Oxford 1998

Taylor, D J *Great Eastern Land* Fontana 1987

— *Real Life* Chatto & Windus 1992

— *Trespass* Duckworth 1998

Theroux, Paul *The Kingdom by the Sea* Penguin 1984

Thwaite, Anthony *Poems 1953–1988* Hutchinson 1989

— *The Dust of the World* Sinclair-Stevenson 1994

— *Selected Poems 1956–1996* Enitharmon Press, Petersfield 1997

Timpson, John *Paper Trail* Hutchinson 1989

— *Timpson's Travels in East Anglia* Heinemann 1990

— *Sound Track* Hutchinson 1991

Tremain, Rose *Restoration* Sceptre 1990

— *The Garden of the Villa Molini* Sceptre 1988

Trollope, Anthony *An Autobiography* Williams and Norgate 1946

— *Can You Forgive Her?* Oxford University Press, Oxford 1948

— *The Belton Estate* Penguin 1993

† Hall, John *Trollope: a biography* Oxford University Press, Oxford 1991

† Glendinning, Victoria *Trollope* Hutchinson 1992

Turner, Judy (*see also* Saxton, Judith) *The Arcade* New English Library 1990

— *Harbour Hill* New English Library 1991

Vine, Barbara (*see also* Rendell, Ruth) *The Brimstone Wedding* Viking 1996

— *No Night Is Too Long* Viking 1994

Wallace, Doreen *A Little Learning* Ernest Benn 1931

— *East Anglia* Batsford 1939

— *In a Green Shade* Lutterworth Press, Cambridge 1950

— *Sons of Gentlemen* William Collins 1953

— *Richard and Lucy* Remploy 1978

Walpole, Horace

† Mowl, Timothy *Horace Walpole, The Great Outsider* John Murray 1996

Warner, Sylvia Townsend *The Corner that Held Them* Virago 1993

— *The Diaries of Sylvia Townsend Warner* ed. Harman, Claire, Chatto & Windus 1994

— *The Flint Anchor* Virago 1997

† Harman, Claire *Sylvia Townsend Warner – A Biography* Chatto & Windus 1989

Weldon, Fay *Growing Rich* HarperCollins 1992

Wesker, Arnold *The Wesker Trilogy* Penguin 1979

— *The Kitchen and other plays* Penguin 1990

— *As Much As I Dare* Arrow 1995

Wilde, Oscar

  † Ellmann, Richard *Oscar Wilde* Hamish Hamilton 1987

Williamson, Henry *The Story of a Norfolk Farm* Faber & Faber 1941

— *Lucifer Before Sunrise* MacDonald 1967

— *Green Fields and Pavements – a Norfolk Farmer in Wartime* Henry Williamson Society, Longstanton 1995

  † Williamson, Anne *Henry Williamson – Tarka and the Last Romantic* Alan Sutton, Stroud 1995

Wilson, Anthony C *Norman and Henry Bones* Methuen 1959

Wodehouse, P G *A Pelican at Blandings* Jenkins 1969

— *Wodehouse on Wodehouse* Hutchinson 1980

— *Yours Plum – The Letters of P G Wodehouse* ed. Donaldson, Frances, Hutchinson 1990

— *Money for Nothing* Penguin 1991

— *Very Good Jeeves* Barrie and Jenkins 1992

  † Green, Benny *P G Wodehouse – A Literary Biography* Pavilion 1981

  † Murphy, N T P *In Search of Blandings* Secker & Warburg 1986

Woodforde, James *The Diary of a Country Parson 1758–1802* The Canterbury Press, Norwich 1996

  † Winstanley, Roy *Parson Woodforde – The Life & Times of a Country Diarist* Morrow & Co., Bungay 1996

Woodforde, Christopher *A Pad in the Straw* J M Dent 1952

Woolf, Virginia *The Complete Shorter Fiction of Virginia Woolf* ed. Dick, Susan 1985

— *A Passionate Apprentice – The Early Journals 1997–1909* The Hogarth Press 1990

— *The Flight of the Mind* The Hogarth Press 1993

  † Gordon, Lyndall *Virginia Woolf: A Writer's Life* Oxford University Press 1984

  † King, James *Virginia Woolf* Hamish Hamilton 1994

Wordsworth, William *Poetical Works, Volume One,* Second edition ed. de Selincourt, E, Oxford University Press, Oxford 1963

— *The Letters of William and Dorothy Wordsworth – The Early Years 1787–1805* ed. de Selincourt, E, Oxford University Press, Oxford 1965

  † Gill, Stephen *William Wordsworth – A Life* Oxford at the Clarendon Press, Oxford 1989

  † Moorman, Mary *William Wordsworth – A Biography. The Early Years*

1770–1803 Oxford University Press, Oxford 1965

  † Reed, Mark L *Wordsworth – The Chronology of the Early Years, 1770–1799* Harvard University Press, Cambridge, Mass., USA 1967

Wright, Adrian *No Laughing Matter* Toto, Poringland Norfolk 1986

— *Foreign Country – The Life of L P Hartley* André Deutsch 1996

Norfolk and East Anglian Guides and Anthologies

Barrett, Elizabeth *East Anglian Trackways* Wimpole Kenton 1990

Berry, Paul ed. *Poets' England 16 – Norfolk* Brentham Press, St Albans, Herts. 1994

Bradbury, Malcolm ed. *Class Work* Hodder & Stoughton 1995

Brooks, Peter *Salthouse* Poppyland, North Walsham 1992

Dixon, Geoffrey *Folktales and Legends of East Anglia* Minimax, Peterborough 1996

Dymond, David *The Norfolk Landscape* Hodder & Stoughton 1985

Durham, Andrew *Langton's Guide to the Weavers Way and Angles Way* Langton 1995

Fendall, Caroline *A Norfolk Anthology* The Boydell Press, Ipswich 1972

Gilchrist, Roberta and Oliva, Marilyn *Religious Women in Medieval East Anglia* Centre of East Anglian Studies, University of East Anglia, Norwich 1993

Goodwyn, E A *East Anglian Literature. A Survey from Crabbe to Adrian Bell* 1982

Hales, Jane *Norfolk Places* The Boydell Press, Ipswich 1975

Harvey, A S ed. *Ballads, Songs and Rhymes of East Anglia* Jarrold, Norwich 1936

Hillen, Henry James *The History of King's Lynn Volumes I & II* EP Publishing, Wakefield 1978

Jesty, Chris *East Anglian Town Trails* Robert Hale 1989

Jones, Elizabeth *Poppyland in Pictures* Poppyland, Cromer 1983

Kellehar, Cecil *The Ranworth Story* David Benham Publishing, Salhouse 1996

Ketton-Cremer, R W *A Norfolk Gallery* Faber & Faber 1948

— *Forty Norfolk Essays* Jarrold Norwich 1961

Malster, Robert *The Broads* Phillimore, Chichester 1993

Marsden, Walter *Resting Places in East Anglia* Ian Henry Publications, Romford 1987

Martins, Susanna Wade *A History of Norfolk* Phillimore, Chichester 1984

Mee, Arthur *The King's England – Norfolk, Fourth revised edition*, Hodder & Stoughton 1972

Pateman, Kerrie *1995 Regional Anthology East Anglia* Poetry Now, Peterborough 1994

Pevsner, Nicholas and Wilson, Bill *The Buildings of England, Norfolk 1: Norwich and North-East* Penguin 1997

— *The Buildings of England, North-West and South Norfolk*

Pocock, Tom *Norfolk* Pimlico 1995

Robinson, John Martin *The Dukes of Norfolk* Oxford University Press 1982

Rye, Walter *Cromer Past and Present*, Jarrold Norwich 1889

Sager, Peter *East Anglia* Pallas 1996

Sampson, Dr Charles *Ghosts of the Broads* Jarrold Norwich 1973

Simpson, Roger *Literary Walks in Norwich* 1983

Skipper, Keith *More Norfolk Connections* Poppyland, North Walsham 1992

Stibbons, Peter and Cleveland, David *Poppyland – Strands of Norfolk History* Poppyland, North Walsham 1990

Tolhurst, Peter *East Anglia – A Literary Pilgrimage* Black Dog, Bungay 1996

Wade-Martins, Susanna *A History of Norfolk* Phillimore, Chichester 1984

Waters, W G *Norfolk in Literature* Jarrold Norwich 1923

Wilson, Angus *East Anglia in Verse and Prose* Secker & Warburg 1982

Yaxley, David *Portrait of Norfolk* Robert Hale 1981

General Reference

Contemporary Poets, Sixth edition, St James Press, 1996

Drabble, Margaret and Stringer, Jenny eds. *The Concise Oxford Companion to English Literature* Oxford University Press, Oxford 1990

Eagle, Dorothy ed. *Oxford Illustrated Literary Guide to Great Britain and Ireland* Oxford University Press, Oxford 1992

Legget, Jane *Local Heroines. A Women's History Gazeteer to England, Scotland and Wales* Pandora 1988

Morley, Frank *Literary Britain, A Reader's Guide to Writers and Landmarks* Hutchinson 1980

Ousby, Ian *Blue Guide: Literary Britain & Ireland* A & C Black 1990

— ed. *The Cambridge Guide to Literature in English*, Cambridge University Press, Cambridge 1988

Parker, Peter ed. *The Reader's Companion to Twentieth Century Writers* Fourth Estate and Helicon, Oxford 1995

Twentieth-Century Crime & Mystery Writers, Third edition, St James Press, 1991

APPENDIX II

Clubs and Societies

Grateful thanks to the following for helping with research and providing material for this guide:

The Jane Austen Society,
Carlton House, Redwood Lane,
Medstead, Alton, Hants. GU34 5PE
Enquiries to: Susan McCartan

The E F Benson Society,
The Old Coach House, High Street, Rye,
Sussex, TN31 7JF
Secretary: Allan Downend

Chaucer Heritage Trust,
Chaucer Heritage Centre, 22 St Peter's
Street, Canterbury, Kent, CT1 2BQ.

The Wilkie Collins Society,
47 Hereford Road, London, W3 9JW
Membership Secretary: Paul Lewis

The Dickens Fellowship,
The Dickens House, 48 Doughty Street,
London, WC1N 2LF

The Gaskell Society,
Far Yew Tree House, Over Tabley,
Knutsford, Cheshire, WA16 0HN
Enquiries to: Joan Leech

Rider Haggard Appreciation Society,
27 Deneholm, Whitley Bay, NE25 9AU
Enquiries to: Roger Allen

The Arthur Ransome Society,
Abbot Hall Gallery, Abbot Hall, Kendal,
Cumbria, LA9 5AL

The Dorothy L Sayers Society,
Rose Cottage, Malthouse Lane,
Hurstpierpoint, West Sussex, BN6 9JY

Robert Southey Society,
16 Rhydhir, Longford, Neath Abbey,
Neath, SA10 7HP
Enquiries to: Robert King

The Trollope Society,
9A North Street, London, SW4 0HN
Enquiries to: John Letts, OBE

Henry Williamson Society,
16 Doran Drive, Redhill,Surrey, RH1 6AX
Enquiries to: Mrs Margaret Murphy

P G Wodehouse Society (UK),
16 Herbet Street, Plaistow,
London, E13 8BE
Membership Secretary: Helen Murphy

Parson Woodforde Society,
Priddles Hill House, Hadspen, Castle
Cary, Somerset, BA7 7LX
Enquiries to: G H Bunting

The Wordsworth Trust,
Dove Cottage, Grasmere,
Cumbria, LA22 9SH

Index of Persons

(Page numbers for main text entries are in **bold**; picture references only are in *italics*)

Index of Places

(Page numbers for main text entries are in **bold**, for black & white plates in *italics*; colour plates are referenced individually)

Acknowledgements & Permissions

Grateful thanks to everyone who provided material and assisted in the research and writing of this guide. Special thanks to Ben, Reuben and Ruth at Ben Cracknell Studios, Norwich, for providing the 'still centre' when everything around was turmoil. Also to Alan Blair, Cromer, Robert Eke, Wymondham, Frances Collinson at Gressenhall Museum of Rural Life, Norma Watt at Castle Museum, Norwich, Rochelle Mortimer-Massingham at Cromer Museum and Clive Wilkins-Jones at Norfolk Studies Library, Norwich.

Every effort has been made to identify the owners of copyright material and to obtain permission for its use in this guide. The authors would be grateful to learn of any unintentional errors or omissions.

Grateful acknowledgements are made for permission to reproduce the illustrations on the following pages. Where there is more than one illustration per page, items are sub-referenced (a,b,c) from top to bottom:

Colour images:
Alan Blair: Front cover, front flap, 66a, 66b, 67, 68a, 101b, 104a, 205a, 206. Malcolm Bradbury (Pamela Bigsby): rear flap. Harry Cory-Wright from *Creek*, Saltwater Publications, Brancaster Staithe:102.Norfolk Museums Services (Castle Museum): 101a. Norfolk Museums Services (Derek Edwards and Norfolk Aerial Photography Library): 170.

Mono images:
Brian Aldiss: 174a. Anglia Television Ltd: 81. Jane Austen Memorial Trust: 124a. Elspeth Barker: 177a. The E F Benson Society: 138a/189. Alan Blair: 58, 198 and 221. Bloomsbury Publishing plc: 20 (Finlay Cowan), 90, 264 (Nigel Parry), 179b (Matthew Donaldson). Malcolm Bradbury (Pamela Bigsby): 74. Elizabeth Brock: 34. Peter Brooks: 214. Alan and Sandy Brownjohn: 233. Kate Charles: 165b, 220. Chaucer Heritage Trust, Canterbury, Kent: 159. Constable & Co Ltd: 59/236a and 151/196b. Angela Coombes and Lindsay Clarke: 30b. Brian Cooper: 281. Kevin Crossley-Holland: 197. Curtis Brown, London: 94. The Dickens House Museum, London: 113c. Gerald Duckworth & Co Ltd: 69. Eastern Counties Newspapers: 53, 54, 71, 108, 116/200, 158, 230 and 280. Faber & Faber: 13 (David Gentleman), 134 (Jason Bell), 149 (Caroline Forbes), 192 (R Snook), 203a (Jerry Bauer) and 177b. The Gaskell Society and Mrs Trevor Dabbs: 124b (Simon Warner). Robert Hale: 251b (Douglas P Cole). HarperCollins: 251a (Isolde Ohlbaum); 268 (Caroline Forbes). The Harvill Press: 78. Hodder Headline plc: 142, 210 (Sean Pollock) and 259. David Holbrook: 62. Angela Huth: 194. Little, Brown & Company (UK): 93/263b (Simon Upton). James MacGibbon: 218. Macmillan Publishers Ltd: 103b (Jane Bown); 249 (Mark Douet). The Estate of Gladys Mitchell dec'd: 96 (S M Crispin Mitchell). Peter Morrow: 279. John Murray (Publishers) Ltd: 253a. Colin Middleton

Murry: 274b, 275a, 275b. National Portrait Gallery, London: 43b, 57a, 86a, 89a/212a, 106, 115, 122a, 126, 126a, 131, 137, 155, 229b, 247, 266, 274a and 290a. Norfolk County Council Library and Information Service (Norfolk Studies): 16a, 18, 21, 43a, 49, 51a, 50a/164, 55, 72, 85, 106/292, 113b, 114, 119, 132, 161, 167a, 176a, 209a, 223, 225a, 234, 267, 286a and 286b. Norfolk Museums Service: 15, 24, 26, 112, 145, 229a, 236b, 261, 264a and 273 (Norfolk Rural Life Museum, Gressenhall); 46, 51b, 52b, 60, 73, 89b, 123, 232 and 242 (Castle Museum, Norwich); 126b, 127, 129a, 150 and 152 (Cromer Museum); 117a, 248, 288 and 290b (Derek Edwards and Norfolk Aerial Photography Library). The Orion Publishing Group Ltd: 183 (Weidenfeld Archives) and 76. Oxford University Press: 184. Penguin Books Ltd: 284b (Jerry Bauer); 117b/128 and 191a. David Pitcher and Borough Council of King's Lynn and West Norfolk: 244. Laurence Pollinger Ltd: 186/255. Random House UK Ltd: 37b/63a, 64/130, 75/246 and 187. Ruth Rendell: 278. Eric St John-Foti: 252. Peter Scupham: 100, 105. June Shepherd: 17. Robert Southey Society: 47. Gerhard Stromberg and Andrew Cowan & Lynne Bryan: 79. Chris Sugden: 152. John Timpson: 237. True's Yard Fishing Heritage Museum, King's Lynn: 245. University of East Anglia: 77. Walker Books Ltd: 88. Anne Williamson: 215. Miss Rachel Wilson: 263a. The Parson Woodforde Society: 181. The Wordsworth Trust, Dove Cottage, Grasmere: 28, 29. Adrian Wright: 37a and 163/227a.

Grateful acknowledgements are made to the following for permission to quote from the stated copyright material:

Brian Aldiss for Brian Aldiss, *Bury My Heart At W H Smith's – A Writing Life.* Elspeth Barker for George Barker, *A Vision of Beasts and Gods, Poems of Places and People, At Thurgarton Church, Eros in Dogma* and *In Memory of David Archer.* Christopher Bigsby

and Weidenfeld & Nicolson for Christopher Bigsby, *Pearl.* Alan Brownjohn for Alan Brownjohn, *The Observation Car* and *Collected Poems.* Jonathan Cape for Lindsay Clarke, *The Chymical Wedding;* Arthur Ransome, *Coot Club.* Century Hutchinson for Arnold Wesker, *As Much As I Dare;* Richard Mabey, *Home Country –* Richard Mabey, 1990. Chatto & Windus for Sylvia Townsend Warner, *Diaries, The Flint Anchor* and *The Corner That Held Them;* D J Taylor, *Real Life;* Daisy Ashford, *The Young Visiters.* Commander Mark Cheyne for Lilias Rider Haggard (ed.), *I Walked By Night, Norfolk Notebook.* Jonathan Clowes Ltd on behalf of the Estate of Andrea Plunkett, Administrator of the Sir Arthur Conan Doyle Copyrights for Arthur Conan Doyle, *Sherlock Holmes – The Major Stories with Contemporary Critical Essays,* – 1996 The Sir Arthur Conan Doyle Copyright Holders. Constable Publishers for Brian Cooper, *The Travelling Dead.* Brian Cooper and Robert Hale Limited for Brian Cooper, *Messiter's Dream.* Kevin Crossley-Holland and Enitharmon Press for Kevin Crossley-Holland, *Pieces of Land: A Journey to Eight Islands, The Painting Room, Time's Oriel, Long Tom and the Dead Hand* and *Waterslain.* Curtis Brown, London for Sylvia Haymon, *Opposite the Cross Keys –* Sylvia Haymon 1988 and *The Quivering Tree –* Sylvia Haymon 1990; on behalf of the Estate of C P Snow for C P Snow, *Death Under Sail –* C P Snow. Gerald Duckworth & Co Ltd for D J Taylor, *Trespass.* Faber & Faber Ltd for George Ewart Evans, *The Days That We Have Seen, The Crooked Scythe* and *Where Beards Wag All;* P D James, *Devices and Desires;* Stephen Spender, *Collected Poems* and *World Within World;* Sean French, *Patrick Hamilton – A Life.* Robert Hale Limited for Edward Storey, *Spirit of the Fens.* HarperCollins for Angela Huth, *Wanting;* Fay Weldon, *Growing Rich.* The Harvill Press for W G Sebald, *The Rings of Saturn.* William Heinemann for J B Priestley, *English Journey.* David Higham Associates for Jack Higgins, *The Eagle Has Landed*, Pan Books; Dorothy L Sayers, *The Nine Tailors*, Hodder & Stoughton. Hodder Headline plc for Henry Sutton, *Bank Holiday Monday*; Kate Charles, *The Snares of Death* and *Evil Angels Among Them*. Hodder & Stoughton Limited for Henry Sutton, *Gorleston*; William Rivière, *Watercolour Sky* and *Echoes of War*. Hogarth Press and the executors of the Virginia Woolf Estate for Virginia Woolf, *A Passionate Apprentice – The Early Journals, 1897-1909*. David Holbrook for David Holbrook, *A Play of Passion*. Alan Hunter for Alan Hunter, *Gently Scandalous*. Hutchinson for Ruth Rendell, *The Copper Peacock*; P G Wodehouse, *Yours Plum. The Letters of P G Wodehouse*, ed. Frances Donaldson. Lutterworth Press for Doreen Wallace, *In A Green Shade*. James MacGibbon for Stevie Smith, *The Collected Poems*. Jan Mark and Puffin Books Ltd for Jan Mark, *Handles*. Methuen for John Betjeman, *Letters Volume Two 1951-1984*, ed. Candida Lycett Green. The Estate of Gladys Mitchell dec'd for Gladys Mitchell, *Wraiths and Changelings*. John Murray (Publishers) Ltd for John Betjeman, *Collected Poems*; Osbert Lancaster, *All Done From Memory*. Colin

Middleton Murry for Colin Middleton Murry, *One Hand Clapping* and *Shadows on the Grass*. Pan Books for George MacDonald Fraser, *Mr American*. Penguin Books Ltd for L P Hartley, *The Go-Between*; Barbara Vine, *The Brimstone Wedding*; Paul Theroux, *The Kingdom By The Sea*; Hilary Mantel, *A Change of Climate*. Picador for John Lanchester, *The Debt to Pleasure*. Katherine Pierpoint and Faber & Faber for Katherine Pierpoint, *Truffle Beds*. Laurence Pollinger Ltd and the Estate of John Cowper Powys for John Cowper Powys, *Autobiography* and *A Glastonbury Romance*. Michèle Roberts for Michèle Roberts *The Mirror of the Mother – Selected Poems 1975-1985*. Tessa Sayle Agency for Percy Lubbock, *Earlham*. Peter Scupham and Oxford University Press for Peter Scupham, *The Ark*. Secker & Warburg for George MacBeth, *Poems From Oby*; Malcolm Bradbury, *Doctor Criminale*. Caroline Sheldon Literary Agency for Judith Saxton, *Chasing Rainbows* and Judy Turner, *Harbour Hill*. Sheil Land Associates for Rose Tremain, *Restoration*, Sceptre Books – Rose Tremain, 1989 – her most recent book *The Way I Found Her* is published by Sinclair-Stevenson and Vintage. Sinclair-Stevenson

for Angela Huth, *Invitation To The Married Life*. The Society of Authors and the Estate of L P Hartley for L P Hartley, *Eustace and Hilda Trilogy*. Chris Sugden and Mousehold Press for *The Ballad of Sid Kipper*. George Szirtes and Oxford University Press for George Szirtes, *Portrait of my Father in an English Landscape*. D J Taylor for D J Taylor, *Great Eastern Land*. Anthony Thwaite for Anthony Thwaite, *A Portion for Foxes*, *The Dust of the World, Selected Poems 1956-1996*. Anthony Thwaite and Elizabeth Brock for Edwin Brock, *Five Ways To Kill A Man* and *And Another Thing*. John Timpson and *Norfolk Journal* for extracts from 'John Timpson's The AngliaPhile'. Ed Victor Ltd for Lisa St Aubin de Teran, *Off The Rails – Memoirs of a Train Addict*. Virago Press for Stevie Smith, *Me Again – The Uncollected Writings*. A P Watt Ltd for R H Mottram, *Autobiography with a Difference*; on behalf of The Executors of the Estate of K S P McDowall for E F Benson, *The Tale of an Empty House and Other Ghost Stories*; on behalf of Graham Swift for Graham Swift, *Waterland*, William Heinemann. Anne Williamson for Henry Williamson, *Lucifer Before Sunrise* and *Story of a Norfolk Farm*.